VENISON:
FROM FIELD TO TABLE

VENISON:
FROM FIELD TO TABLE

John Weiss

Drawings by Harry Schaare

 OUTDOOR LIFE BOOKS

STACKPOLE BOOKS

Published by

Outdoor Life Books
Grolier Book Clubs, Inc.
380 Madison Avenue
New York, NY 10017

Distributed to the trade by

Stackpole Books
Cameron and Kelker Sts.
Harrisburg, PA 17105

Library of Congress Cataloging in Publication Data

Weiss, John, 1944–
  Venison—from field to table.

  Includes index.
  1. Cookery (Venison) 2. Game and game-birds, Dressing
of. I. Title.
TX751.W45 1984   641.3'91   84-7365
ISBN 0-943822-24-6

Second Printing, 1987

Manufactured in the United States of America

This book is dedicated to Ernestine Gillespie Weiss, a very special lady.

Contents

17. Soups and Stews

18. Casseroles and Meat Pies   277

19. Liver, Heart, and Other Variety Meats   300

20. Cooking Your Venison Outdoors   322

21. Go-Withs

Man's Ageless Taste for Venison

THE TIME is 32,000 years ago. It is the Last Ice Age. The bow and arrow are not to be invented for another 22,000 years. Pilgrims will not wade ashore in Massachusetts for roughly another 310 *centuries.*

On this particular day, a small group of future Americans finds themselves camped on the Siberian tundra. They are near the northern shores of the Kamchatka Peninsula and there are 21 of them in the band—men, women, children. Although they have no knowledge of their ancestry, a modern anthropologist would probably label them as descendants of the Asian race Mongoloids. But members of the tribe merely consider themselves big-game hunters, and they are hungry.

Their destination is uncertain to all but those who will later study archaeology and their fossilized remains. They know only that for countless generations their people have lived nomadic lifestyles, following immense herds of caribou, bison, and mammoth as they migrate northward during summer, then south again at the approach of winter. During the summers tribe members supplement their meager diets with flower buds and bird eggs, and during the winters they grub for roots. But year around, meat is their primary staple, and animal hides serve their clothing and shelter needs.

Bones and other artifacts retrieved from fire sites indicate these early hunters ate more caribou than anything else, and this leads us to speculate that they found the meat of the big deer more flavorful and tender than that of other north-country creatures. Also, undoubtedly, 600-pound caribou were much

1

easier to kill than 2,000-pound bison or two-story-tall mammoths.

On this day, the strategy of these deer hunters is fairly well defined. Wearing robes of animal skins and antlered hoods to make themselves less conspicuous, the men split into two groups. One group begins to mingle with the caribou as they innocently graze upon lichens and moss. When the opportunity is right, the second group of hunters diverts the attention of the animals with loud shouts, allowing the others to rush unsuspecting, nearby deer and plunge long spears into their bellies and ribs.

In short time, three caribou fall from their wounds and the hunters quickly butcher the meat with flint knives. Meanwhile, the women and children of the tribe use the sharp edges of clam shells to scrape flesh from the hides before rubbing them with a mixture of tallow and brains to prevent the skins from hardening. Later, they will huddle inside their skin tents, passing the time by chewing the hides soft and by using bone needles and strips of sinew to fashion boots and knee-length parkas.

Fuel wood is scarce on the tundra, so much of the meat must be eaten raw. Small quantities that are to be saved for the journey ahead are smoked over a smudge of smoldering dry moss.

These early nomadic hunters are not aware that this year they will not be completing their return trip south, for they are about to become actors in a drama of discovery. The wandering herds of big-game animals continue onward still farther north, entering a narrow isthmus of land later to be named Beringia, and the hunters follow. It is a dry-land bridge, newly created when glacial activity reached its peak and locked up in ice millions of cubic miles of precipitation that would normally have gone into the oceans. The absence of this water lowered the level of the Bering Sea more than 300 feet, enough to turn the shallows of the Bering Strait into a dry corridor connecting the continents of Asia and North America.

As the migrating herds of caribou and mammoth pass through the narrow 56-mile land bridge, their numbers are squeezed together and the hunters find little difficulty sandwiching small groups of animals between men armed with spears. Fuel, in the form of driftwood washed ashore, is now plentiful, and after the kill entire haunches are roasted over crackling flames in a community fire pit.

It is now 5,000 years later. The wheel will not be invented for another 22,000 years. Christ will not be born for another 27,000 years. And Italian, Spanish, and Portuguese sailors will not make various claims of "discovering" the New World for another 230 centuries, yet already the northern hemisphere of that continent is being populated by the first true Americans. They are descendants of the nomadic hunters from Asia and upon completing their journey across the Beringia land bridge they find a landscape of wide and varying characteristics. To the north there are polar seas and vast sheets of ice more than a mile thick. To the west there is subarctic tundra, and to the south a combination of rain forests, fjords, and expansive mountain ranges. In time, far into the future, these early people will come to call themselves "Eskimos" and "Aleuts" and they will call their land "Alaska." And they will continue to subsist by means of big-game hunting.

Now, however, in this richly endowed land they are able to supplement their caribou meat with fish, shellfish, seal, musk oxen, ptarmigan, and many species of berries and wild greens. For the first time, man is using crude clay pottery in much of his cooking and the New World's first, primitive stews are given birth.

Over the course of the next 10,000 years, many tribes of these early men continue to infiltrate interior Alaska. Some are destined to remain permanent residents; others, still following migratory herds of caribou, are gravitating in southerly directions during the winter months. In time, many of them will skirt the unglaciated foothills of what is now called the Brooks Range, and from there they will press onward down the valley of the MacKenzie River and into the broad plains east of the Rockies. Still others will follow the later-named Yukon Valley southward through British Columbia and into what are now Washington and Oregon. Their common bond is that none of them know the steadily retreating glaciers behind them are now melting and clogging northern river systems that drain into the ocean. Nor do they know that the Bering Sea is slowly rising once again and thereby swallowing the dry-land bridge Beringia, sealing their fate and forevermore preventing them from returning to their ancestral homelands in Asia.

Daily life is still foremost a matter of "hunt or starve." And for the first time since he left the tundra of Kamchatka, early man is finding competition, for he is not the only "hunter" in the New World. He must share the bounty of the land with saber-tooth tigers and early predecessors of wolves, bear, fox, and lynx.

By the year 12,000 B.C. man the hunter has continued to drift still farther south into what will later be California and the desert Southwest. In canyon cliffs he is beginning to build multi-story housing complexes his Navajo descendants will later call *pueblos*. Other hunters, still restless from their ingrained nomadic heritage, push eastward onto the plains, where they live in huts fabricated from bark and grass. Still others penetrate what will later be Idaho, Montana, Wyoming, and the Dakotas. From there, their great-grandchildren will push into the lush Missouri, Mississippi, and Ohio River valley regions and then on to the Atlantic Coast.

By now, there is scant evidence of mammoths, mastodons, and saber-tooth cats. As the glaciers continue to retreat, the landscape of the Americas, once two-thirds covered with water, is with each century becoming drier and drier. Creatures previously acclimated to expansive miles of bogs and marshlands seem unable to adapt to their changing environments, and over the next several thousand years hundreds of species succumb to nature's timetable and become extinct. In their places other species, previously fewer in number, begin to thrive as the changing habitat now becomes conducive to their particular needs.

In those marginal wetlands still remaining, there roam *Cervacles*, an ancestor of our present-day moose, along with beaver and otter. At times, hundreds of thousands of plover and other waterfowl species form living blankets on these waters. On prairies vast herds of bison, elk, and antelope graze upon sedges and broomgrass, and woodlands develop inhabited by bears, foxes, turkeys, and coyotes.

Man is still a hunter, but in his travels he has begun to relish the comfort of the warmer southern climes; with the arrival of each summer he finds himself more and more reluctant to follow the caribou herds back to the polar regions of the far North. In making this decision, he finds his acquired taste for deer meat not to be sated except for those infrequent times when he and numerous others succeed in driving *Cervacles* up to its withers in deep swamp muck where the hapless creature may then be dispatched with spears.

To be sure, there have long been other types of deer on the hoof—mule deer, blacktails, and whitetails, all of which developed sometime in the Miocene Epoch more than 700,000 years ago—but with the majority of the landscape now either deeply wooded or open prairie, the habitat is not attuned to the browsing tendencies of these species and this keeps their numbers to a minimum. Also, the hunters quickly learn that *these* deer are so swift, alert, and elusive that attempting to sneak close enough to fell one of the cunning animals with a thrown spear is largely a futile endeavor.

For the time being, man therefore contents himself with the pursuit of bison. Their numbers are prodigious, the meat is good, the hides are warm, and the animals have poor vision, making them relatively easy prey. Hunting is still largely a cooperative effort, and entire herds of bison are stampeded over the edges of cliffs and into deep gulleys. The first animals to go over are soon crushed by the weight of others coming down on top of them, and the last are killed with spears and heavy rocks as they flounder on top of the heap with broken legs.

It is still a time of prehistory, a slice of early man's life for which there are no written records. What we know—and there's often heated debate among scientists as to exactly what happened, when, and where—has been pieced together through carbon-dating examination of man's rudimentary hunting tools, kill sites, and the camps he established.

The time is now 10,000 years ago. Man still depends heavily upon the killing of animals for food but instead of tirelessly pursuing herds of big game he is spending much of the year living in semipermanent communities. Anthropologists will later refer to these people as Paleo-Indians, although individual tribes such as the Llano, Folsom, Clovis, and Plano cultures become as widespread geographically as they are diverse in customs. Following, in thousands of years, will be the Archaic-Indians, and these in turn will be followed by the predominant Adena and Hopewell cultures of the Woodland-Indian period. Not until sometime around A.D. 1500 and thereafter, will these hunters and gatherers be regarded by modern scholars as "American Indians."

It is during the Paleo-Indian period that man reacquaints his tastebuds with deer meat. The reunion comes about through the birth of the *atlatl,* an ingenious device that allows him to throw his spears far greater distances and with greater speed than previously was possible with strictly hand-thrown weapons.

An atlatl is a two-foot-long wooden handle with a bone hook on one end and counterbalancing weights (stones tied in place with sinew) midway along the length of the shaft. The butt of a six-foot-long spear is then hollowed out to accept the atlatl's hook. By grasping the atlatl's handle in the palm, and supporting the spear above with two raised fingers, the Indian achieves an extension of his arm—gaining a distinct mechanical advantage—that allows him to take a much wider arc in swinging his arm and thereby propel the spear three times faster than otherwise and with surprising accuracy.

The invention of this unique device comes at an opportune time because herds of bison, while still in evidence, are very steadily diminishing in number. The Indians subsequently shift their interests to elk, antelope, and deer, which now, through the aid of the atlatl, can be taken with a higher degree of regularity. Indeed, it is the whitetail and mule deer that begin receiving the focus of attention, for the hunters quickly learn that elk and antelope prefer open prairie ground where they are difficult to approach, and if unduly molested they will run for miles. The deer, on the other hand, cling to the edges of thick cover, so they can be ambushed from close range by hiding hunters; and if the Indian misses his target, the animal is likely to run only a short distance before coming to a halt and resuming its feeding.

Another interesting aside has to do with the so-called flint "arrowheads" one commonly sees today in museums and sometimes even finds during the course of outdoor adventures. They're not really *arrow*heads at all, for the bow and arrow, while in full use in Europe and throughout the Middle East, is not destined to arrive on the North American scene for yet another 9,000 years. Thus, such "arrowheads," which typically are much too large to have been used to tip arrows anyway, should more appropriately be referred to as "spearheads," as they were initially used to tip hand-thrown weapons and then later those hurled through the assistance of an atlatl. True arrowheads, used by American Indians much later, were very tiny, seldom more than one-half inch in length, as anything heavier and larger would have greatly impeded an arrow's flight.

The time is now A.D. 1290 and various forms of the word "veneison" begin appearing in common use among English sailors. Derived from the Latin *venatio*, meaning "the fruits of the hunt," the first known incidence of its use is found in a ship's log dated May 10. On that date, the Captain of the *Seahawk*, bound for Madrid, penned a notation in the provision's ledger to *Huy nomen with heom into heore schip i-novz bred and wyn, venesun of heort and hynd, and of wild swyn*, reminding himself to take onboard for his journey enough bread and wine, venison of male and female deer, and wild boar.

For the next 100 years there is no uniform spelling of the word, nor specific definition, and its pronunciation varies: *uneysun, venysoun, wenysoun, venson,* or *vinzun*. Sometimes the reference is to deer, but other times it is variously applied to boar, hare, rabbit, or indeed the red meat of almost any other wild animal.

The year is now 1400 and "venison" is gradually being refined to mean solely the meat of deer. The first of these explicit references comes from the rural English countryside where Squire Lowe Degre, after a successful hunt, describes the eating *of Storkes and snytes and venyson freshe of bucke and do*. Then, in 1598, an author known only as "Manwood" writes in the English journal *Lawes Forest* that *Amongst the common sort of people, nothing is accompted* [equal to] *the venison fleshe of Red and Fallow Deere.*

Meanwhile, in the Americas, various Indian cultures from coast to coast have almost entirely abandoned the use of the atlatl for throwing their spears. During the previous several hundred years, they found that much smaller shafts only two feet in length can be propelled with astonishing speed and accuracy by using a flexible length of wood drawn tense with sinew stretched between the opposite ends. When the end of a notched spear is placed on the "string," drawn back its full length, and then released, the "bow" quickly returns to its former shape, generating powerful energy, and this has the effect of throwing the "arrow" a long distance. The result of the invention allows hunters to begin enjoying deer meat more frequently than ever before in the collective history of man. The weapon also provides a new means of defense, and sometimes aggression, among tribal communities that perchance encroach upon each other's hunting grounds.

The year is now 1620. It was 128 years ago that Christopher Columbus landed his ships Santa Maria, Pinta, and Nina on the shores of the Bahamas.

This is the year William Bradford and his Pilgrim followers establish Plymouth Colony on the shore of Cape Cod Bay in Massachusetts. They find the countryside profusely wooded and inhabited by "savages" and numerous wildlife species.

The Indians—Delawares, Penobscots, Iroquois—have long since become quite proficient with their bows and arrows, but deer are not plentiful in the climax forests east of the Appalachians, so the Indians often employ gang-hunting tactics for acquiring their venison. Sometimes they form long lines that advance through miles of wooded tracts, the drivers beating hollow gourds against tree trunks to make whitetails flee in the direction of other hunters waiting in ambush farther ahead. Another ploy is setting fire to the woodlands, and as the wind fans the blaze, the hunters wait along downwind vantage points for alarmed deer to come racing their way. Still other times deer are driven into lakes or wide rivers where they are helpless and duly clubbed by Indians in canoes. Many of the deer are roasted whole over enormous fires to feed entire villages where all are clothed in durable, lightweight buckskin.

The Pilgrims, as well, quickly learn to savor the New World's venison, using a forerunner of the shotgun, called a *blunderbuss*, which has a flared muzzle that sprays a lethal charge of lead balls when an ounce of black powder is ignited by a spark.

While Indians are cooking their venison over open fires, and occasionally in clay jars filled with water, the colonists use heavy, black implements they call "cast iron," which they have brought with them from the Old World. Three types seem to be the most prevalent. There are high-sided frypans and bowl-shaped, three-legged pots with capacities ranging from only one quart to huge vessels holding 25 gallons. The Dutch oven also is in use, or at least its namesake in the form of the high-sided skillet covered with a dome lid. But the classic Dutch oven, fitted with a wire bail and a concave lid with a flange for holding coals, will not gain widespread fame for another 150 years when pioneers begin heading west in Conestoga wagons.

It is now 1752. The province of Pennsylvania has just purchased a one-ton "Liberty Bell" from England for the grand sum of $300. It will be rung to call citizens together to announce the adoption of the Declaration of Independence, which is now being drafted but won't be officially signed for another 24 years. New colonies are spreading from New England down the Atlantic Coast and westward into the raw wilderness of the Ohio Valley. The country does not yet have a president, as George Washington is surveying new territories in the Virginias and is not destined to hold that high office for another 37 years.

As individual family units and small groups of settlers sever their umbilical ties with the New England colonies in order to pioneer the new frontier, the eastern whitetail population begins a slow and steady increase — a direct result of positive changes brought upon its habitat. For the first time ever, deciduous forests hear the ring of the axe and the clang of plowshares as log cabins are built and wooded tracts cleared for agricultural purposes. Even the continued burning of woodlands as a hunting method by the Cheyenne, Shawnee, and Cherokee is beneficial to the whitetail, for the random, checkerboard elimination of high-canopy forests promotes a variety of regenerative vegetation and understory. As the food dramatically increases, so do the numbers of deer.

By now, the blunderbuss has been replaced by the Kentucky long rifle, and several decades later these flintlocks will yield to percussion-cap rifles. Men with names such as Boone, Bridger, and Crockett are gaining national acclaim for their hunting exploits and shooting prowess.

In 1816 Eliphalet Remington founds the Remington Arms Company, and 15 years after that smokeless powder is born. In 1867 the first rifle bearing the name "Winchester" appears on the market after a period of years during which Oliver Fisher Winchester acquired controlling interests in the Volcanic and New Haven Arms Companies. Soon, the Winchester Model 73 and then the Model 94 are among the frontier's most popular arms. Venison continues to play an incredibly important role in the diets of explorers and pioneer families, who rely heavily upon stews as a means of stretching their precious meat.

In 1893 Benjamin Harrison is elected the 24th President of the United States. This is also the year a 30-year-old genius by the name of Henry Ford invents the first gasoline engine, and within the next 24 years he will build and sell more than 15 million automobiles. Sixty years after that man will make use of another type of vehicle, called Apollo, to visit the moon. In 1893, however, frontier families, trappers, traders, and cowboys are still struggling to tame the wild lands west of the Mississippi. Passage of the Homestead Act 30 years earlier has been encouraging them by the thousands to steer their wagons westward in search of cost-free farmlands.

For several decades buffalo herds have been diminishing at an alarming rate. It is said that a person can walk alongside the Northern Pacific Railroad tracks in North Dakota and never put his foot on the ground for a distance of 100 miles, walking solely on buffalo bones instead. The buffalo's decline adds to the reliance many place upon venison: East of the Continental Divide it's mostly whitetail venison but as westward-bound pioneers penetrate the foothills of the Rockies, mule deer, previously utilized only by Indians, become subjected to intense pressure almost overnight. For 40 years, gold-mining camps from Oregon to California have already been making a serious dent in the blacktail population, consuming tons of the venison every year.

Meanwhile, throughout the East, small settlement towns have long since been transformed into burgeoning cities and trade centers. America is entering an age of unprecedented development and industrialization, and its appetite for venison as a tasty and inexpensive meat source seems to have no bounds.

Numerous states, sensing the venison bubble is about to burst, have been attempting correctional measures for many decades. In Virginia, a law has been on the books for a century that prohibits the killing of does. Pennsylvania, Connecticut, and New York have almost simultaneously adopted laws that regulate the seasons during which deer can be harvested. In most cases, seasons are closed from February through August to ensure maximum reproductivity of the animals. Yet although such laws are well-intentioned, they are largely unenforceable. Adding to the growing plight of the deer, there are no limitations on the numbers of animals that can be harvested during the "open" seasons.

There is no way to know exactly how many deer the nation possessed before the great decline. Since no hunting licenses were required, and game management agencies were only in their infancy, there simply were no viable means of record keeping. Further, the consensus for the previous 200 years was that the virgin land of the New World had unlimited wildlife resources. However, many records, such as trading company logbooks, do exist, that give at least a vague idea of the enormity of the deer kill during the years 1830 to 1900.

One New York hunter living in the Adirondacks, Thomas Meacham, is known to have killed at least 2,500 deer over a span of 29 years. For 11 consecutive years, an average of 80,000 deer were killed annually in Michigan. A Delaware hunter brought to a trading post 18 deerskins per week for 47 consecutive weeks. Hundreds upon hundreds of barrels of venison and tall stacks of hides arrived almost daily in growing eastern cities by freighter canoe, river barge, wagon, and mule train.

To make matters even more tenuous, lavish hotels, restaurants, and boarding houses in New York City, Philadelphia, St. Louis, and other major cities demanded only prime cuts of venison to please their wealthy clientele, and they were willing to pay top dollar. Adding to the whitetail's trouble in the East and Midwest, and the mule deer and blacktail's predicament in the West, meat buyers in France, Great Britain, and other foreign countries began taking their toll, thereby aggravating an already serious situation. Indeed, eating venison no longer was merely a necessity for poor people living off the land in the Americas but was rapidly becoming a popular pastime in the richest palaces of the world.

Thousands of men found they could earn a better living as market hunters than by remaining in factories or behind horse-drawn plows. They became known as superior marksmen with shooting skills honed to perfection. It became a matter of personal pride to take 20 shells hunting and return with 20 deer and not a pound of the choicest cuts damaged.

It is now 1900 and the majority of the country's deer have been either exterminated or pushed into remote regions. In Pennsylvania, New York, and New Jersey, news that a hunter has succeeded in killing a deer makes front-page headlines, for most people have not even *seen* a deer in these states for many years. States have just begun keeping records and enacting surveys; it is estimated that the entire whitetail population, nationwide, is less than 350,000. Many states, in fact, begin announcing that for all practical purposes deer have been extirpated in their regions.

Yet amidst this ominous news there is a glimmer of hope because this is the year the hunter-financed conservation movement is born. Market hunting is promptly outlawed and the states begin implementing wildlife management programs spearheaded by competent biologists. Prominent naturalists begin coming to the forefront of national attention. Men such as Teddy Roosevelt, his Chief Forester Gifford Pinchot, George-Bird Grinnell, and John Audubon and organizations such as the Sierra Club, the Boone and Crockett Club, and even the Army Corps of Engineers call loudly for the establishment of strict seasons and bag limits. Hunters begin purchasing licenses to fund the work of their state agencies and their required equipment and personnel. Game wardens are hired by the hundreds to ensure that new regulations pertaining to wildlife are obeyed to the letter.

A new era is dawning in which man, for the first time in his history, no longer chooses—or is allowed—to hunt indiscriminately or as a means of subsistence. Hunting is destined to become a "sport," strictly governed by the laws of the states and the unwritten rules of fair chase.

With this startling turn in the hunting history of man, deer populations begin to increase slowly in select regions. In those few states where they even begin to flourish, it becomes feasible to live-trap surplus animals the range cannot support and use them for restocking states where the herds are so depleted they are unable to sustain themselves through natural succession alone.

It is now 1937. The federal government has just implemented the Pittman-Robertson Act (also known as the Federal Aid to Wildlife Restoration Act), partly in response to the requests of sportsmen. Hunters want to do more, and not just for deer or other game species but for all wildlife. They realize that many regions have become so depleted of wildlife that greater financial help is needed than that being generated through the sale of hunting licenses alone. Another growing threat to wildlife is also becoming apparent: Man's incessant expansion of cities. Each year, tens of thousands of acres of prime habitat is bulldozed away and permanently paved over for housing developments and industrial uses.

Through the Pittman-Robertson Act, dollars contributed by hunters purchase more than 4 million acres of wildlife habitat in the next 45 years. An additional $1 billion is raised through special excise taxes that hunters pay when purchasing firearms, ammunition, and archery equipment, with the money subsequently channeled into management programs that benefit game and non-game species alike. These efforts by hunters and their conservation agencies begin having a tremendous impact upon deer populations nationwide.

It is now 1983. From a low of 350,000 whitetails at the turn of the century, their numbers have gradually multiplied to an astounding 17 million, which is far more than when Indians and Pilgrims sought their venison. Pennsylvania, which was one of the states that only 50 years ago had to request transplanting stock from other regions due to its virtually nonexistent herd, now boasts a population of over 750,000 deer! Ohio's deer population has quadrupled in just the last three decades! Texas leads all other states with over 3 million deer—nine times as many as existed in *all the states combined* less than 75 years ago!

As further testimony to the success of the conservation movement, many states are beginning to lengthen their seasons and also are allowing—even encouraging—hunters to harvest does. With deer populations exploding almost everywhere, and causing extensive crop damage in many states, biologists recommend that in the best interests of the animals we must ensure that their numbers do not exceed the carrying capacity of the available habitat.

In the 30,000 years that have passed since early man first stepped into the New World, he has experienced dramatic cultural and technological changes. Instead of wearing clothes made from caribou hides and sleeping on the dirt floor of a grass hut, modern man wears a three-piece suit of synthetic fibers and lives in buildings of concrete, steel, and glass. Instead of a daily philosophy of "hunt or starve," he has become almost totally reliant upon the agricultural pursuits and livestock-raising efforts of others to provide him with food.

Yet despite these major transformations in his lifestyle, he's never lost his hunting instinct, for man is fundamentally a predatory animal and no predator's genetic urges can be entirely dulled by time. As social situations require, he may succeed in repressing such drives, yet somewhere below the surface of his personality they remain an integral part of his very being.

How else to explain the fact that each year a wide cross-section of our modern society (the U.S. Fish and Wildlife Service estimates that in 1983 the number was 18 million) ventures afield to hunt deer? How else to explain their willingness, in fact eagerness, to endure weather extremes, physical discomfort, and other hardships with no assurance their efforts will culminate in success?

On an individual level, any hunter's motivations for deer hunting can be examined from still other perspectives, and this brings me full circle back to the subject of venison.

Nutritionists have found venison higher in protein and lower in fat than any domesticated meats one can name. For example, 100 grams of trimmed, prime-grade beef has 17.4 grams of protein and 25.1 grams of fat. In comparison, an equal quantity of venison has 21 grams of protein and only 4 grams of fat. Because venison is low in fat, it is consequently also low in cholesterol.

And of special importance to health-oriented families, venison is not pumped full of artificial coloring dyes, flavor enhancers, preservatives, and numerous other chemical additives that we are just beginning to discover may have possibly damaging future effects upon ourselves and our children.

Aside from the nutritional benefits of venison, a family realizes substantial savings when a hunter brings home a deer. Of course, deer vary widely in body sizes and therefore in how much meat any particular hunter receives from his kill. But according to the Wildlife Management Institute, in the early 1980s hunters nationwide annually took home over 128 million pounds of boneless venison. Assuming that deer meat is equivalent in price to ground beef, hunters' yearly harvest has a monetary value of at least $185 million. So even if a hunter ends up with a minimum of 50 pounds of meat packages for his freezer, in these days of spiraling inflation the savings on the family's grocery bill is nevertheless impressive.

This book deals with all of these aspects, and more. We'll begin by joining you, the hunter, in the field at the very moment you are sizing-up your quarry, and we'll walk in your shadow all the way to the dining room, offering helpful suggestions to ensure your prize is properly cared for and affords maximum pleasure on the table.

A good deal of the information in this book is the result of many years of trial and error during which I've cooked dozens upon dozens of deer in as many different ways. I've also consulted closely with numerous meat specialists, nutritionists, and respected cooking authorities associated with major universities, wildlife departments, and government extension agencies. My thanks to those experts for their contributions. I hope that all our efforts will help hunters nationwide get greater enjoyment from their venison.

JOHN WEISS
Chesterhill, Ohio

CHAPTER 1

How to Judge Deer on the Hoof

Throughout man's history from prehistoric times to the present, it is clearly evident that both his philosophies and methods of hunting have changed.

Foremost, early man was an opportunist when it came to killing a deer. This is understandable, and justifiable, for when you're hungry and must rely upon the use of a spear or bow and arrow in order to avoid starvation, it simply is not prudent to be fussy about what you kill. You take what comes along, and you're grateful for it.

Archaeological excavations of early hunting camps bear this out by revealing the bones and skulls of both male and female deer and of animals ranging in age from just-born fawns to mature adults. The sheer numbers of bones uncovered at such camps and villages also indicate that early man killed far more animals than he could have possibly eaten. We can speculate that the reason for this was his lack of equipment or facilities for preserving the meat, except of course during the cold winter months when nature offered instant refrigeration. But during all other months of the year, it's likely early man killed a deer, ate his fill, crudely smoked whatever small amount he could comfortably carry, moved on, and perhaps only a day or two later was hunting in earnest once again.

Later-day Indians and Pilgrims solved their venison-storage problems by either smoking the meat or merely distributing it among neighbors, friends, or tribal members to be eaten almost immediately. Still later, pioneer families used more refined smoking techniques and also salting and pickling methods to preserve their venison.

Today, a hunter's situation is entirely different. His home freezer is fully capable of preserving his kill in excellent condition for many months and that is a distinct advantage his predecessors did not enjoy. Hunting has evolved in certain other ways as well, giving birth to problems that could not possibly have been imagined thousands or even hundreds of years ago.

For one, conservation laws have drastically curtailed the amount of time a hunter may spend in the field each year. Instead of diligently pursuing deer 52 weeks of the year for subsistence, a hunter is restricted to strictly enforced season dates set by the states.

Throughout much of the North, East, and Midwest, where whitetails predominate, the deer-hunting season lasts approximately one week, although there are a few exceptions where 10-day or two-week seasons exist. In portions of the deep South—again, whitetail country—and westward into the domain of mule deer and blacktails, seasons may extend over a month or more, but even in these regions the "allowable" hunting time does not even begin to approach the year-round hunting our forefathers engaged in.

Also, bag limits everywhere are very closely regulated these days. In the North, a hunter generally is allowed to harvest one deer per season, regardless of the method used to take that deer. In the South, hunters may be allowed to take several deer, but again, this small liberty (due to the presence of far more animals than the habitat can support and the difficulty of successfully hunting in swamp and tropical growth regions) does not even begin to match the dozens of deer stone-age men and later-day Indians commonly killed during the course of a calendar year.

The results of these changes in hunting laws over the years have been manyfold. First and foremost, since modern man does not have to hunt in order to eat, he no longer needs to be an opportunist. Likewise, since he's generally allowed to harvest only one or two animals per year, he'll want to be very selective in making his choices, to ensure that the animals he does take offer the best possible eating.

The "Catch 22" is that with the reduction in season lengths and in the numbers of animals any particular individual may harvest, many hunters have forgotten, or never learned, many fundamentals governing the proper killing of animals and the handling of the meat. This is not meant to imply criticism, but is merely a cause and effect relationship arising from modern hunters' lack of continual experience outdoors on a day-to-day basis. When a hunter is not used to killing large numbers of animals in a routine manner, he slowly acquires certain voids in his knowledge of what to do and how to do it. And with this sometimes comes a bit of apprehension, followed by guesswork, which in turn often leads to rituals, myths, and fables duly passed along from one generation to the next.

The next several chapters, therefore, review the techniques of selecting a tender deer, killing the animal properly, and handling the venison afterward. Much of this information is very basic and straightforward and intended to benefit young hunters or, indeed, those who have never hunted before. Much of this advice also is intended to refresh the memories of older, experienced hunters. Added to this, many new findings and tips related here for the first time are sure to tweak the interests of the most serious veterans of the buck-brush and thereby increase their level of skill, too.

How to Select a Tender Deer

One of the most popular misconceptions passed down through the generations is that grizzled old bucks are as tough as shingles, and if you want a tender-eating deer you're advised to shoot a "dry" doe or a yearling spike or forkhorn buck. It may come as a shock to many old-timers, but nothing could be further from the truth.

The age of an animal has very little to do with the tenderness of its meat. Admittedly, I have eaten some ancient bucks that chewed like recapped truck tires, but I've also eaten a good many that were as tender as butter. Similarly, one year I killed a nine-month-old spike buck and almost needed a linoleum knife just to slice the tenderloins. Another year, another spike buck had meat so delicate my friends and I almost felt compelled to eat with our heads bowed in reverence.

What determines the quality (tenderness) of virtually any animal is a combination of (1) the health of the animal at the time it was killed, (2) the diet of the animal throughout the year, (3) the amount of stress the animal was subjected to just prior to its demise, (4) the meat-handling techniques used from field to kitchen, and (5) the cooking method, since different cuts of meat require different cooking techniques. Under favorable circumstances, even an old barnyard rooster that has seen the passing of a dozen years can, in the hands of a skilled chef, be transformed into mouth-watering fare beyond description.

There's nothing a hunter can do to control the diets of deer, since they are inclined to eat just about anything at one time or another. But over the years I have noticed that deer taken from rich agricultural regions, where they undoubtedly fed regularly upon corn, soybeans, alfalfa, oats, orchard fruits, and truck-garden vegetables, have been hog fat and consistently more tender than generally leaner animals killed far back in the hinterland where they subsisted mainly upon twigs, buds, leaves, weed species, wild grasses, and similar native foods. A hunter who is more concerned about delicious meat for his storage locker than about a trophy rack might do well to forego his usual trip to some wilderness camp and, instead, concentrate his efforts upon those lush farmlands just beyond most city limit signs.

Two other things a hunter can certainly do at the outset is evaluate the health of any animal in question before squeezing the trigger or releasing the bowstring, and ensure as much as possible that the animal is not subjected to unnecessary stress during the moment of the kill. I'll reserve the subjects of meat-handling techniques and cooking methods for future chapters.

The health of a deer can be quite accurately determined by merely spending some time examining its various body features. Sometimes this is easier said than done because few deer are enthusiastic about posing long minutes before a hunter wielding a .270 caliber rifle. And, of course, impulsive hunters who are more interested in shooting and getting their animal on the ground any way they can, and as quickly as possible, obviously have no way of evaluating the quality of their venison until after the fact. By then it's too late, and they must hope for the best because their hastily made decision is now irreversible.

But many times (I'm talking now about the careful, methodical hunter who plans his strategy and is *very* selective about what he takes home), it is indeed possible to watch a deer for quite a while before deciding whether or not to try and collect it. By doing this, the hunter gains a valuable education for future hunts when he perhaps does not have so much time to look over a particular animal; then his accumulated experiences from the past allow him to merely take a quick glance at a deer and instantly know its worth. If and when a particular animal does not measure up to his expectations, he withdraws back into the shadows and continues to hunt, hoping to come across something much better. There is immense pride and satisfaction in this type of hunting philosophy, once a sportsman has acquired it through careful nurturing over the years.

In evaluating a given deer, first check the color and condition of the animal's coat. This should take only a few seconds. Through the warm spring and summer months a deer's coat is made up of thin, solid, light-reddish-colored hairs that allow body heat to readily escape and thereby render somewhat of a cooling effect. Later in the season, about the time leaves are just beginning to reveal their first splashes of autumn color, deer exchange their summer coats for grayish-brown coats of thick, hollow hairs that efficiently trap body heat and provide them with warmth during the approaching bitter cold winter months. These coats, in turn, will be shed sometime the following spring as daily average air temperatures once again begin to climb.

Naturally, therefore, if you spot a deer during the fall or winter hunting season and it still is sporting a reddish-colored coat, something is wrong. That animal is not in good health and may not even make it through the upcoming winter. Unless you like using a carpenter's crosscut saw to slice your steaks, better wait for something better to come along.

Even a deer that has its characteristic gray-brown winter coat may be in poor health if that coat looks dull, lusterless, and ruffled in places and overall has a scraggly-looking appearance. This occurs when the coat hairs are no longer being supplied with naturally produced lanolin and other body oils normally secreted by the skin and hair follicles. In any species this dysfunction is a beginning sign of malnutrition or other ill health.

A deer in prime condition, on the other hand, has a coat that is smooth and thick, of uniform coloration or very gradual blending as you pass your eye over the body, and with a rich, glossy sheen. There is no mistaking such deer. In fact, from the picture window of my southern Ohio farmhouse, my family and I have a perfect view of our south meadow. And when the angle of the sun is just right, healthy deer seen from a distance actually appear to "shine" like bright lights, as the luster of their coats have distinct reflective qualities to them. There are often as many as a dozen whitetails on that meadow at the same time, attracted to the lush red clover I keep well fertilized, and I cannot recall ever taking a single deer there that was not butterball fat and utterly scrumptious.

After learning to evaluate the condition of a deer's coat as a benchmark relating to the animal's health, next study the contours of the animal's musculature to determine whether the deer is "on the mend" or "on the skids."

Unlike livestock, which generally gain weight continually, wild animals frequently go through periods of ups and downs during their lives. Winter, for example, is terribly hard on many species living in the North, and spring is generally a recovery period. In the deep South or arid western states, however, midsummer may be difficult as well, due to unrelenting heat waves, droughts, and insects and parasites that torment wildlife species. Cool weather usually is the tonic that revitalizes them. In any of these situations, some animals may never recover from their setbacks, while others recover slowly, and still others bounce back almost immediately. But whatever the case, their present states of health are always reflected in their coats and the contours and shapes of their bodies.

Deer that are slowly and steadily gaining in weight are unanimously far more tender than those that haven't yet recovered from their setbacks or are slowly deteriorating in both physical health and body weight. A partial explanation for this is that anytime a living organism begins losing weight, fat stores are always the first to go. And it's the fat (called "marbling" by livestock

At first glance, this looks like a fine buck. But look closer and you'd probably decide to pass him up. He is in poor health, as evidenced by a somewhat scraggly coat, ribs showing through the hide, protruding brisket, and thin, sinewy legs.

growers), layered in muscles and woven interstitially through the fibers of the meat, that, during cooking, helps to break down those tissue fibers and thereby make them tender. Deer, compared to livestock, are quite lean even when healthy, and losing what little interstitial fat they do possess is disastrous to the final eating experience.

A good rule of thumb is to keep the word "round" firmly planted in your mind. Deer by their very nature are active animals and consequently never larded to extremes like livestock. Nevertheless, vigorous, healthy, well-fed, tender-eating deer reveal distinctly padded, rotund curvatures no matter which particular area of the anatomy you're looking at.

Animals on the skids are equally easy to recognize. You'll be able to see clearly the animal's ribs through its skin, its vertebrae along the spine, some-

This buck with a smooth, glossy coat is in prime condition. Moreover, the word "round" comes to mind as you examine his many body features. The size of the antlers indicates he's 3½ to 4½ years of age.

times even the vague outline of its pelvis. Likely, the animal's neck also will be thin, its muzzle may appear long and narrow rather than short and blocky, and its breastbone, where the lower neck joins the brisket, will protrude sharply outward.

Bucks, Does, and Fawns

Many times, a deer's antlers also give clues to his health because food intake always goes first into body growth and maintenance and only after these requirements have been satisfied are excess nutrients channeled into antler growth and development. Consequently, a buck carrying a rack that is thin, spindly and whitish colored may not have been feeding well for one reason or another. Look for thick, well-proportioned main beams and tines that are dark mahogany colored and perhaps white at the tips. You'll see these characteristics on healthy bucks of all ages, not just on trophies.

Regarding antlers, however, there are a few exceptions worth mentioning. Once a buck—whether whitetail, mule deer, or blacktail—reaches an age of approximately five or six years, it gradually begins to decline in sexual virility and each succeeding year this is reflected in antlers that grow progressively smaller and are misshapen. The animal may still be in excellent health for another several years and therefore prove tender beyond belief. It is just that his reproductive capabilities have gradually begun to wane.

Similarly, antler growth and development is greatly influenced by trace mineral elements (phosphorus and calcium) in the water deer drink. Some regions of the country are quite high in these nutrients while others are quite low. This explains why many specific regions continue, year after year, to produce large numbers of trophy bucks while other areas apparently equal in habitat and food value rarely produce impressive racks. Deer in these latter regions may be just as healthy, overall, and just as tender, but simply do not have that "little something extra" in their diets that is especially conducive to large antler growth.

So don't let antlers alone fool you when ascertaining the health and eating qualities of any particular deer. Give the antlers a cursory inspection, to be sure, but let your final judgment be governed by the color and condition of the animal's coat and the appearance of its musculature.

A lot of ballyhoo has also been circulated about killing only "dry" or "barren" does—those not presently lactating or beyond the age of bearing offspring—as their meat is supposedly more tender than that from a doe still capable of reproduction or one that has recently been nursing fawns.

I cannot verify if this is true because it's virtually impossible for anyone other than a biologist to determine if a doe is barren, and even *he* is incapable of such magic when the deer is on the hoof. Members of the scientific community tell me they'd very much like to know how some hunters profess to shoot only barren does. Moreover, how some hunters identify dry does is something else, if the claim could be proven, that would quickly find itself printed in the scientific journals. In actual hunting situations, things like this are just not verifiable. It's a moot point, anyway, at least with regards to dry does, because by the time late fall and early winter hunting seasons arrive, the vast majority of does that produced young in the spring have long since weaned their fawns and ceased lactating. Some fawns may continue to follow their mothers around, at least until she goes into estrus during the rut and chases them away, but almost none of them are still suckling at this time.

So it's my opinion, and it's one that's shared by most other hunting authorities, that a hunter should forget entirely about the dry-doe/barren-doe controversy and, instead, take the time to study the animal's physical features as described earlier.

Another matter of debate has to do with the eating qualities of bucks in rut. Many deer hunters stalwartly maintain that rutting bucks are virtually inedible, but the issue is not so cut and dried.

During the rut, male deer become so amorous they spend little time eating and resting. They're almost constantly on the move with pent-up, wild-eyed sexual energy coursing through their systems, the result of a sudden increase in the sexual hormones released by their endocrine glands. In addition to territorial disputes with other bucks, a mature male may successfully breed with and impregnate as many as 35 does during the brief mating period. It should come as no surprise that this amount of continual courtship leaves him gaunt, worn, and exhausted!

One study has shown that a healthy buck weighing 185 pounds just prior to the rutting period may be down to only 145 pounds at the conclusion of the rut only two weeks later! It is this very phenomenon that accounts for a high degree of winter kill among bucks in the far northern states. Often, the deer simply do not have enough time to gain back their substantial weight loss before the onset of bitter cold weather, and this makes them not only subject to malnutrition and disease but also weak and vulnerable to predation. Such bucks, toward the tail end of the hunting season, are "on the skids"— far below their normal body weight. Their musculature may be stringy and almost blue colored, because it has no interstitial fat whatever, and therefore is not very good eating.

Yet bucks living in warmer climates, especially in agricultural regions where prime foods are in abundant supply, may not be so adversely affected because the delay or even total absence of cold weather allows them to begin a speedy and almost immediate recovery. Before the hunting season is only half over, they may already be "on the mend."

Generally, therefore, good advice is this: *The earlier in the season you kill your deer, the better.* If this is not feasible, I again emphasize, study the animal's general outline, its coat, its antlers, its musculature and other body features, looking for distinctive clues that tell in advance what type of meat you're likely to end up with if you take that animal.

Does, by the way, are not subjected to the same degree of exhaustion and weight loss as bucks because their peaks of sexual activity are very brief. While a buck may be rut-crazed from daylight to dark for an entire two-week period, does come into estrus (heat) for a single 24-hour day. If they do not conceive during this period, they lose heat, return to a normal lifestyle, then come back into heat for another brief period 28 days later.

Fawns are a bit different. Actually, I dislike using the word "fawn" in a book designed primarily for hunters because too many quickly associate a fawn with meaning a just-born deer with a spotted coat and wobbly legs. I prefer using the word "yearling" instead, which means a deer that is at least seven months of age, weighs from 60 to 80 pounds, and can be, if necessary, and often is totally independent of its mother's care. These little buggers are often just as crafty and elusive as fully adult deer. Likewise, their venison is many times exceedingly tender but other times as tough as bark.

Fawns born early in the spring are weaned early. And since they've been on "solid" food for several months they've had time enough to acquire modest fat stores and therefore are quite tender. Fawns born late, as a rule, prove just the opposite. A hunter who desires to take a yearling should therefore pick one that appears unusually large in size—a sure giveaway the deer is somewhat older—and then quickly shift his attention to the various body features described already.

I've discussed these various points at length so that any hunter, once he has firmly seated in his mind what to look for, will be able to judge the quality of any given deer at a quick glance. I've seen wholesale buyers of beef cattle walk into a stock lot filled with steers and in scant minutes "grade" dozens of individual animals and their respective values. They've trained themselves to know what to look for—which animals have prime carcasses and which are below standard and best shipped to the sausage factory. Deer hunters who take the time to acquire similar skills can accomplish the very same thing.

Avoid Stressed Animals

Hunters can control to a certain extent the stress that any particular animal is subjected to just before being killed. And it stands to reason that deer that have been stressed minimally are destined to provide far more delicious eating than those stressed excessively.

An explanation for this comes from food technicians, microbiologists, and wildlife specialists at Texas A & M University where, through the cooperation of the Texas Parks and Wildlife Department, the subject has been studied intensively.

"Stress" can be defined as an unusually high metabolic rate resulting from significantly increased bodily functions. In other words, the organism's operating level has been strained far beyond its range of normal activity. In deer, this commonly occurs when the animal is chased long distances by dogs, pushed hard by hunters participating in drives, or is crippled or superficially wounded and is diligently attempting to escape.

In these circumstances, adrenalin begins rapidly flooding the blood stream. Simultaneously, oxygen deprivation in the musculature allows the build-up of lactic acid and other waste residues. If the deer in question is not injured and is able to escape and rest, the adrenalin flow eventually subsides, blood oxygen gradually increases and cleanses the animal's circulatory system of lactic acid and other wastes, and the animal very shortly returns to a nonstress state of being.

However, if the animal is killed during the peak of its stress response, adrenalin and various acid wastes, instead of eventually being purged from the system, remain in the musculature. This not only causes the meat to be less tender than normal but even gives it a strong, sour, acidic taste that many not too fondly refer to as a "gamey" flavor.

At the opposite extreme, a deer taken under nonstress conditions typically proves to offer tender, sweet, succulent meat. Normal heart rate, endocrine gland secretion, blood flow, kidney and liver function, and overall body chemistry are such that the meat is not subjected to excessive acid contamination. This is precisely the reason why ranchers, before butchering beef or hogs, place them in holding pens or tightly confined feedlots, where the animals are not allowed to move around.

One time—I'm happy to say this was long ago—I was invited to South Carolina to participate in a deer drive using dogs, being duly informed such hunts were steeped in rich southern tradition and I would never forget the experience. I haven't.

For almost a solid hour I sat on a hillside listening to the baying of redbones and blueticks as the pack relentlessly pursued a deer through deep swamp palmetto. Eventually the baying grew louder and louder, almost pounding in my ears, and suddenly a forkhorn buck came by with the dogs almost nipping at his heels. The deer, obviously exhausted, was running quite slowly and its tongue was hanging out and wagging from side to side. I shot quickly and luckily brought the deer down, and I will testify the venison tasted absolutely awful. In fact, I'm ashamed to admit that after two or three meals we took the remainder and made dog food of it.

Another time, just recently, I was in the Land-Between-the-Lakes region of western Kentucky, sitting in a blind watching the intersection of two deer trails. Far in the distance I could hear the shouts and hollers of numerous hunters staging a massive deer drive. About 20 minutes later, a nice six-point buck, which apparently had eluded the hunters, came loping by, and it was easy to see that the deer had been running hard for a long distance. He was panting heavily, his head rising and falling from exertion as he tried to catch his breath. The deer's body was in splendid condition, and under any other circumstances I would not have hesitated to fill my license right then and there. But I wanted a winter's supply of tasty steaks and roasts—

not another 75 pounds of dog food—and reluctantly but determinedly let him go about his business. Lesson learned.

This is not meant to be a blanket condemnation of deer drives, because when they are executed properly the animals are not overly stressed. By "properly," I mean using a small group of skilled, well-organized hunters who move through the woodlands without a great deal of commotion in an attempt to slowly "push" deer a relatively short distance to partners stationed ahead. In these cases, the deer seldom line out like jackrabbits heading for the next county. Instead, they generally slink and sneak along, trying to circle and dodge the drivers and standers, and they frequently provide easy shots at either slow-moving or stationary targets. It's the huge, raucus gang hunts covering miles of terrain with spooked animals running hither and yon that typically result in stressed deer, wounded deer, and venison that is not fit to eat. As for using dogs to chase deer, I can only surmise that some hunters are more interested in honoring tradition than dining upon succulent venison.

CHAPTER 2

Notes on Shooting Your Deer

J ERRY BURROWS is a friend of mine who earns his living as a professional meatcutter for a large packing company. And like many of us caught up in times of spiraling inflation, he does a little "moonlighting" on the side to try and make ends meet.

The interesting thing about Jerry's particular sideline is that he works at it only two weeks out of the year, by converting his garage into a temporary butcher shop and processing deer for local hunters. For only $50, a hunter can have his deer expertly cut up and packaged for the freezer in as little as two hours, and that includes having burger ground or sausage stuffed into casing links.

"It's enjoyable work," Jerry recently explained as I watched him tying string around rolled rump roasts, "but dealing with hunters sometimes takes a lot of diplomacy. Over the years I've had plenty of hunters get steaming mad and actually accuse me of stealing some of their deer meat. This usually happens when two pals bring in deer of almost identical body weights and shortly thereafter walk out with very noticeable differences in their number of neatly wrapped packages of venison. The reason is because close to 50 percent of the deer brought to me for processing have some of their best cuts totally mutilated by shots either passing through the hindquarters, high along the backbone which destroys the tenderloin steaks, or penetrating the front shoulders. In cases like these, I could be perfectly frank and tell the two hunters that one of them was an expert marksman while the other was a boob who just plain ruined a lot of his meat because he didn't know how or where to aim his rifle, but things like that are usually best left unsaid."

To be sure, the vast majority of deer hunters are respectable sportsmen who would never purposely misplace their shots and thereby turn prime roasts into dog food. But since this does indeed happen so often, there are several inescapable conclusions: Most of us should probably spend more time practicing with our chosen firearms and studying the anatomy of the game we're hunting; most important of all we should be far more selective in picking acceptable shots and turning down all others that do not measure up to our rigid, self-imposed standards.

A good deal of honesty and personal discretion also enters any discussion of shots taken at deer, for the stark truth is that some hunters are far more proficient with firearms than others, and some have stacked up many more years of in-field deer-hunting experience. As a result, two hunters who are evaluating the same shooting circumstances may come to entirely different conclusions as to whether a given shot can be attempted with a high level of confidence, whether the shot should be delayed until the animal's position changes, or whether the shot should be passed up altogether.

At a processing plant, meatcutters examine two deer. It should be obvious that these whitetails are not going to yield equal quantities of wrapped packages of venison. The buck is in prime condition, with not a bit of meat wasted. But the doe's hindquarters have been ruined by an ill-placed shot.

However, regardless of any individual hunter's shooting skills, there are some shots that never should be attempted. One is when numerous deer are running together in tight formation and all that is visible through the sights are blurred glimpses of antlers partly obscured by flashes of doeskin. Another is the extremely long shot, beyond 250 yards, that the hunter has never practiced on the target range. And still another is when a deer is only partly visible behind a screen of cover through which there are no clear shooting alleys. No matter what type of firearm is being used, a certain amount of bullet deflection is bound to occur, and the end result of shooting in dense cover may be a crippled animal that gets away.

One shot no hunter should attempt is into a group of animals that are running close together.

Knowing when, exactly, to take a shot is another paramount consideration that depends chiefly upon the existing circumstances, for, like fingerprints, no two encounters with deer are ever precisely alike. If I could set the stage and actually dictate perfect conditions for you, here's what I'd write into the script: The deer would be as close as possible, yet completely unaware of your presence; it would be broadside to your line of aim; it would be standing still or moving very slowly while either feeding or looking in some other direction; and, there would be little or no intervening cover.

Admittedly, such ideal conditions seldom occur on a regular basis. But the point to be made is that if you know what constitutes perfect shooting conditions, and diligently strive to set them up, you are then better able to make discriminatory judgments when less-than-ideal conditions prevail. This is the hallmark that separates the skilled, veteran hunter from the amateur and bungler. Instead of impulsively blasting away with the attitude of "when there's lead in the air there's hope," the experienced and conscientious hunter uses at least half of the fleeting moments awarded him to use his brain before his trigger finger.

I should probably also express a few thoughts about taking shots at running deer: I'll say without hesitation that I am unequivocally against such behavior. Since many readers may flatly disagree and begin thinking I've got a rip in my marble bag, consider the following:

Another shot that should be passed up is an animal in dense cover that is likely to deflect the bullet.

To begin with, it is admittedly a compelling sight to see a trophy buck bounding pell-mell through the woodlands, and if that deer was of record-book status and the hunter was only interested in the horns and nothing else, there might be a *slight* justification for attempting the shot. I emphasize the word "slight" because shooting conditions would have to be such that there would be a reasonably good chance of bringing the animal down. Otherwise, there's just too much risk of such a fine animal only being wounded, escaping, and eventually winding up as crow bait, and that would be a sorry ending for a deer that had such a unique gene pool and took so many years to achieve such proportions.

More realistically, it is extremely unlikely any hunter will ever come across a record-book buck no matter how many years he diligently puts into the effort. On the average, less than ten of the deer killed annually are of such magnificent dimensions that they qualify for the record book, yet *millions* are harvested every year, so go ahead and calculate the odds of any particular hunter stumbling into a new record deer. Even if a deer sports a rack an inch or two wider than anything the hunter has previously taken, it is still, undoubtedly, only a so-so deer by trophy standards. Given this, the overwhelming majority of hunters should probably be more concerned about the quality of the venison they take home than whether the antlers will "measure up."

Another reason for willingly passing up shots at deer that are high-tailing it for the next county is the distinct possibility of such animals being in a high state of stress. Since this is ground I've already covered, readers should know that such animals are not likely to provide good eating due to the adrenalin, lactic acid, and other waste residues saturating their musculature.

In the last analysis, it is extremely difficult—and for many, impossible—to aim accurately enough at a running animal to score a hit in a vital region that kills the deer quickly and yet damages a minimum of meat. There are just too many unknowns involved, too many variables beyond the control of even the most proficient marksman. In short, shooting at a running deer is an iron-clad guarantee of taking home only half a deer, and since the deer was not a record-book candidate anyway, what was gained? (Anyone who answers, "half a deer was gained" is beyond help and not worthy of the title "sportsman.")

Shooting Ethics

Historically, market hunters who plied their trade from 1830 to 1900 are looked back upon as scoundrels and plunderers of wildlife because, nationwide, they almost entirely obliterated our deer herds as well as many other game species. Yet I feel we can and should temper our ill feelings with a bit of compassion.

After all, those who lived during the market-hunting era sincerely believed there was no limitation to the bountiful wealth of natural resources in the virgin wilderness of the New World. They had no reason to suspect deer populations could be severely depleted by overhunting; wildlife biologists were almost unheard of, few studies of game populations had been conducted, and there were no viable means of record keeping.

In many ways, the market hunters' attitudes toward the apparently never-ending supply of game were virtually identical to our own later-day opinions about crude oil. Until about 1970, we had no reason to suspect oil was less than plentiful. It was there for the taking and we used it liberally, without concern or worry about conservation measures, until suddenly one day the roof fell in and we woke up to reality.

Moreover, during the 19th century market hunting was an entirely legal and accepted way of earning a living. And as such, the practices that prevailed are relevant to modern sport hunting and demonstrate that hunters who acquire certain shooting skills can collect antlers, hides, and prime venison with virtually nothing wasted. For very practical reasons, a market hunter had no desire whatever to bang off a salvo of shots at a running deer from far away. He knew in advance that ammunition was expensive or hard to come by, or both, and that sending a fusillade at any given animal would greatly cut into his profits. He also was aware of the high probability of only wounding a deer, having to spend hours tracking it down, maybe not even finding it and thereby having to start all over again. And even if a crippled deer could be recovered, likely as not a good deal of the "money meat" would be damaged and not bring him a good return in the market place. Indeed, he might have to kill and butcher *two* deer in order to acquire the same total amount of meat otherwise available from a single animal.

Market hunters therefore knew it was not in their best interests to hunt in anything even beginning to approximate a reckless manner, and this led to a very specific code of ethics: Expend as little ammo as necessary to get the job done, recover every deer shot at as quickly as possible, and ruin absolutely not an ounce of the prime venison destined for sale. In short, the market hunter was a one-shot artist with immense pride in his accomplishments. He was a sniper who carefully planned his strategy, waiting for just the right opportunity to present itself before making his move.

Modern hunters should emulate their early market-hunting counterparts. Foremost, they should ensure that their rifles are properly sighted in and that they are intimately familiar with their operation. Surprisingly, however, every year there are hunters who buy new rifles and take them hunting right out of the box, never even reading the directions and mistakenly assuming the guns are already sighted in and ready for use. Incredibly, still other hunters borrow rifles just before opening day, with no idea where slugs will impact when the target is at various distances. In either of these cases, the hunter's efforts are almost doomed to failure from the outset. And as for the safety factor involved, and the staggering number of deer only crippled, just thinking about the whole sordid affair makes me wince.

No hunter can make a wiser investment than buying several boxes of ammo and spending time practicing on the target range, and here is where a conservation ethic does not apply. Shoot up all the shells—preferably over a span of many days rather than all at once—and in addition to shooting at various distances, practice shooting from prone, sitting, kneeling, and squatting positions. Many hunters use these practice sessions for getting rid of their old or mismatched ammo, reserving their new shells for the actual hunt, but this too is patently unwise, as the two may offer wide differences in performance.

When hunting, and preparing to level the sights on a nearby deer, another critical concern is making use of some type of "rest." By this, I mean somehow steadying the rifle to eliminate any subtle "wobble" that may otherwise arise from unsteady hands, hard breathing, normal body tremor, or just plain excitement. Early market hunters often carried with them a pair of three-foot-long sticks tied together one-third of the way down from the top. When the sticks were spread and the legs anchored into the ground, they formed an X, providing a rock-solid crotch into which the forearm of the rifle could be laid for incredibly steady aiming. Other hunters bought or fashioned lightweight bipod arrangements that strapped onto the forearms of their rifles so they were always available for instant use. Some variations of these bipods are available today in sporting-goods stores.

For pinpoint accuracy, always try to use some type of "rest" to stabilize your sights. Old-time market hunters frequently used forked sticks like these.

Modern hunters may want to consider various types of lightweight bipods now on the market that make precise shooting accuracy a cinch.

Other types of rests can be contrived just before taking a shot at a deer. Nearly always, the steadiest positions are prone or sitting, with the forearm of the rifle cradled in the crook of a hat or on top of a rolled-up coat lying on a log or rock. If the only way to take the shot is from a standing position, lean slightly to one side and brace your upper torso and arm against a boulder or tree, or lay the hand holding the forearm of the rifle over a tree limb. Just keep in mind that any type of rest is immensely more accurate than none at all and some way to achieve the advantage of a rest always is possible if you take a moment to look around and think things through.

Even with these factors taken into account, no hunter should be so eager to take a shot that he risks only wounding a deer or mutilating many choice cuts of meat. The deer, of course, must be one that is in prime condition and therefore acceptable to the hunter. If the deer is not exactly what he's looking for, he unhesitatingly passes up the shot in hopes something better eventually will come along. Similarly, if the deer *is* one he wants, but the shooting circumstances are not to his liking, he again defers, hoping the position of the animal or its relation to surrounding cover will soon change. In other words, the hunter insists that he and he alone is in control of the shooting atmosphere, not the deer.

Many hunters may be inclined to say, "but what if it's the last day of the season," or "what if this" or "what if that?" Well, there may indeed be a season in which a hunter does not collect a deer, but that is certainly no rationalization for irresponsible shooting. Nor is it an excuse for taking a poke at the very first deer that may come along on opening day. There are 17 million deer out there walking around and any hunter who has practiced his craft and honed his skills should therefore be able to be at least moderately selective in the various shots he takes. He owes that much to the quarry he's pursuing.

Where to Aim

A century ago, those market hunters who were the most successful at their trade, and the best paid, were ones who learned to pick their shots. They were aware of the stark reality that those specific shots that were the surest and deadliest were also, happily, the ones that left virtually all of the venison undamaged.

Actually, deer of all species possess many vital regions that, when penetrated, will result in the animal's demise, either sooner or later. However, many of these vital regions are quite small, which makes hitting them a questionable matter. And many others, although larger, require penetrating prime meat to reach them. Others are within such close proximity to prime meat that they're risky as well; if the shot is just a bit off, valuable venison is lost because in many cases, usually depending upon the caliber and bullet design, the shot may strike the desired aiming point but the shocking impact of the bullet may damage nearby meat.

Ballisticians frequently demonstrate this point by firing bullets through blocks of gelatin and using high-speed cameras to record the action. But you can demonstrate the same phenomenon to yourself sometime by investing two bucks in a watermelon and shooting at it on a target range. Prop the melon up, so your bullet will travel from one end to the other, spang through the middle. The length of a watermelon is about the same distance as the width of a deer's body when the animal is standing broadside, and the inside of the melon fairly well simulates the organs, tissues, and fluids in a deer's body. You'll quickly see, upon shooting, that the slug does not merely pass through the melon's length, leaving small entrance and exit holes. On the contrary, the very instant the slug touches the melon's skin it begins expanding and from there plows a large pathway the remaining distance. Furthermore, the speed of the slug generates massive shock waves that literally cause the melon to violently explode with large pieces flying in all directions.

A rifle slug passing through the body of a deer is not quite so dramatic, but it is indeed sufficient to cause extensive tissue damage entirely surrounding the bullet's path.

With this in mind, I've never understood the logic behind so many of the shots touted in magazine articles and other books. I distinctly remember seeing one drawing in a deer-hunting book, by a leading author no less, where recommended aiming points were indicated on a deer running directly away. One aiming point was the root of the tail, the claim being that a slug hitting there would bring the deer down instantly by paralyzing its central nervous system, which is entirely true. But imagine the slug continuing to plow its way forward through the entire length of the loins lying on either side of

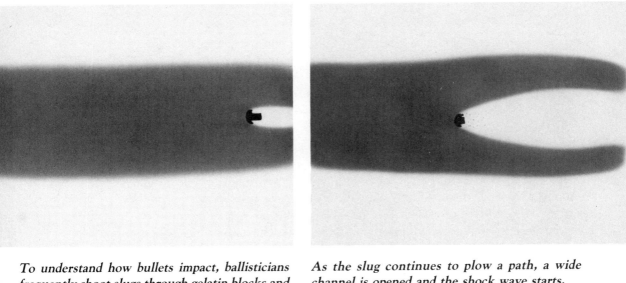

To understand how bullets impact, ballisticians frequently shoot slugs through gelatin blocks and then photograph the action with high-speed cameras. Here, the slug is entering the block and beginning to mushroom.

As the slug continues to plow a path, a wide channel is opened and the shock wave starts.

the backbone. The other recommended aiming point for a deer running directly away was squarely in the middle of one hind leg or the other, about halfway down from its attachment at the pelvis. A slug entering here, it was said, would sever the femoral artery, and the deer, if it didn't fall from a shattered leg bone, would bleed to death almost immediately. True again, but the author never mentioned that in taking such a shot you could kiss that entire hindquarter good-by.

Almost as bad, I've seen recommendations about shooting for the spine when a deer is standing broadside. Again, the integrity of the central nervous system is so disrupted that the deer immediately hits the dirt like a sack of potatoes. But you can virtually forget about treating your family to tenderloin steaks or chops.

Another shot I cannot recommend is the heart shot. A slug that hits the heart proves almost instantly fatal. If the deer does not drop on the spot, it will make a dash for 50 yards or so and then suddenly go down like it fell into an abandoned well. But the heart lies much lower in the chest cavity than most hunters realize, and there's a good chance, if the slug is placed just a bit too far forward into the brisket region, or too far to the rear and therefore in the paunch, that the deer will escape and not die until it is far away. Even if the heart is squarely penetrated, the hunter may lose a good portion of both front legs, which are situated directly in front of that organ.

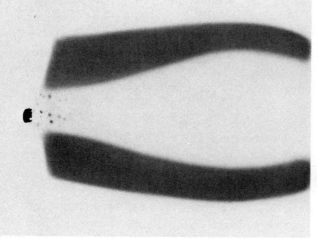

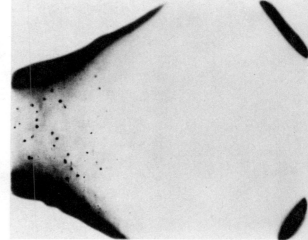

In this photo of the slug exiting the gelatin block, note how the bullet by now is almost completely flattened and the shock wave is spreading.

In this final photo, 1/1000th of a second after the slug has passed all the way through the gelatin, massive shock waves are in full progress. That's why you shouldn't aim for the heart, neck, or spine. Too much prime meat surrounding the bullet's point of impact is destroyed.

Head shots are also instantaneous in their results but I rate them out of the question as well. The target is small and often moving just enough to greatly increase the risk of only wounding the deer.

Neck shots are "iffy." When the vertebrae of the neck are broken, the deer falls right in its tracks. But the neck is a relatively large target, and too many hunters have a tendency to aim right for the middle, not realizing that the actual vertebral column is situated in the upper one-third (toward the back of the neck). The esophagus and major arteries feeding the brain are located in the lower one-third, and a shot here will result in a flesh wound from which the deer will eventually die, but often not then and there.

So neck shots are one of those dubious affairs. Many times the deer goes right down, and just as often, even though vital regions are not directly contacted, shock waves emanating from the bullet are sufficient in themselves to disrupt adjacent vital areas and this prevents the animal from traveling far. But I've seen many deer suffer only superficial neck wounds that allowed them to go long distances, never to be found. Furthermore, those deer that are recovered, either on the spot or sometime later, usually have a good deal of damaged neck meat. It's not prime meat, to be certain, but it is a major cut for making burger, stew meat, or sausage.

If a deer is standing directly facing you, another neck shot possibility is aiming for the white throat patch just below the animal's chin. So hit, the deer is instantly dead; but again it's a small target and a shot that strays only two or three inches off-center may result in a deer that escapes and dies elsewhere.

Hunters should also be aware that either head shots or neck shots predictably ruin the hide, skull, or antlers. This can be quite discouraging if the hunter wants to have his prize sent to a taxidermist because the damage may be irreparable.

This brings us to the lung shot, which is the one I've always recommended to beginner and expert alike. It is instantly fatal, or nearly so, and therefore the animal does not experience a prolonged period of stress. Moreover, the lung is the largest vital target the deer possesses, which increases the chances of a successful shot.

The lung region is about the size of a basketball and it lies directly between and slightly behind the two front shoulders. I always suggest aiming just a tad behind the front leg, as there is still plenty of lung material for the slug to penetrate and you avoid the otherwise regrettable loss of one or both front shoulders. If you study a deer's anatomy, you'll see that this aiming point appears almost as a slight depression in the curvature of the ribs. That is, going forward from the short ribs, where they begin just forward of the rear legs, the rib cage begins to bulge out somewhat until just before it reaches the rear of the front legs, at which point the ribs begin to sink in concavely, so they take a somewhat shallow appearance. This is the animal's "boiler room." It's the surest shot I know, and one that results only in a small loss of inconsequential rib meat. Since this aiming point also is quite far removed from contiguous musculature, there's rarely any bullet-shock damage to any of the prime portions of venison.

So if you remember nothing else from this chapter, it should be this: Aim for the lungs—three inches behind the front leg, six inches up from the bottom line of the chest, and about 12 inches down from the line of the back—and you've got your deer, and your deer meat!

The curious thing about this matter of "where to aim" is that a methodical, careful hunter who wants to facilitate a quick and merciful death of his deer, with no wasted meat whatsoever, simply does not need a number of shot-placement options. If he is in control of the shooting situation, and patiently waits until the animal is standing broadside or nearly so, as he should, he'll logically never have to consider anything but the lung shot.

It should be mentioned that there may be times when deer are not standing perfectly broadside but are just slightly quartering-away or quartering-forward. Shots such as these can be justified if the angle is not too acute, but the hunter will have to aim just a bit forward of the usual point or just a bit farther back, to ensure that the slug in turn angles forward (or backward)

The lung shot is the best bet of all. Not only does it prove almost instantly fatal, but it is the largest vital target a deer possesses. Also, little prime meat surrounds the lung region so bullet-shock damage to your venison is minimal.

into the lung region. However, if the angle is acute, it's better to pass up the shot. If not, the slug, once it has passed through the lungs, is sure to seriously damage one of the offside front legs or one of the offside hindquarters.

In summary, no hunter should be so eager to kill a deer and fill his license that he willingly accepts poor shooting conditions and thereby ends up sacrificing a good deal of his venison. This philosophy may take a bit of concerted restraint at first, particularly for young or beginning hunters who are anxious to kill their first deer. But once acquired, this restraint is worth its weight in good eating and serves as an irrefutable mark of the sportsman's skill.

CHAPTER 3

Easy Field Dressing

ONGRATULATIONS! Less than one minute ago you were tired, discouraged, and convinced that in this supposed oasis of deer country you alone had mistakenly chosen to hunt the desert. For days on end you patiently maintained your vigil on stand, never once even catching a glimpse of buckskin. Then suddenly, just when you least expected it, there he was! Slinking along, craftily, using every primitive sense to its fullest in monitoring his surroundings. Taking one cautious step at a time with an air of such secrecy even the most sagacious CIA official would blush with envy. A truly magnificent animal. Not a record-book candidate by any stretch of the imagination but nevertheless a handsome deer indeed, and best of all in absolutely prime condition.

Now he's lying at your feet. Your face is flushed with honest, well-earned excitement and your heart is still going like a trip-hammer. The memory of this day will remain more firmly planted in your mind than acid etched in steel plate.

However, something else is also happening. Other feelings are now beginning to rumble around in your gut. You feel just a slight twinge of apprehension. You know the fun is over and now the real work begins.

Before the kill, things were much easier because whenever the going got tough you could pace yourself. But now, you're in a race against the clock. Lying before you is an animal that weighs 180 pounds. Sixty pounds of that consists of prime steaks and roasts, and there is another 35 pounds of venison that will make excellent stew meat, sausage, and burger. And you know for sure you'll lose every ounce if you don't immediately prevent it from spoiling. You have to cool that meat as quickly as possible, then get it out of the woods and safely to home or camp. What you do in the next hour or so will largely determine the quality of the meat you and your family will be eating during the next nine months.

It's a good thing you gave the matter some thoughtful consideration before the hunt. In your pockets you have all the necessary equipment to do a professional job. You know what steps to follow. And back in camp, or at home, still other logistics have been attended to and remain waiting for the arrival of your animal.

Knives and Other Field-Dressing Equipment

Hunters commonly make use of many tools. The most important, undoubtedly—be it a rifle, shotgun, or hunting bow—is used to quickly and mercifully bring the animal down. The second most important are his knives, for they are used almost continually from the very first step in field dressing until the final moment of ecstasy when he begins slicing the steak on his dinner plate. Yet it is an unusual quirk that many hunters invest prodigious amounts of time in deciding upon precisely the right rifle, or mulling endlessly over whether to use aluminum arrows or fiberglass, then almost as an afterthought reach for just any knife when it's time to perform some cutting chore or another.

This is regrettable because there are innumerable knife designs and sizes, each intended for given tasks, and nowadays you don't have to fork over a sheik's ransom to avail yourself of them. Thanks largely to the innovations of custom-knife makers in the last two decades, many previously unheard of features are now even available at a reasonable price in mass-produced factory-made knives. By taking advantage of at least several models, the hunter, like the master mechanic with many different tools, can enjoy far more versatility and efficiency in performing sundry cutting tasks.

The five times a deer hunter is likely to need a knife are during *field dressing, skinning, caping, rough butchering,* and *meatcutting* (final reduction of various cuts into freezer-ready portions). In most of these cases, distinctly different knife sizes and blade designs are sure to prove superior to anything else. Some are even mutually exclusive. A skinning knife, for example, calls for a wide, upswept or backswept blade, the round cutting edge thereby suiting the sweeping or rotary stroke used in hide removal. A caping knife must be small, slender, and acutely pointed for working in very tight places. Knives for boning, butchering, or slicing meat, on the other hand, should be much longer and straight-bladed.

In the realm of field-dressing knives, although many models may be suitable for this particular operation, "short and light" are sound principles to abide by. Indeed, it's almost a truism that the more experienced a hunter becomes over the years, the shorter grow his knife blades. Friend and professional big-game guide Joe Brunneti, who works out of Steamboat Springs, Colorado, commonly relies upon a mere two-inch stockman's knife for dressing out most of his deer. Throughout the Rocky Mountain states, in fact, it's becoming almost faddish for outfitters to pull some dainty little thing out of their pockets, set to the task of dressing a deer, and often to the astonishment of their less-accomplished clients do very commendable jobs.

The average deer hunter will probably not want to go to such extremes to demonstrate his knife-handling prowess. But the point to be made is, absolutely forget about long, saber-type knives, especially those reminiscent of the "Bowie" genre or similar ones that look better suited to cutting sugar cane than field dressing deer. These tools, sheath ridden and sagging down almost to one's knee, have no practical purpose other than declaring to all onlookers that the wearer is a first-class greenhorn.

Gargantuan knives are simply too heavy to use for more than a few minutes at a time and increase the likelihood that your hands will tire, which leads to sloppy work at best or accidently cutting yourself at worst. Moreover, any manner of venison cutting can be somewhat delicate at times and requires a bit of finesse if the final product is to have a neat, pleasing, well-manicured appearance. Yet with any knife possessing a blade much more than four inches in length, your wrist and fingers find themselves too far away from the actual cutting site to accurately control the blade.

A look at any surgeon's array of scalpels confirms this; while he may have six or more different blade designs, none are more than 1¼ inches in length! Deer hunters who therefore opt for something in the neighborhood of three to 4½ inches maximum—the additional length needed more for leverage and faster work than anything else—are in the right ballpark.

As to cutting-edge design, straight, trailing-point and drop-point blades are the three most commonly preferred for field dressing; while I personally prefer drop-point blades, there is no advantage in any hunter being a conformist. Pick the one you enjoy using most and can handle with the greatest dexterity. This might be a fixed-blade sheath knife, a mid-size folder that goes into your pocket, or a slightly larger folder that rides in a lightweight belt pouch.

Pros and cons regarding the comparative functional aspects of fixed-blade knives and folders are relatively minor. Folders can be frustratingly difficult

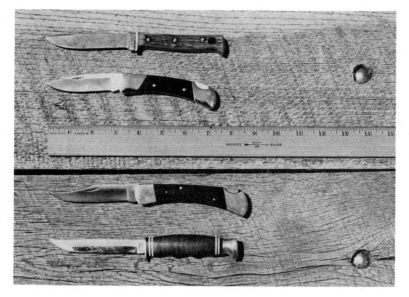

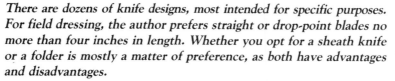

There are dozens of knife designs, most intended for specific purposes. For field dressing, the author prefers straight or drop-point blades no more than four inches in length. Whether you opt for a sheath knife or a folder is mostly a matter of preference, as both have advantages and disadvantages.

to clean after each use because all kinds of gunk can work its way down into the knife housing and hinges, yet it is imperative this be removed to ensure a sanitary cutting tool. Conversely, fixed-blade knives can be cleaned in a jiffy, but sometimes it is cumbersome to have their sheaths hanging on one's belt, particularly when repeatedly getting in and out of a Jeep or squatting down into the narrow seat of a portable tree stand.

The only practical solution is for the hunter to try different models and decide what works best for him, staying within the range of "short and light" knives. I like and use both knife designs, maintaining a special affection for Buck's folding Duke knife with a 4-inch drop-point blade, Buck's folding Ranger with a 4¼-inch upswept blade, Puma's Hunter's Pal with a 4-inch straight blade, and Kabar's Hunter with a 4-inch straight blade. Other quality, factory-made knives are produced by Schrade, Case, Kershaw, Gerber, and Camillus.

In addition to folders and fixed-blade knives suitable for field dressing deer, one other design some hunters show a liking for is the "Wyoming" knife. Its appearance is similar to a pair of brass knuckles in that there are finger holes for holding onto and wielding the device, but then two short blades that stick out in opposite directions. Technically, this is not a true knife but rather a gadget for holding replaceable, scimitar-shaped razor blades. In the hands of an expert, a Wyoming knife can be used to unzip a deer's abdominal region in a flash. But since its other cutting applications are very limited and impractical, I invariably reach for other types of knives when planning a hunt.

Going back to conventional fixed-blade knives and folders, there was a time many years ago when I was in favor of blades made of relatively soft carbon steel such as C-1095 because I could easily hone them razor sharp. Then, during the course of field dressing, all that was necessary was taking an occasional swipe across a whetstone to touch it up a bit. Now, I'm no longer content with such knives but prefer those of much harder steel that hold their edges through the duration of most cutting chores. Typically, this means a blade made from stainless steel alloy or high carbon steel. These knives can be awesomely difficult to sharpen if the hunter neglects them for prolonged periods. But otherwise, their edge-holding ability is impressive and allows the hunter to leave his whetstone in camp or at home, thereby eliminating just one more weighty nuisance bulging his already overloaded pockets.

In fact, once you've achieved a scalpel-sharp edge on a stainless or high-carbon-steel blade, and don't find immediate need to use it, it will remain sharp until you do get around to necessary cutting work. Less expensive, regular low-carbon steel suffers from gradual oxidation (rust), which causes it to slowly lose its edge even when just sitting around.

I've spent a lot of time discussing knife features because they play such an important role in the handling of venison. What I've said here applies in part to other knives that are considered in subsequent chapters, although different blade lengths and designs may be more suitable for specific cutting applications.

In addition to proper knives, there are several other essentials a deer hunter will need minutes after his deer is down. One often forgotten item is a long, rectangular plastic bag for the liver and heart. I recommend two discarded bread wrappers, one slipped inside the other for added strength. They're free and perfectly suited to a unique trick I devised long ago, but I'll keep the reader in suspense as to how they're actually used.

Another crucial item is a 20-foot hank of quarter-inch nylon rope with a tensile strength of not less than 400 pounds. Compared to hemp, nylon is impervious to rot or other deterioration. It's also stronger per diameter, and therefore lighter in weight, than ropes made of natural fibers. With this specific type of rope a hunter can accomplish three functions. He can use it to raise and lower his firearm or bow from a tree stand, to hang his deer if there will be a slight delay before it can be removed from the woods, or to drag the animal to camp.

Finally, the hunter should have made provisions in advance for hanging his deer at camp or home. This might be in the form of the venerable camp meatpole, but it can also be a handy tree limb, the rafters in his garage, or even the roof joists in an open-air shed. The hanging mechanism obviously must be strong enough to support the weight of a heavy animal, and the location should be shaded and breezy. Of critical concern, there should be no danger of birds or the neighbor's pets enjoying samples of your venison.

My pal and regular hunting partner Al Wolter not too fondly recalls how he learned this the hard way. After hanging his deer in his garage, he neglected to close the door, an apparently minor oversight, one might think. The following day, when preparing to butcher his deer, he went to the garage and immediately several *very* fat dogs waddled quickly past him. His deer, almost a skeleton, hung in mute testimony to what had happened, and ever since the memory has been a grim reminder of precautionary steps that must be taken to safeguard hard-earned venison from freeloaders.

Myths About Field Dressing

Perhaps no other aspect of deer hunting is so riddled with misconceptions and misinformation as the process of field dressing the animals. Every year millions of respectable, well-intentioned people—the kind who salute the flag every morning and help old ladies cross the street—seem to become villains when it comes to field care of their deer.

The majority of these vile practices perpetrated upon innocent venison are no reflection upon the hunter's integrity but are born of past conditioning. We're all products of our accumulated experiences, and when a young hunter is taught by his father that a deer's musk glands must be removed to prevent the meat from spoiling, why should that young hunter believe otherwise? And why shouldn't he, in turn, pass along the same absurd pearls of wisdom when the time comes to teach field care to his own son?

Fact of the matter is—and here is the paradox—many such wives' tales cause many problems and even wasted venison. It is important, therefore, to dispense with many such fables before considering proper field-dressing procedures.

The tarsal glands—those moist, dark tufts of hair located midway on the hocks of each hind leg—cease functioning when a deer dies. They also are situated a good distance from the prime venison of other body parts. Consequently, there is only one way for the tarsal glands to cause tainted or spoiled meat and that is when unskilled hunters begin slashing away at the glands with their knives, trying to remove them, and in so doing inadvertently cause oil from the gland ducts to come in contact with other parts of the deer.

I once watched in dismay as a young Colorado hunter feverishly attempted to remove the musk glands of a mule deer. By the time he was finished, sticky gland-scent stains randomly adorned the front of his jeans, one sleeve of his shirt, and both hands. His knife blade verily dripped of the stuff. Next he began quartering the meat, handling much of it close to his body as he then stuffed portions into cloth game sacks. I'd bet a nickle that venison later tasted like turpentine.

No doubt, millions of words of advice about tarsal glands will continue to echo through the mountains, but the entire subject can be summed up in one sentence. Exercise a bit of precaution to avoid touching, cutting into, or otherwise disturbing the musk glands and you'll have no trouble with them whatever.

At the top of the list of myths about field dressing is the one about cutting off a deer's various leg glands. Leave them alone because it is impossible for them to spoil the meat.

Neither is it necessary to plunge your knife blade into a deer's neck or throat to supposedly bleed an animal. What blood it does not lose on the ground moments after the shot will pump quickly into the chest cavity. You'll notice this when you open the deer up and the stuff literally pours out.

Cutting open the animal's neck region therefore accomplishes only two things. It ruins the hide, which right then and there cancels any plans you might have later to send your deer to a taxidermist. It also creates an unnecessary entrance into the body cavity through which blowflies, dirt, and other contaminants may enter and eventually spoil the meat.

Laughably, I've even read of hunters chopping off all four hooves of their deer before commencing field dressing, believing that not to do so invites a serious risk of cutting oneself. Were there any logic to this, why not also promptly cut off the antlers, which pose a far greater hazard to careless hunters?

Leave the hooves alone. They're actually not sharp at all but quite rounded at their edges due to constant abrasion from the earth. Besides, you don't want to hear a lot of snickering behind your back at the deer-checking station when you present an animal that has no feet.

Yet another horrendous practice I've witnessed on many occasions is opening up a deer "from stem to stern." What I mean is, after making an abdominal incision, many hunters continue cutting all the way through the chest, bearing down on their knife handles with both hands to cut through sternum and ribs, then continuing yet onward until they reach the base of the lower jaw. After that, they about-face, reach for an axe or saw, and literally do a hatchet job on the deer's pelvis.

Opening the chest region in such a manner, again, unnecessarily exposes too much meat to contamination. And attempting to split the pelvic arch, sometimes called the aitch bone, chiefly results in the bladder being punctured, the hindquarter roasts being at least superficially damaged, and jagged remnants of splintered bone telling all the world of the hunter's ineptness.

Many such methods of handling deer in the field culminate in venison that is absolutely horrible. Indeed, whenever I hear someone lament over his dislike for deer meat, claiming it is too "gamey," too strong, overly pungent, or too tough, I know instantly why the meat tasted so. Someone bungled one or more of the steps from field to kitchen. That someone either didn't take the time to pick out an animal in prime condition, botched the field-dressing procedure, transported the deer improperly, wreaked havoc during the butchering, or had no idea how to prepare various cuts of meat for the table, and therefore resorted to either guesswork or what grandpa taught him 30 years ago.

Basic Field-Dressing Steps

When your deer is down, there are two fundamental considerations. The first is reducing the temperature of the carcass in order to cool all those precious steaks and roasts until such time as they are secured in wrapped packages for the freezer. The second concern is all the while keeping the meat clean and free from contamination by dirt or insects. If these two matters are carefully attended to, nothing but smiles will grace your dinner table.

Field-dressing deer is the same no matter whether the species is a whitetail, mule deer, or blacktail since all have virtually identical anatomy. And the basic four-step procedure I recommend involves slitting open the belly, allowing the warm blood in the body cavity to drain away, removing the abdominal and chest organs, then removing the reproductive/excretory tracts.

1. To keep the animal and your work area as clean as possible, roll the deer onto its back, then maneuver the animal so that its head and shoulders are slightly elevated. Swing them around so they are on slightly higher ground than the lower body region of the deer, or use several rocks or pieces of deadwood to prop up the front shoulders.

Taking a minute to do this before opening the animal's body cavity will allow blood, intestines, and internal organs, as they spill out, to flow downhill and away from the carcass. If propping up the head and chest region of the deer is not possible and the ground is perfectly flat, use your hands to lift the deer's head after making the abdominal incision to facilitate drainage of blood. Then drag the animal forward six or eight feet onto clean ground so it is away from the pool of blood left behind.

1. To field-dress your deer, roll it over onto its back with its head slightly uphill if possible. If the animal starts to roll, brace with logs or rocks.

2. Making the abdominal incision is no more difficult than grasping between your thumb and forefinger a clump of belly hair and lifting. Simultaneously, use just the tip of your knife blade to slice a small "starter" hole about two inches in length. This should allow you, as you straddle the deer and face

2. Pinch a bit of abdominal skin between your fingertips, lifting, and making an inch-long slit.

the head, to insert the first two fingers of your left hand. Next, spread your fingers and lift them sharply upward. Then, between your spread fingers insert just the forward first inch of your knife blade, edge facing up, and guide the blade from the base of the reproductive organs down the centerline of the animal to the sternum (the breastbone, just where the ribs begin). It's an easy, one-minute operation. The reason for lifting the abdominal wall and using the knife with the blade edge facing up is to ensure that you do not inadvertently slice into the intestines lying directly below and perchance cause messy digestive matter to spill all over. If the animal tends to flop over onto one side or another, a partner can steady it by holding the two front legs upward. If no one is available to help, brace one side of the animal against a boulder, or brace both sides with dead logs.

As the abdominal incision is completed, the paunch and intestines will begin to bulge up and out. You can now set your knife aside briefly and pull them the remainder of the way out of the body cavity with your hands until you come to the diaphragm. This is a sheetlike wall of thin skin inside the body cavity that separates the lower intestinal organs from those higher up in the chest region. Use your knife to cut the diaphragm free by running the blade around the entire inside perimeter of the chest cavity to expose the lungs and heart.

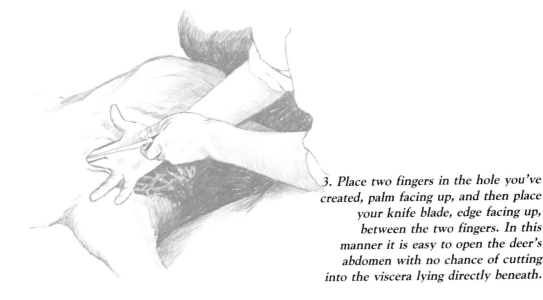

3. Place two fingers in the hole you've created, palm facing up, and then place your knife blade, edge facing up, between the two fingers. In this manner it is easy to open the deer's abdomen with no chance of cutting into the viscera lying directly beneath.

3. The next step is equally easy but just a tad messy, so take off your wrist watch and roll up your sleeves, as you'll be inserting your arms full length into the chest cavity. Those who are a bit squeamish about this might want to buy what's called a "gut kit," available from any sporting-goods store that carries deer-hunting supplies. It consists merely of lightweight, disposable, arm-length plastic gloves.

With the abdominal organs lying on the ground beside the deer, yet still attached to the pelvic region, extend one arm up into the chest cavity to the base of the neck and feel for the windpipe and esophagus. These will feel like two tubes, a soft, ¾-inch-diameter tube lying on top of a rigid, 1½-inch-diameter ribbed tube. Grasp the twin-tube assembly with your hand, then insert your knife (very carefully!) with the other hand and sever the tubes as high up in the neck as you can reach.

Withdraw the knife-holding hand and, still grasping the tubes with the other hand, begin pulling backward. As you continue pulling, the esophagus and windpipe will easily tear from their thin attachments and with them will come the heart and lungs. Pull them entirely free of the body cavity.

4. Sever the heart from its various restraining ligaments and set it nearby on clean grass, moss, or ferns to cool and drain. Then do the same with the liver, which is attached to the intestines from the abdominal region. Contrary to what you may have read elsewhere, deer do not have a gall bladder; hence, there is none to remove.

4. After freeing the diaphragm from the chest wall, reach far up into the neck region and sever the windpipe; then pull it back and out, along with the heart and lungs, which will come with it. Next, separate the heart and liver from the offal and set them aside.

5. Remove the reproductive/ excretory tract by using just the tip of your knife to encircle the anus; then carefully begin working deeper into the pelvic canal. Take care not to cut into the bladder, which is deep within the pelvic canal. See text for details of removing remainder of excretory/reproductive tract.

5. When you began field dressing, you were straddling the deer, facing the head. Now, turn around and face the opposite direction to facilitate the removal of the remainder of the lower intestines and the reproductive organs.

Extend your abdominal cut to the base of the penis (or, if it's a doe, make an oval cut around the udder and remove that flap of skin). Since the penis and testicles lie on top of the abdomen, a very shallow cut will allow them to be removed. Lift the penis gently and simply slice the skin around both sides of the organ, taking as little skin as possible, as this protects the valuable hindquarter meat lying directly beneath. Continue lifting and cutting, next going around the testicles; where the penis tubes enter the bladder cavity there is a bit of soft cartilage you can cut with your knife to increase your work area, but be careful not to puncture the bladder or related tubes. As you finally go around both sides of the testicles, your two knife cuts will briefly join together again, but an inch farther toward the rear they will have to separate once again to go entirely around the anus.

Going around the anus in such a manner will create a flap of skin around the orifice that you can grab with your fingertips. Because of the location of this part of a deer's anatomy, it can be a bit awkward to work on. Ideally, a hunter should have a partner on hand who can straddle the deer facing the rear while lifting the hind legs and pulling them forward, to fully expose the anal region as you face it. If no help is available, try to raise the animal's rump by placing a log beneath it or cradling it between rocks on either side.

After grasping the flap of skin you've cut around the anal orifice, use just the tip of your knife blade to begin cutting around the rectum, working progressively deeper and deeper into the pelvic canal just like coring an apple. However, the deeper you go, the closer you approach the bladder and care must be exercised not to slice into it or you'll have a flood of urine gushing all over. This is one reason why so many expert hunters prefer field dressing with knife blades no longer than four inches; a limited blade length prevents them from going too deeply and perhaps rupturing the bladder.

When you reach the point in which the rectum has been entirely encircled and cut free as deep as you can go, stop working from this direction and begin coming in the remainder of the way from the other (abdominal) side.

Gently push away as much lower intestine as possible with one hand, while with the other holding your knife begin to carefully separate the bladder from inside the pelvic canal. Usually, the bladder is a small, soft, pouchlike affair only partially filled with urine and therefore presents no problem. But if it seems quite full and distended, good advice is to pinch the ureter (the tube connecting the kidneys to the bladder) tightly closed with your fingertips, slice it free, aim it away from the deer, and then exert gentle hand pressure on the bladder to release the urine spray away from your work area.

Continue making your gentle knife cuts deeper and deeper into the pelvic canal. Soon cuts made from this direction will meet those previously made from the other side, and you'll be able to pull out the entire reproductive/excretory tract easily in one long, undamaged string.

All of this may sound terribly complicated and difficult but it's actually quite easy and quickly accomplished, once a hunter has learned the anatomy of a deer. Consider your first effort, even if a little less than professional, a learning experience. From that time on, subsequent deer can typically be field-dressed in less than ten minutes.

Your deer's entire insides have now been removed and if the weather is a bit cool you'll see steam rising from the body cavity, a sure sign your venison is beginning to rapidly cool. It's best now to grab the animal's legs and flip him over onto his belly so all four limbs extend outward in spraddle-legged fashion. This allows any remaining blood or body fluids to drain away. Leave the animal in this position for a full five minutes, meanwhile further trimming the heart and liver, cleaning your knife and hands, and taking a moment to catch you breath.

6. After the deer's insides have been removed, flop the animal onto its belly so it is spraddle-legged. This will allow remaining blood and body fluids to drain away quickly.

There are slight variations to the field-dressing method just described, and each hunter in time seems to find his own unique preferences and sequence of operation. Some like to have a small hank of cotton string in their pockets, which they use to tie off the urethra and lower intestine as added insurance these will not spill their contents in some unwanted place if accidently nicked by the knife blade. Other hunters also take the time to retrieve the kidneys from the offal on the ground if they are not still attached to the fat under the backbone. Others even delay field dressing altogether until the deer has been removed to camp; this is not so preposterous as it may initially sound.

I once participated in a deer hunt in North Carolina, as a guest of a large hunting club, where it was customary to stage deer drives. It also was standard procedure, when a deer was brought down, for all hands to temporarily suspend the drive, pick the deer up and bodily carry it to the meatpole at the nearby clubhouse. Usually within ten or 15 minutes the deer was hanging by its antlers from an overhead beam, with a large washtub placed on the ground between the deer's hind legs. It was an amazingly easy and quick matter, then, to open up the deer and have everything inside immediately avalanche out and into the washtub, a tactic designed to keep everything, including the venison, immaculately clean.

Assuming you're hunting alone, however, and you're still in the woods with your deer, and it has had ample opportunity to drain, now flip it back over onto its back again. Use several handfuls of dry grass or moss to wipe the inside of the body cavity of any remaining blood clots or other debris. Don't be too fussy about this as you'll be cleaning up the carcass to a greater extent later in camp. If there will be some delay before you or your partners can begin dragging your deer out of the woods, insert a stick crossways in the body cavity to spread the loose abdominal walls and further speed cooling of the meat.

7. After the deer has been drained, drag it a few yards away from your clearing site, turn it over onto its back, and place a stick in the field-dressing incision to speed cooling.

I mentioned earlier that having a plastic bag for the heart and liver is essential. The reason I recommend a discarded bread wrapper is because of its long, narrow shape. Place the heart and liver inside, then place the bag

8. Before dragging your deer out, secure the heart and liver in a plastic bag inside the body cavity, with the tail of the bag coming out the bullet hole and tied in a knot to hold it.

inside the chest cavity of the animal. Next, twist the long tail of the bread wrapper and poke it out through the bullet hole in the lung region. On the outside, grab the visible tail, pull on it until the liver/heart bag inside is snug against the rib cage, then tie a large knot in the tail on the outside of the hide. Your liver and heart now ride out of the woods inside the body cavity of the deer, which sure beats having to carry the bag separately or trying to cram the odd-shaped, heavy glob of meat in your coat pocket!

CHAPTER 4

Getting Your Buck Out of the Woods

I T CAN BE a heart-wrenching experience to hunt long and hard without even glimpsing an acceptable buck worth taking, and then when you finally do level your sights upon some monster, come to the decision to pass up the shot. This is exactly what happened one fall in the rugged mountains of Teton County just outside of Jackson, Wyoming. I was looking for one very special deer that would give me the best of both attributes most hunters diligently search for: heavy antlers and prime venison.

On the sixth day of my hunt with outfitter Burt Enterline we finally saw such a buck not more than 100 yards away. The only trouble was, that 100-yard distance was a vertical drop pitching straight down into the bowels of a rocky chasm bordered by sheer walls. For five minutes my rifle sights were on the buck's lung region, as he passively nibbled at shoots of buffalo grass in the bottom. I could have nailed him easily, and undoubtedly the deer would have proved to be my largest to date.

My mind was changed when Burt slowly leaned in my direction and brought me to my senses by whispering, "What in the hell are we going to do after you kill that deer? How in blazes will we ever get him out of that hole?"

If we'd had a Jeep with a winch mounted on the front, I could have ridden the cable down into the chasm and hooked onto the deer, then Enterline could have hauled the two of us out. Or, if we'd had 100 yards of stout rope, we could have cut the deer up and lifted it out piecemeal in gamebags. But since we had neither rope nor winch, the only prospect, if I shot that handsome deer, would be to hand-and-toe-hold our way down the sheer walls and then sit down and begin eating, without the foggiest notion how we'd ever climb back out again.

Naturally—reluctantly—I passed up the shot, and once I was mentally committed to that decision actually sighed a bit in relief.

A key element in any deer-hunting adventure, as I learned on this outing, is don't shoot what you can't bring in, no matter how impressive any given deer may be. This is by no means a suggestion that hunters should be so intimidated by upside-down real estate they never venture far from roads or trailheads.

But it is important that savvy sportsmen constantly size up the territory in which they are pursuing big game, with an eye upon how a deer eventually taken can best be removed to camp or a waiting vehicle. This evaluation can involve a good deal of personal restraint upon occasion, particularly when the final day of the season is rapidly approaching and your license still remains unfilled. Yet consider the even less propitious alternatives. One sure way *not* to win a popularity contest among your hunting partners is to wander into deer camp late at night with the news that you've just slain the heaviest buck ever taken in Potter County and that he lies only six miles back in the hinterland, in the bottom of a canyon and on the other side of a river. The excessive delay that is certain to follow in removing such a deer from the field may even result in damaged or spoiled venison.

What, then, are the limits? How far is a reasonable distance to transport a deer from the kill site to camp or vehicle? Well, an instant before squeezing the trigger, mentally examine all factors involved, such as access to roads or trails, the possible use of a four-wheel-drive vehicle, packhorse, or backpack frame for at least a portion of the journey, the rugged nature of the landscape, how many hunters are available to assist, and of course the existing temperature and weather conditions. Depending on the circumstances, as little as 100 yards may be too far, as we learned on our Wyoming hunt. Yet in other situations, lugging a deer carcass across several miles of countryside may be entirely justified.

Just remember, while it's true that the biggest deer generally are taken far in the backcountry, and while it's high adventure to be an explorer, no advantage is gained by killing a deer in such an idiotic location that the joyous camaraderie of your deer camp turns immediately sour (and perhaps your venison, too).

Carrying Methods to Avoid

As in field dressing deer, reams of misinformation seem to be perennially circulated about suitable methods of removing deer from the field to home or camp. Getting a deer out of the woods invariably takes more than just a strong back and a weak mind. Since I've always been adverse to hard work, I've tried every conceivable method of transporting big game home in the hopes of lucking upon small tricks that might make life easier. Most of what I've learned is what *doesn't* work very well. Since those ineffective methods only add to one's labor they are worth mentioning here in hopes the reader may save himself some of the agony and bone-weary hours of trial and error I've endured over the years.

One ludicrous idea that never fails to appear in at least several sportmen's magazines every year has to do with two hunters carrying a deer that is trussed upside-down to a long pole that they support over their shoulders. It's a classic hunting scene that makes the hunters look like macho woodsmen, but it's totally impractical. No matter how high the pole is lifted, or how high the deer is tied to the pole, the antlers predictably grab every bush or branch tip. Even more critical, the high center of gravity of the deadweight mass causes the carcass to shift and sway around, a tendency which is further aggravated by the irregular footfalls of the hunters carrying the weight. Figure that with a 180-pound buck to tote, plus the weight of the pole, each man has over 100 pounds of bouncing weight on his shoulder. The end result eventually proves to be shoulders and necks rubbed raw and unrelenting lower-back pain.

There are only two situations for which I recommend this procedure. One is when a deer is killed far back in tropical habitat and therefore must be carried bodily to avoid being dragged through water and swamp muck. The second instance, even more rare, is when a hunter must ensure his deer hide is entirely undamaged because he plans to have a full-body mount made of a special trophy.

I'm sure you've also seen the so-called Indian travois method in which two long poles are tied together at one end, the deer cradled in the middle, and the apex of the poles then supported over the hunter's shoulders while the opposite, widespread ends are allowed to drag on the ground. I decided to try this method once and began by cutting the required three-inch-diameter saplings (about eight feet in length). Jeepers, the saplings themselves were so heavy I instantly knew there was no way I could then load a deer onboard and heft the weight to my shoulders.

Two other methods of removing deer from the field may actually get you shot! One involves tying all four of the deer's feet together, lifting it by the hooves, and then carrying the deer almost like a big purse or shoulder bag. This is particularly dangerous on public hunting lands but even unwise on private property as well, because trespassers and poachers never heed posted signs. Suddenly, some trespassing dummy sees flashes of buckskin and a flopping white tail through a screen of cover and begins blasting away, not knowing there's a partially hidden hunter (you!) carrying a deer behind that cover.

The other insane method is the so-called fireman's carry in which a deer is draped around the hunter's shoulders as he holds onto the legs. It is difficult for me to understand how national outdoor magazines can eternally preach hunting safety, then actually publish pictures recommending the fireman's carry when deer hunting. When using the fireman's carry, a man from the waist up is unrecognizable as anything but a deer and this is a dandy invitation to draw gunfire. It's a moot point anyway because no one ever tells you how to get that heavy, floppy deer carcass up onto your shoulders in the first place (or how to later remove the blood and body oil stains that are sure to ooze onto your new jacket). Another question is, what happens if the hunter should somehow succeed in lifting that 170-pound deer carcass onto his shoulders but then, during the hike to camp, stumbles and falls? Likely as not, an antler tine will go into his body like a dagger, or the enormous weight of the animal crashing down on top of him will snap his neck like a piece of dry spaghetti. Next time you see a picture of the fireman's carry, merely chuckle and file it in your "not for me" department.

One other method commonly used by hunters that is not quite so dangerous is the simple matter of grabbing a deer's antlers with both hands behind the back and dragging it. Although this practice is widespread, I cannot recommend it without due words of precaution.

Simply grabbing a deer's antlers and beginning to drag is a common way of removing a buck from the field. But this is recommended only for short distances and only for hunters who are in good health.

If the drag is a long one, and one's youth has long since slipped over the mountain, all kinds of back and shoulder problems may ensue. The reason for this is that the deadweight of the animal on the ground presents a very low center of gravity, requiring the hunter to bend low to grab onto it and remain in this crouched position through the duration of the drag. This results in tremendous strain upon both the vertebrae of the back and its contiguous musculature, often causing you to remember the dragging experience far longer than you would have liked. Also, should you slip on wet leaves or snowpack, there's at least a fair possibility of sharp antler tines going into your calf muscles.

Carrying Methods That Work

I noted the absurdity of tying a deer carcass to a long pole which is then carried on the shoulders of two hunters. However, a variation of this technique does indeed work well if, for some reason, it is imperative that the deer not be allowed to touch the ground.

Turn the deer over so it is lying on its back with its legs up in the air, and then lay a two-inch-diameter pole, about seven feet in length, along each side of the deer. Next, lash the carcass between the poles. In this manner, two hunters can easily lift the load to waist level and carry it just like a stretcher, and they can just as easily set the load down to rest occasionally if need be. The deer doesn't flop around because it now has a much lower center of gravity and its weight is stabilized between two poles instead of swinging from one. Further, the poles themselves don't wreak destruction upon one's shoulders or neck, although I do recommend wearing gloves to avoid inevitable abrasion of bark from the poles against one's hands.

A reversed travois technique is another neat trick. Make a travois in the usual method and then lash an additional cross-member between, and extending beyond, the widespread legs. When two hunters are present, each can grab the convenient handles afforded by the cross-member with the apex of the poles (ordinarily at one's shoulders) dragging on the ground.

Two hunters can also drag a deer by the antlers. This is much more sensible than a single hunter attempting this particular drag method with his hands behind his back, as each hunter can stand at almost full height without bending over much. And since they are positioned somewhat to either side of the deer's head, this lessens the possibility of the antlers wounding the lower anatomy if one of the hunters should momentarily stumble.

A lone hunter has fewer options, of course. One is using some type of shoulder harness. These are available in sporting-goods stores and are made

The stretcher method of carrying out deer is good if you don't want the carcass to touch the ground.

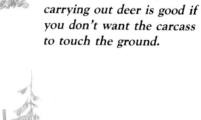

Another option for moving a deer is the reversed travois. With the carcass raised somewhat, two hunters can easily transport it over very rough ground with a minimum of effort.

Special shoulder harnesses for dragging deer are available, but the author has found that the animal's antlers tend to snag in trailside brush.

of the same type of webbed seat-belt material used in automobiles. The most common designs have a belt that buckles around the waist, a diagonal shoulder strap, and a somewhat longer strap going off the backside that can be secured to the deer's head.

Not too long ago I tested one of these devices by dragging a heavy log around my backyard and found the going surprisingly easy. Then, later in the season, I killed a fat doe and found the dragging easier still. I was pleased as punch, until the following year when I killed a buck and ran into all kinds of difficulties. The antlers kept digging into the ground or grabbing roots, stobs, and brush, continually and annoyingly jerking me to a halt. To extricate the deer from its hold, I had to back it up several feet. There has to be a way of solving this dilemma. One possibility I aim to try as soon as possible is dragging a buck backwards by the hind legs, so the natural curvature of the antlers allows them to slide right over tangles and obstacles. I just wonder whether dragging against the grain will spoil the hide.

Meanwhile, until something better evolves, there is one way of dragging a deer that is best of all, that I and most other experienced hunters rely upon most often. It's no more complicated than using a short length of rope and a stick of deadwood that is about two inches in diameter by two feet in length.

First raise the deer's front hooves and place them behind the antlers (or behind the ears if it's a doe) and lash them to the neck so they are up, out of the way, eliminating their resistance against the ground and giving you a somewhat pointed object to pull through the cover. Next, tie the other end of the rope to the center of the deadwood stick and begin wrapping it around until the stick is about two feet from the deer's head. At this time, take a half-hitch around the stick with the rope so it won't have a tendency to begin unwinding.

Now place your hands behind your back, one holding either side of the drag stick, lift the head and front shoulders of the deer slightly off the ground,

The easiest drag method is to tie a rope around the deer's neck and the other end around a stick. Two hunters can easily drag the deer, as can one with his hands behind his back. To prevent front hooves from dragging against the ground, tie them behind antlers.

and begin heading for camp. Compared to grabbing onto the antlers and heaving-ho, this method allows you to stand almost at full height while dragging. And since there is about a 1½-foot distance from your backside to the antlers, there's little chance of them ever gouging your own hide.

Ideally, the best thing is using this drag method with a partner, each grabbing onto one side of the stick. It is amazing how easy this makes the job, especially if you have gloves to protect your hands. When your right hand and arm get tired (your partner will be on the opposite side, using his left hand and arm), merely stop to catch your breath and then switch places for a while.

This unique method of dragging deer is so much easier than any other method, in fact, that two not overly large deer that happen to be killed in the same vicinity can be dragged simultaneously!

One brand-new gadget now on the market seems to have a good deal of merit. It's a molded-handle affair joined to a length of heavy-duty aircraft cable. The cable is looped around the base of the antlers and then secured in a slot in a block of aluminum. The hunter then has a handy, comfortable handle he can use to drag his deer.

This ingenious device for dragging deer has a wire cable that fits around the base of the antlers.

When secured, a comfortable handle allows the hunter to drag his deer easily.

When dragging a deer by any method, take it slow and easy, particularly if you're over 40 years old. Pace yourself. Stop every 50 yards or so, even if you do not feel overly tired. This "rest time" allows you to scout ahead a bit for the easiest drag route. In this manner you can spot and then take advantage of slight variations in the terrain, avoiding even short uphill drags and following the best trail to skirt rock formations, blowdowns, or other obstacles. Nearly always, it's best to take a slightly longer route if it enables you to stay on level ground or drag downhill. I've even been known to briefly drag my deer in the *opposite* direction of camp if it means eventually coming to dry, powdery snow, damp leaves, pine needles, or some other terrain surface that allows the remainder of the drag to see the deer carcass effortlessly slide along.

If there are four hunters in the group, all the better. Two can begin dragging the deer. The third carries all the rifles, binoculars, and other heavy gear. The fourth works farther ahead, finding the best trail, pushing aside logs, and clearing away brush or branches. Then, every 200 yards or so, they alternate positions.

At this point I should probably backtrack for just a moment to describe what to do if a deer cannot immediately be removed from the field. Often, this is the case with animals that are so heavy the hunter must return to camp for assistance. Or it may simply be too dark, after the animal has been field-dressed, to risk dragging until the following morning.

Before the hunter leaves his animal, he should ensure that it will have maximum opportunity to begin cooling, while remaining protected from birds or animals.

Hanging the deer is the best bet, and the easiest method is to find a stout limb, tie a rope around the antlers, and lift the animal as high as possible. Likely as not, all you'll succeed in doing is getting the forward part of the deer off the ground, with the rear hooves still touching the earth, but this is okay since the cooling night air can still circulate entirely around the carcass.

Or use three stout saplings about eight feet in length. Lay them, forming a pyramid at their ends, over the deer's head and lash them tightly to the antlers. Then begin raising the poles to form a teepee by alternately lifting and pushing inward the base of each pole one foot at a time.

If neither of these means is practical, at least try to place deadwood logs or rocks beneath the deer carcass to allow air to circulate underneath. And always, before leaving, ensure that sticks are placed crosswise in the belly to spread the abdominal walls and allow cool air to enter the body cavity.

To keep birds or animals at bay during your absence, lightly covering a deer on the ground with pine boughs or branches is very effective, although

If a hunter cannot remove his deer from the field until the following day, he should try to lift it off the ground. Hang the deer from a tree limb or fashion a tripod from lightweight poles.

there is no logical reason for this to deter predators. Another guile that is especially well suited to protecting a deer hanging from a tree limb or sapling pyramid is tying some article of your clothing to the antlers. A well-fermented t-shirt works as well as anything. It flaps around in the breeze and also exudes a strong man-scent into the night air, discouraging even the most desperate wildlife creatures from bothering your cache.

Horse-Packing Your Deer

Nine times in ten a hunter who has successfully collected his deer will find he's within relatively easy dragging distance of a road or trail. This is typically the case when whitetail hunting. There are some situations, however, in which whitetails are taken in remote places, especially in the northern border states and the Canadian provinces. And mule deer and blacktails taken in the western and Pacific coastal states characteristically fall in rough terrain far from even the thin threads of cattle trails.

In any of these situations, dragging a deer all the way to camp or a waiting vehicle may be impossible and this leaves only three choices. You'll probably not seriously consider the first option, hiring a helicopter to fly in and hover overhead while dropping a sky-hook to you and your deer. Don't laugh. I heard of a millionaire Hollywood movie producer doing that very thing!

The other alternatives—far more realistic approaches—are using either your back or a horse's back to transport your venison.

The easiest, of course, is leading a packhorse to camp with your deer meat aboard. Most hunters obviously don't own horses (or mules), but in those states where they are most likely to be needed for hunting work they are widely available for rental. Check the Yellow Pages of a phone directory, the classified ads in local newspapers, or ask the nearest rancher.

Even though horses or mules may not be playing a day by day role in your hunting activities, it's wise to learn which particular ranchers in your vicinity have them available. Most likely you'll be able to navigate your jeep fairly close to the kill site and can retrieve your deer by dragging it the remaining distance. But it's nice to know, if your deer runs into jumbled real estate before dropping, or if you sprain your ankle, just where to go locally to obtain help in bringing out your animal.

Rarely do ranchers simply hire out horses or mules and let strangers drive away with them in transport trailers. In other words, it's the rule, when you rent a horse, that you hire the owner for a few hours as well; he knows exactly how to bridle the animal, which type of saddles or packcarriers to use and how to cinch them in place, how to load game meat, how to tie diamond hitches, how to control the animal (which is sure to be unfamiliar to you), and all the rest. It will cost more than just a couple of bucks to remove your deer from the outback in this manner, but at the same time you save worry, hassle, and responsibility because the owner of the animal does all the loading, packing, and lashing.

However, in the event that you and your partners are deer hunting on a private ranch, or have hired an outfitter to take you into the high country, and horses or mules are a daily part of your camping, travel, and hunting activities, knowing a few basics about horsepacking is well worthwhile.

Probably the most crucial thing to keep in mind is that while horses and mules do a splendid job of carrying out their appointed tasks, and are incredibly sure-footed even in upside-down terrain in pitch darkness, I have never met a single one that even remotely enjoyed having some species of wild-game animal strapped onto its back. In fact, stories abound in western big-game camps about packhorses spooking and tearing off down the mountain, running wild-eyed for miles all the way to the barn while dragging a ragged array of hides, antlers, and meat bags behind them.

It is imperative, therefore, that packhorses never be unduly disturbed or alarmed or given reason to suspect danger. The most common way of accomplishing this is by covering the horse's head and eyes before walking toward it with animal parts or attempting to load such things on the horse's back. A lightweight hunting jacket is ideal for this. It can be used to cover the upper part of the horse's head, without impairing its breathing, and if the sleeves are tied lightly beneath the animal's chin, it will hold the blinders in place.

While extremely large animals such as elk and moose are almost always quartered before being loaded onto packhorses, deer generally are loaded whole. This can be an exercise in frustration even when two hunters are attempting to heft the load, but a few tricks of the trade make the job easier if not entirely fun.

First, tie the animal's reins to something to discourage it from sidestepping away during the loading procedure. Then, after blindfolding the critter, drag the deer up to the side of the horse and with your partner use the "Armstrong" method of lifting the deer head-first/belly-down so it drapes equally over either side of the animal's back.

Another ruse is to position the horse as close as possible to a rock outcropping or some other terrain feature that is as high as the animal's withers; then drag the deer a short distance around and come in from the topside so the deer can be easily scooted from the ledge a few feet sideways onto the horse's back.

Getting a heavy buck onto a horse's back requires ingenuity, hard work, and a knowledge of horses and their behavior. The horse should be tethered and blindfolded while loading a carcass on its back.

A third and even easier tactic in timbered country is to hoist the deer aloft with a rope or small block and tackle so it is hanging several feet above the ground from a tree limb. Then, move the horse in close and begin slowly lowering the deer as a partner carefully guides it downward to settle equally upon either side of the horse's back.

Whatever the logistics allow, the next thing to keep in mind, as the deer is being lashed down, is to ensure that the antlers are tied up and out of the way so there is no chance they will gouge the horse's back or ribs during the ride out. It may even be necessary to pad the antlers with burlap or someone's hunting coat.

Backpacking Your Deer

In situations in which horses are not available, or cannot be used due to the inhospitable nature of the terrain, you must become the beast of burden yourself and carry the deer out on your back. This is why I always have in camp, or back in my vehicle, the following items: a tubular packframe made of lightweight magnesium or aluminum, several muslin gamebags, a 20-foot length of thin nylon lashing cord, a heavy-duty folding knife with a small saw blade in its housing, and a canteen of water. Seldom are these ever needed on an average deer hunt, but when that fateful day does come along (it will, sooner or later) they are worth their weight in gold.

With your deer hanging from a tripod arrangement as described earlier, or from a tree limb, or lying on its back with its body cavity walls propped open, hike to your vehicle to obtain your packing-out essentials. This allows you to carry out the deer liver and heart on the first trip and to simultaneously relieve yourself of your rifle, ammo, binoculars, and other gear. You can also exchange your heavy hunting coat for a lightweight jacket but be sure, when returning to your deer, that you continue to wear your safety orange hunting vest.

After returning to the kill site, use your knife's saw blade to remove the deer's four lower legs at the knee joint to lighten the carcass by 12 pounds. Next, cut your deer in half. This will allow you to pack the animal to your vehicle in only two trips, carrying a maximum weight of about 65 to 75 pounds per trip. To split the animal into front and back halves, cut both sides to the spine between the second and third ribs from the rear, then use your saw blade to sever the backbone.

Should the deer be an especially large one, it may be prudent to reduce it to even smaller carrying portions. If there's any doubt as to how much you can carry, it's always recommended to make three easy trips rather than trying to do it in two and finding yourself so physically drained you begin stumbling and become accident-prone on the hike back to camp.

There are several ways to reduce a deer to three loads, depending upon the weather, logistics of the hunt, and personal preferences. One method is hanging the deer (if it's not already) and removing the entire hide and head (a considerable weight!), then halving the deer in the usual manner. This leaves the back half of the deer for one trip out; the front half for the next; and the rolled-up hide, head, and horns for the final journey.

Or, do not skin out the deer but merely remove the head and neck where they join the body at the front shoulder. The first trip out, while you're still fresh, should see you carrying the slightly heavier back half of the deer, with the lighter weight front half and head/neck parts reserved for the second and third trips.

Over the years, any hunter will find the packing-out procedure that suits him best, but whenever possible I always try to leave as much hide covering the venison as possible. The hide protects the deer meat from precipitation, trail grime, bumps and bruises, and other unknowns that can result in damaged venison.

Whenever it is indeed necessary to remove the hide from all or large portions of meat, leaving them exposed, gamebags come into use. I prefer tightly woven muslin bags, which allow air circulation to cool the meat, yet they are quite durable and offer complete protection from dirt and insects.

Another tip I've found useful, if the weather permits, is to hang your deer in the field and begin packing out until the following day. The cold night air will rigidly firm up the meat, making it far easier to handle than when it is warm and soft. Obviously, hot weather—higher than 55 degrees during midday—precludes this approach; when it's hot you'll want to get your meat back to camp as quickly as humanly possible.

No hunter should experience much difficulty tying the front half, rear half, or head/neck portion of a deer to his packframe, but a few words of advice are nevertheless in order.

To begin with, take whatever amount of time is necessary to balance the load before tightly lashing it down. You don't want to find yourself carrying a lopsided load, as this invites a sprained ankle on the greater-weight-bearing foot. Try to distribute the meat evenly, so it is shoving straight down on the centerline of the packframe.

Also, try to position the weight as high as possible (within reason) on the packframe. This will allow you to maintain a normal upright stance while hiking, rather than being hunched over. The advantage here, particularly if you have a waist belt on your pack, is that your hips and strong upper leg regions can help bear the brunt of the weighty load rather than the back alone having the entire responsibility.

In wilderness regions, there may be no alternative except to cut up your deer in the field and pack it out 60 pounds at a time on your back. When hunting such areas, bring along a lightweight packframe, gamebags, and nylon rope.

Lashing muslin gamebags to your packframe poses a greater problem, since the lumpy, irregular loads will tend to flop around and throw you off balance with each step. I like to twist the neck of each gamebag, slip a rope noose around the neck, then tie the neck as high as possible on the packframe (if you have two such bags, position them evenly to balance the load). With the necks of the bags tied off and holding the weight as high as possible, then criss-cross your rope back and forth to hold the middle and bottom portions of the bag in place. If you want to go to the trouble of packing additional gear, a lightweight roll of wide duct tape is perfect for lashing odd-shaped meat bags to a packframe. The stuff is sticky and super tough, easily conforms to irregular shapes, and holds them securely in place.

Any time you're carrying venison parts in which deer hide is exposed (especially the head or antlers!) on your back, take additional precautions so that some dolt doesn't mistake you for a buck sneaking through the puckerbrush. This is why I always save (at home) old fluorescent orange vests that have fallen into disrepair and no longer can be used for hunting. I use scissors to cut the bright plastic into wide ribbons and always keep at least several stowed in one of my coat pockets to later be tied to my packframe or a deer I'm dragging out of the woods. During the big-game hunting seasons, many ranchers even adorn their packhorses and mules with these highly visible streamers so their animals are not mistaken for elk or big deer.

When packing out, it also does no harm to continually belt out the chorus line of your favorite Broadway tune (if you ever hear someone singing "Oklahoma" in Colorado's high country, it's me!).

CHAPTER 5

Camp Care of Deer Meat

OUTSIDE your mountain cabin the dark chill of night is beginning to settle like a shroud over the landscape and sparkles of frost are littering the ground like broken glass. The wind is howling ominously and there are spits of sleet in the air, but at this precise time and moment nothing in the world could possibly dampen your spirits, for you are more content than you've been since this time twelve months ago. Only a dozen paces from the front door a single handsome buck hangs from a birch limb in testimony to your hunting skills, the discomfort you've endured, and the long days of just plain hard work you've willingly surrendered. It's the first deer to arrive in camp and you're both proud and satisfied that you've earned every ounce of your winter's supply of venison.

Inside the rustic log cabin a crackling fire is invitingly warm; in stocking feet, you lean back in your chair and have yet another sip of your hot toddy. The smug look on your face begins drawing a rapid-fire burst of good-natured ribbing from your partners.

"I didn't know there were any retarded deer in these woods," one hunter laughs.

"Or blind ones," another adds, peering out the window at your buck.

"How many shots did you need?" someone else asks. "Seems like we heard at least a dozen."

"Too bad you've filled your tag already," another partner coyly laments, "because now you don't have a chance at that real monster we've been seeing on King Mountain."

"Oh well," still another partner banters, "at least now we've got a full-time camp cook and someone to chop wood and haul water."

You take it all in stride, the smile on your face stretching even wider; it's all part of the close camaraderie of your annual deer camp and you wouldn't trade these precious memories for all the oil in Prudhoe Bay.

Besides, although your *shooting* is officially over for the season, the total hunting experience still is far from concluded. Legally, you can continue to tramp through the popple thickets working as a driver to try and help your partners collect their deer. And you can lend a hand field dressing and then dragging out other animals that are sure to be harvested before the week is over. And as soon as another deer is taken by someone else, you can begin dishing out a little playful ribbing yourself.

Meanwhile, your own deer hanging outside is going to require a good bit of attention during upcoming days. You'll want to ensure that the venison remains cool and protected from flying and crawling marauders, and you'll want to clean the carcass for the trip home. Your mind is buzzing with things to remember and steps to follow, but right now other things take precedence. Like throwing another log on the fire, graciously accepting another congratulatory slap on the back, and sipping once more from your hot mug, for these are among the rare things in life that keep men from growing old.

Hanging Your Deer

As soon as deer have been transported back to camp they are traditionally hung from some type of overhead device. I prefer a stout tree limb because little work is involved compared to fabricating a horizontal meatpole supported by upright pilings driven into the ground. Also, if it's still early in the season and the weather is warm, leaves on the trees will help to shade your animal carcass from bright sunlight. A similar tactic is to lay a horizontal pole between two trees, supported by crotches in their trunks or limbs. If suitable trees are not handy, an alternative is to fashion a tripod of long sapling poles lashed together at the apex.

Whatever the specific design of the hanging mechanism, however, their purposes are all the same: Namely, to get the animal up and off the ground so it can more conveniently be worked upon, so the carcass will remain clean of dirt, so ground-crawling critters won't bother it, and so air can better circulate to facilitate cooling.

Visit almost any camp and you'll see many deer hanging by their heads while others are hanging by the hind legs, their owners claiming the matter is no more than personal preference.

There are several reasons why I distinctly prefer hanging deer by the hind legs. With the carcass in this position, remaining body heat is free to rise and easily escape. Conversely, if you hang a deer by the antlers, rising body heat has a tendency to be trapped in the chest cavity, which prevents cooling of the neck and front shoulder areas as quickly as otherwise would occur.

Also, the vast majority of a deer's blood, lymph, and other body fluids are located in the front half of the body. Most of these fluids have been removed during earlier field-dressing activities, but there may still be just a bit remaining in the deer's smaller veins and arteries and in some intramuscular spaces. When the animal is hung, these liquids will begin to slowly drain away. This is all to the good, but you'll want these fluids to exit as quickly as possible, not slowly seep down over and through the carcass and perhaps cause spoilage or impart the venison with objectionable flavors.

If you'll recall, during field-dressing operations the windpipe and esophagus are severed high up in the neck region. Therefore, if the deer is hung by the hind legs, any residual body fluids wanting to drain away will simply follow a natural course downhill through the now wide open windpipe/esophagus region and quickly pass out through the nostrils and mouth without contacting any valuable cuts of meat. In fact, a day or two later you'll notice a small puddle on the ground directly beneath the animal's head.

To hang a deer by the hind legs, first make a two-inch-long slit with a knife through the thin skin separating the hock of each rear leg from the Achilles tendon. Then insert through these two holes the opposite ends of a gambrel, tie a rope to its top-center, and hoist the deer aloft.

My favorite gambrel is one made for me long ago by my pal and hunting partner Mike Wolter. He constructed it in his workshop by using an acetylene torch to heat and then bend a length of cold-rolled steel rod and then welded meat hooks on each end. In sporting-goods stores you can also buy big-game gambrels made from aluminum rod. They are not terribly sturdy but they're inexpensive (about five dollars) and they get the job done. Other hunters I've known have made their own gambrels from scraps of reinforcing rod, steel pipe, and even bar stock. If none of these approaches suits you, buy a heavy-duty livestock gambrel at a feed or farm supply store (obtain the smaller size intended for hogs, not the jumbo model designed for beef steers).

Always use a woven or braided nylon rope (with a tensile strength of at least 400 pounds) with your chosen gambrel for hanging a deer. Ropes made of natural fibers are not to be trusted because they deteriorate quickly by rotting from the inside out, making them look deceptively strong until suddenly they part, which may cause your deer to come crashing down to the ground.

In a camp shared by several hunting partners, deer can easily be hung by merely throwing a rope over a high limb or meatpole and then heaving-ho

Best way to hang deer is from the hind legs, by making slits through the skin just beneath the Achilles tendon and then inserting a gambrel.

Inexpensive factory-made gambrels, like the one at top, do a good job. The bottom gambrel is the author's favorite, a heavy-duty model custom-made by Mike Wolter.

to raise the carcass until the head is approximately two feet off the ground. However, if you're alone, you might want to use one of those miniature block and tackle affairs that are advertised in mail-order catalogs (price tag, about ten bucks). Typically, they consist of six-inch-long aluminum sidewalls with a series of nylon pulleys inside and about 25 feet of nylon rope. All advertising claims to the contrary, you cannot use one of these gizmos to lift 1,000 pounds with one hand, but using two hands to lift a deer off the ground is indeed a piece of cake.

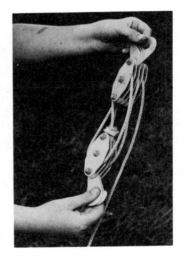

Lifting a deer onto a meatpole, or hanging it from a tree limb, is not difficult if several strong backs are available to help. Otherwise, a lightweight block and tackle makes a one-man job much easier.

Initial Meat-Care Procedures

At this point I'm going to discuss various venison-care activities every hunter sooner or later must attend to. The sequence in which these tasks are performed may vary, depending upon average daily air temperatures, prevailing weather conditions, and so on.

Generally, when my deer arrives in camp, the first order of business, even before hanging the animal, is removing the heart and liver from their plastic bag and placing the two organs in a clean pail filled with water and one cup of salt. It's even wise to cut the liver into two or three large pieces to expose the inside, although this is not necessary with the much smaller heart.

Slosh the organ pieces around in the water to remove surface debris, such as bits of dirt or pieces of moss or leaves, as well as large exterior blood clots. In a few minutes the water will turn bright red. Dump this water out and add a fresh quantity of salted water. Rub the liver gently with your hands and poke your fingers inside the large arteries of the heart to further loosen and dislodge blood clots from inside. When the water turns bright red again, discard it and replenish the supply with clean salted water once more.

Now, allow the heart and liver to soak at least six to eight hours. This soaking will thoroughly purge both organs of any remaining traces of blood. Likely as not, you'll want to change the water again after three or four hours.

It's unfortunate but many hunters leave the heart and liver in the woods when field dressing their deer. This is a shameful waste of meat that, nationwide, undoubtedly amounts to millions of pounds of delicious food each year. Even if you do not personally care for liver or heart (later, I'll reveal some special recipes that may very well change your mind!), there are sure to be others in camp who would appreciate having them.

After the liver and heart have undergone a minimum six-hour soaking period, remove them from the water, set the organs on a drainboard for 10 or 15 minutes, then place them in a plastic bag in your refrigerator or camping cooler. Traditionally, liver and heart are consumed in camp for dinner the first night or the very next morning for breakfast. They also can be properly wrapped and frozen for later use, although fresh liver always is far superior to that which has been frozen and then defrosted.

At this time, I also like to remove the tenderloin steaks. These should not be confused with the long backstraps located on either side of the backbone and which require removing the hide to obtain. Rather, they are much smaller, only 1½ or 2 inches in diameter by about 12 inches in length, and they are located along both sides of the backbone *inside* the chest cavity.

I call them mini-tenderloins; but whatever they're called, they are the tenderest venison any deer possesses. In fact, they are so delicate a hunter must exercise care in removing them so they do not fall apart in his hands. The easiest way to remove these prime strips of meat is by using a small knife, even a pocketknife, to separate one end or the other from attachments along the backbone and then filleting them the remainder of the way out. When the deer carcass is hanging by the hind legs, with the body cavity open and exposed, removal of the mini-tenderloins is far easier than when the deer is hanging by the head, which prevents you from easily seeing your work—another advantage of my preferred hanging method.

Strangely, many hunters leave the mini-tenderloins in their deer until they begin full butchering operations at home, but I advise against this practice. By that time the tenderloins will have acquired a "glaze" or hard casing on their exposed surfaces, which must then be trimmed away, resulting in a significant loss of the prime meat. A much better approach is to remove the mini-tenderloins as soon as possible, trim them of bloodied areas and fat, then quickly refrigerate them.

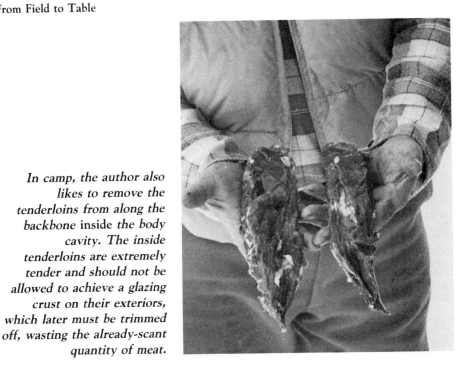

In camp, the author also likes to remove the tenderloins from along the backbone inside the body cavity. The inside tenderloins are extremely tender and should not be allowed to achieve a glazing crust on their exteriors, which later must be trimmed off, wasting the already-scant quantity of meat.

Another thing in favor of removing the mini-tenderloins in camp is to please the one or two partners who absolutely refuse to eat deer liver or heart and yet would nevertheless like to share in the celebration of eating venison on the eve of the first deer brought into camp.

With the heart, liver, and mini-tenderloins attended to, your next chore is cleaning the deer carcass still hanging outside. Use a small knife, preferably with a drop-point blade, to trim away fat globules, damaged bloodshot areas, torn skin, and whatnot. Allowing these to remain on the carcass, especially in warm weather, may foster the growth of bacteria that will spoil the meat.

If enough water is available, I like to then wash out the inside of the body cavity. Many hunters consider this anathema, claiming water should never be allowed to touch exposed meat or other parts of the carcass, but this is merely another wives' tale someone started long ago that bears no truth whatever. Washing facilitates the removal of debris that may not have been entirely removed during field dressing or that found its way inside the body cavity when the deer was being dragged out of the woods. Removal of these potential contaminants is imperative if the carcass is to properly age without spoiling. Just remember to use your water sparingly (most of it will drain downward and exit through the nostrils and mouth) and afterwards use clean rags or paper towels to completely blot up any remaining moisture.

Be sure to take time to clean your deer. Trim away bloodshot regions and fat globules, and slosh out the inside of the body cavity with water. Here, at the author's mountain camp in Colorado, two deer have already been reduced to primal cuts and are chilling in the near-zero air.

Be sure as well to clean any chunks of meat that have been packed out on your back. Again, a rag soaked with warm water then wrung out serves nicely. Dried blood that is too stubborn to remove with a damp rag alone will easily come away by occasionally dipping the rag in a small bowl of vinegar.

All of these measures result in a nice deer carcass that is far more presentable and easy to work with than one that is dirty and stained with dried blood smears. And that, in turn, results in far more venison eventually finding its way to your dinner table.

Protecting Your Deer Carcass

Every year untold numbers of deer are wasted due to a variety of usually unforeseen events. Warm weather and infestation by blowflies are the two leading culprits that venison must be guarded against.

Ideally, deer hanging in camp until the week's hunting is over should not be subjected to air temperatures below 25 degrees at night or higher than 45 degrees during midday. If either situation is anticipated or arrives without forewarning, special measures should be taken to prevent the meat from freezing or becoming too warm and spoiling.

Begin by hanging the deer in a location that is shaded during the better part of the day. In this manner, the carcass will undergo sufficient chilling during the night hours to keep the meat cool during the daylight hours.

One hunter I know bought a used sleeping bag for next to nothing at a rummage sale and ingeniously "bags" his deer whenever it's bitter cold. By cutting out the bottom of the sleeping bag, he doesn't face the problem of trying to slip the deer inside. All that's necessary is merely to wrap the bag around the deer and close the zipper; this insulation prevents his venison from freezing overnight. He also does this during extremely hot weather, allowing the deer to chill overnight and then first thing in the morning wrapping it with the sleeping bag to retain its cool temperature throughout the day. At the end of each hunting trip he merely tosses the sleeping bag into his washing machine, so it's clean for next year's outing.

Other hunters who may not want to go to this much trouble should at least have a piece of canvas tarpaulin in camp that can be draped over their deer either at night to prevent freezing or during the heat of midday to prevent the venison from overheating. If a sudden, unexpected cold snap occurs and there is no tarp in camp, consider lowering the deer to the ground and covering it with pine boughs to prevent freezing. Or, do anything else you can think of so that the carcass is not exposed to the direct assault of the wind. Naturally, you'll want to do the opposite if a sudden heat wave occurs, because then the carcass should be subjected to breezes.

Blowflies are the bane of deer hunters. Anyone who would like to study blowflies at work need only go out and kill a deer anywhere in North America where the daytime temperature is in the upper thirties or higher. The critters will swarm to your location.

Blowflies are similar in size and appearance to common houseflies but are easily distinguished by their metallic bluish or green colors. They enact their dastardly deeds by landing on fresh meat or the hide of a recently killed animal and laying thousands of eggs. The eggs look like tiny grains of white rice and in two or three days hatch into maggots, which feed upon the meat until the larva eventually turn into more flies to complete the cycle. Ordinarily, by the time a hunter first notices the presence of blowflies, it is too late to save the venison. Consequently, strict measures must be taken right at the outset to prevent as much as a single fly from ever touching your deer.

In consistently warm states throughout the South and Southwest, but most notably in Texas where the invention was first contrived, many hunters build special deer-hanging houses to protect their animals. In size, these buildings resemble large outhouses except that all three walls and the front door are made of screen nailed to two-by-four studs. A conventional roof overhead shades the deer hung inside during midday and also shelters them somewhat from inclement weather. These buildings are permanent affairs in annual deer camps and they do a yeoman's job of preventing insects from contacting the deer while at the same time allowing fresh air to circulate around the carcasses.

Just keep in mind that the door and roof, as well as all corners and edges where screening is joined to wood framework, must be very tight fitting. Blowflies have a special talent for finding the single ¼-inch hole you've overlooked somewhere and using it to gain entrance as swiftly as if you accidently left the front door wide open.

If your regular hunting party has a cabin almost anywhere, there is no better insurance for safeguarding your venison than having everyone chip in to buy the required materials (total cost is about $50) and then investing perhaps eight hours of labor time to construct a deer-hanging house.

On public hunting lands where the building of any structures is prohibited, or in remote areas where tent camps are established for the deer season, other remedies must be sought.

First, forget the worn-out advice that seems to appear constantly in deer-hunting books and magazine articles about sprinkling a deer carcass with black pepper. From my experience, thoroughly peppering a single deer requires about two quarts of the spice if every square inch is to be covered. Otherwise, blowflies will merely land and deposit eggs on those tiny places where there are no specks of pepper. Moreover, there also is the difficulty of getting the pepper to adhere to any part of the deer that is not moist, such as the hide. The first strong breeze will likely blow much of the pepper away from such areas, and blowflies will eagerly search out and infest the exposed meat. In short, then, the old "pepper gambit" is about the world's worst waste of time and money.

Gamebags, on the other hand, can do an excellent job of protecting deer carcasses from blowflies and other insects, provided they are the right kind and used properly.

Don't give a minute's consideration to the one-dollar cheesecloth gamebags you see in many sporting-goods stores. Their thin, fragile, wide-mesh construction is about as effective in warding away flies and insects as waving your arms and cursing.

What you want are heavy-duty gamebags made of porous but tightly woven cotton or muslin. They're shaped like long tubes with a drawstring closure at one end and they cost plenty (up to $25 apiece, depending upon brand name and exact dimensions), but they do the job well and can be washed and reused for many, many years.

The other alternative is to have a willing seamstress in the family custom-make several gamebags for you from old bedsheets. They must be large enough to slip over the antlers and also over the hind legs, which will be widespread when the deer is hung with a gambrel.

There are two aspects to using such gamebags that are so critical to success that I'm surprised they've never been mentioned before in other hunting books or magazine articles. Foremost, the *entire* animal, not just the main body torso, must be enclosed in the bag.

I know one hunter—so embarrassed by his oversight he doesn't want his name mentioned here—who committed two cardinal sins that cost him plenty of prime venison. First, he hung his deer by the head, then slipped a gamebag over the animal, bringing it up to the chin region and then tying the neck of the bag securely shut. When he later began butchering his deer at home, he verily gagged when he discovered most of the venison was ruined because blowflies had entered the body cavity by crawling through the mouth and nostrils. As I said, the critters will use whatever entrance is available to make their way to your deer meat.

The second canon of deer care when using a gamebag is to ensure that no damp or moist portions of the carcass or exposed meat are allowed to directly contact the bag. I learned this lesson the hard way one season when I hung a skinned and quartered deer (that had been backpacked out of a canyon in pieces) in several gamebags. When I opened the bags two days later I both cringed and curled my lip at the sight of big ugly gobs of white blowfly eggs here and there. Strangely, however, there were no holes or tears in the bags, and no flies actually inside, and for a long time I was at a loss as to how they had gotten to the meat. Finally, I figured out that flies had landed on the outside of the meat bags and then shot their eggs right through the thin fabric at various moist areas where the bags were plastered to the venison.

The way to avoid this is by filling your gamebags—whether they hold meat parts or encase an entire deer—with a number of small branches so the meat and the actual fabric of the bag do not touch each other.

Other Deer-Care Methods in Camp

There may be an occasion in which a hunter wants to protect his venison from pestiferous insects but finds he does not have a suitable gamebag with him. Or perhaps he has remembered to bring his own gamebag, but one or more of his partners have forgotton theirs.

One neat trick that seems to discourage even the most determined blowflies is making use of a smudge fire. Build it directly beneath your meatpole or beneath a tripod arrangement from which a deer is hanging. Since you don't want to cook your venison, keep your fire small and your deer hung high, and allow only small wisps of smoke to waft up and around the carcass. Begin with a fire made of dry hardwood and once you've established a good bed of coals lay green branches on top. Not a lot of smudge is needed but it must be continual.

I came by this idea for warding off pests while fishing. For years I've been an inveterate cigar smoker and whenever my Dad and I shared a boat I noticed he was always relentlessly besieged by mosquitos and black flies, even though he liberally doused himself with insect repellent, while I was seldom bothered. Finally it dawned on me that the cloud of cigar smoke constantly swirling around my head was responsible for my protection and to this day, whenever fishing the North country, I always have a box of stogies somewhere onboard. Anyway, I reasoned the same principle should likewise apply to protecting a deer's anatomy, gave it a try, and found it works like a charm.

Going back to the subject of deer care in warm weather—no, make that *hot* weather—another matter of dire necessity is getting the hide off your deer as quickly as possible. The coats deer wear during the hunting season consist of hollow hairs with superior insulating qualities in the event of cold weather. So if rapid chilling of the meat is to take place whenever the temperature is high, off the hide must come.

I go into detail regarding hide removal in Chapter 8, so suffice to say here that if the hide is removed it becomes even more critical that a gamebag be used to protect the now fully exposed carcass. Don't be alarmed if the carcass seems to become hard quickly and dry on the outside. This is normal and is called "casing," which is the formation of a very thin, durable crust that once acquired gives still additional protection to the meat beneath. Later, during butchering operations, this casing will be trimmed away.

CHAPTER 6

Taxidermy Tips
for the Trophy Hunter

WELL BEFORE a successful hunter gets on with the important business of actually butchering his deer and wrapping packages of venison for the freezer, he'll predictably find himself facing another problem.

He'll have in his possession numerous, inedible body parts he may wish to preserve for future enjoyment. Perhaps, he'll want to have a taxidermist make a head mount of his buck, particularly if it's of trophy proportions. If the antlers are not all that impressive, however, he may wish to mount them himself upon some type of decorative wall plaque.

The hunter with an even stronger inclination toward craftsmanship may wish to use individual antler tines to make knife handles, or he may saw the antlers into discs to make attractive garment buttons or jewelry. The deer's lower legs and hooves can be fashioned into a handsome gun rack, or bookends. Or, all four can be arranged close together and standing upright, to make an intriguing lamp base.

Then there is the deer hide itself. It can be tanned with the hair on for an attractive wall hanging, rug, or tabletop covering. If the hide is tanned with the hair removed, a sizable rectangle of leather is created, which has innumerable uses.

In any case, the time to consider any of these possibilities is not after your deer is on the ground but well before the season opens. There are two reasons for this. First, it is imperative that a hunter have a reputable taxidermist lined up, to whom various deer parts can immediately be delivered without delay. Second, there are certain aspects of field care and camp care that must be carefully thought out in advance.

Deciding on a Taxidermist

Decades ago the work of taxidermists was not highly regarded. A "stuffed" deer head was usually just that: a deerskin fitted over a crude framework of wire and wood, the cavity then filled with sawdust, straw, or excelsior. The result was not only an abominable, even grotesque representation of the original quarry but one that often began deteriorating the minute it left someone's garage workshop.

Today all of that is changed and taxidermy studios are manned by skilled artists using the latest techniques and space-age materials to produce animal mounts that last indefinitely (given proper care) and look so real you almost expect them to bound away any minute. Nevertheless, as in any business, there are a small percentage of taxidermists who produce poor work and it's the hunter's responsibility to separate the bad from the good.

Before you begin butchering your deer, consider whether you'll send parts to a taxidermist. A trophy animal like this deserves wall-mounting, but that will be impossible if you haven't given it proper field care.

Midsummer is a perfect time to look around for a reputable taxidermist. Since a deer-head mount takes an average of six to nine months to complete, midsummer generally sees a taxidermy studio filled wall to wall with finished mounts ready to be picked up by hunters who took them the previous season. This makes it quite easy to compare the quality of workmanship different taxidermists are capable of producing.

Above all, make sure the taxidermist you decide upon is one who specializes in working with deer heads and related body parts; some may actually specialize in mounting birds or fish, for example, but will agree to handle your deer head, which should be warning enough that you'd later be disappointed with the finished product.

Shop around for a taxidermist before the hunting season opens and let quality work, not price, dictate your choice. There are an infinite variety of options, with the most expensive being a full-body mount as was done with this magnificent deer taken not far from the author's own backyard in southern Ohio.

As you are examining the work of a prospective taxidermist, be sure to obtain as much information as possible. Those who earn a full-time living at this profession have nice printed brochures that describe the types of projects they specialize in, the price of each type of work, the amount of the required deposit, when you can expect to take delivery of your mount, and so on.

Invariably, the taxidermist will also hand you some type of flyer or instruction sheet describing the particular way he likes to receive animal parts. Consider deer heads for example. Rarely do taxidermists like hunters to skin out and remove the cape (the hide) from the head of the animal because this requires special knives and plenty of experience in meticulously cutting around the antler bases, eyes, lips, and other facial areas. A majority of hunters do not possess this know-how. The end result, sadly, is accidental cuts and other mistakes that the taxidermist will have to try to repair, usually at added expense; even then the final mount is unlikely to be top quality. So a good rule of thumb, after deciding upon a particular taxidermist, is to follow his instructions explicitly.

As of 1983, a quality deer-head mount costs an average of $150 to $200, and as noted earlier, it will usually take from six to nine months for the work to be completed. But there are other alternatives. Some of the most inspiring mounts display a buck and doe together on the same wall plaque, at roughly double the price. Then there are positively stunning full-body mounts that may cost a grand or more; they also require ample space in which to be displayed, which often means an expensive glass case.

Whatever the specific nature of the mount, the hunter usually will be expected to make a 25 percent deposit at the outset, with the balance to be paid when he picks up the finished mount. He'll also be expected to pay any shipping charges involved, and possibly other costs as well. For example, if the neck or head skin of your deer has somehow been inadvertently damaged and cannot be repaired, you can buy a replacement cape from the taxidermist. Hunters commonly sell entire deer hides and capes to taxidermists, which they in turn tan and maintain in inventory by various sizes. These can then be used to properly fit capes to damaged heads. The average price for this service is $25 to $50.

When you're talking with your chosen taxidermist, also look over the many different poses available in deer-head mounts. In the most common pose, the head is held high and looking straight ahead. But you can also have the head turned and looking to the right or left, if there is a particular wall best suited to this pose. Another option is the so-called "sneak" pose with the head low and alert. When you see many such poses in advance of even taking your deer, you have plenty of time to mull over which you like best.

This visit with a taxidermist also provides a good opportunity to look around his studio for other projects you may eventually like him to undertake, such as creating a handsome-looking gun rack from your deer's hooves, or perhaps making a throw rug from the tanned hide. Just be sure, before commissioning such work, to get all prices and other details spelled out in advance.

But do not allow the price alone to dictate the type of work you'd like to have done or, indeed, the taxidermist you choose to do the work in the first place. Years after you've long forgotten the price you paid for a superior mount you'll continue to proudly display it and relive the memory of that special hunt.

Field Care of Deer Parts

When that impressive buck is finally lying at your feet, you first think about field dressing in order to lower the temperature of the carcass quickly. Yet as you begin this work, you should keep in mind any specific instructions given by your taxidermist. Therefore, it's necessary to backtrack momentarily and reemphasize several points covered in an earlier chapter.

Foremost, be sure not to damage the cape by cutting the deer's throat. And do not allow your field-dressing incision to travel all the way from the pelvic region to the base of the chin. Both of these common mistakes are entirely unnecessary in proper field dressing, and both inflict such grave damage upon the hide that the taxidermist will be unable to use it. All that is required in proper field dressing, to obtain your steaks and roasts and ensure that the hide and cape remain in good condition, is to run your incision just to the base of the sternum (breastbone, where the ribs begin) and no farther.

Next comes the matter of removing the deer to camp or home. Great care must be exercised to prevent the hide from being ruined. Actually, hide damage is most likely to occur in the Rocky Mountain states, where the terrain is typically a combination of dense forestland, torturous rocky ground, and brittle sagebrush flats, any of which can destroy a deer hide in short order. Many times, I've seen hunters drag their deer scant yards only to discover large bald patches where the hair has been rubbed from their deer hides. Once the hair is removed by the abrasive action of the ground, additional dragging incurs still more damage by gouging and cutting the hide itself. In the most severe cases, the prime meat beneath the hide may even be bruised.

The situation generally is not so serious when deer hunters ply their efforts east of the Continental Divide. The terrain here rarely is so harsh and most often is a combination of dry weedy fields, grassy meadows, forests carpeted with pine needles, and woodlands revealing a soft floor of fallen leaves. There also is a good possibility of snow cover. Consequently, it is not unusual to drag a deer as much as a full mile and yet incur minimal hide damage if any at all.

So good advice, before dragging your deer a single yard, is to size up the situation. If the dragging distance is relatively short and the ground terrain seems not at all foreboding, go ahead and heave-ho. However, if you are uncertain about the results of doing this, consider any and all viable alternatives.

Can you get any type of four-wheel-drive in close to your deer? If not, is there in camp some type of all-terrain vehicle such as a dirt bike, three-wheeler, or snowmobile? Or, is there any possibility of paying a farmer a few bucks to haul out your deer with his tractor? Is there a nearby rancher for hire, who has a horse or mule to bring your deer in from the hinterland?

But wait! Even if none of the above possibilities is feasible, there may be still other solutions. If three partners are available to help, the four of you can each grab one of the deer's legs and bodily carry the animal to camp. Sure, it's tiring, and you'll need to make frequent rest stops, but it *is* a possibility if it is imperative that your deer hide not receive a single scratch. If only one partner can assist, fashion a makeshift stretcher that the two of you can carry at waist level.

Still another option is using a large-capacity contractor's wheelbarrow to carry your deer home. I've seen many camps where wheelbarrows or similar homemade contraptions with bicycle wheels are common equipment. Around the camp itself, they're extremely handy for hauling firewood and large containers of water, and because of their big rubber tires they roll easily over rough ground while transporting deer from places that cannot be reached by any other means.

Finally, if it's you and you alone, with no one to lend a hand and no way other than dragging to remove your deer to camp, here's a nifty trick I've used many times. Return to camp or your parked car to relieve yourself of heavy hunting gear such as your rifle, ammo, and binoculars. Then return to the kill site with your drag rope and a rectangular piece of heavy-duty polyethylene.

Lay this plastic sheeting flat on the ground, roll your deer onto it, tie the leading edge of the plastic around the deer's neck, then attach your drag rope and have at it. This plastic is terrific stuff as it allows your deer to literally slide across the ground with ease. You may even have to be careful going down gradual slopes, especially if the ground is snow covered, or the entire thing will just take off like a runaway sled! Best of all, it's an effortless way to transport your deer to car or camp with no damage to the hide whatsoever.

Camp Care of Head and Cape

There's no question about it. Over the years you've debated having a deer head mounted and in the final analysis always vetoed the idea. But now you've finally succeeded in collecting a deer known to locals as Hue (short for "humongous") and your decision is final. You're going to have a splendid head mount created for a certain wall in your den that has been vacant much too long.

Congratulations! But help ensure that your taxidermist will be able to do a commendable job by doing your job first. This means immediately removing the head and cape from the animal while the hide is still "green." When it is in a fresh, recently killed state, the hide is soft and pliable and comes off the animal quite easily, with minimal risk of damage. Conversely, if the deer is allowed to hang for several days, the hide begins to dry, harden, and adhere so strongly to the carcass you'll think it is attached with Super Glue. Not only is it then quite difficult to remove but instead of using mainly your hands you'll have to rely upon quite a bit of cutting with your knife, which drastically increases the chances of accidently slicing or nicking the hide.

Aside from not removing the hide at the earliest opportunity, another common error many hunters make is not removing *enough* hide. If a head mount is to be produced, many hunters simply cut the head off in the vicinity of the lower-neck region. Taxidermists wince at such a head because it leaves them no additional cape for any patching or mending that may have to be done. It also gives the finished head mount an inferior "amputated" look.

The most admirable head mounts reveal not only the entire neck region of the animal but also the brisket and beginning contours of the front shoulders and back, giving the trophy much greater presence and dimension.

So always cut the hide *behind* the front shoulders as you encircle the chest region with your knife cut. Next, from the sternum, carefully make a cut just to the beginning of the insides of the forelegs, with subsequent cuts going down the insides of the legs to the knees. Never continue the brisket cut down the entire length of the front of the neck because this part of the deer is clearly on display and difficult to mend.

With these cuts made, now make another cut down the center line of the back of the neck to the base of the skull, with additional cuts then going to the base of each antler as shown in the accompanying diagrams. On the finished mount these cuts, which later will be sewn together by the taxidermist, will be out of sight.

Now carefully begin peeling the hide down and away from the shoulder/neck region, using your knife blade as little as possible. The goal is to expose the entire neck so that the meat may be salvaged, but at this stage it is not necessary to actually remove the meat from the carcass; it can remain intact and age with the remainder of the deer. As the hide is gradually removed around the outside of the neck and up to the chin area, go no farther. Simply cut through the neck bone so the head will fall free with its attached cape intact. Your taxidermist will undoubtedly prefer to attend to the remainder of delicate skinning around the eyes, mouth and other head parts.

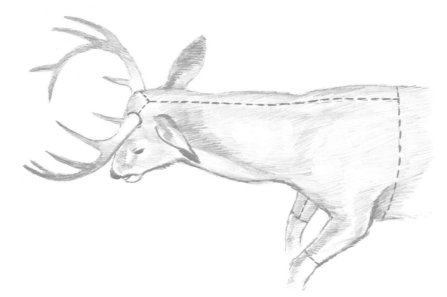

Many hunters unknowingly ruin their deer hides for taxidermy purposes by cutting the throat during field-dressing operations, or not removing enough hide for the taxidermist to work with. Shown here are the cuts taxidermists recommend. The hide should be cut well behind the front shoulder to allow ample cape, and removed from the head by cutting down the centerline of the back of the neck.

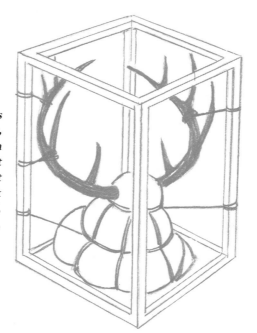

To transport the hide and antlers a long distance to a taxidermist, particularly when you're using a commercial carrier, you'll want to ensure the antlers are not damaged. A wooden framework like this, covered with cardboard, usually is sufficient.

Finally, thoroughly salt the inside of the cape, rubbing the salt well into all parts of the hide. Then pour additional salt into the neck opening and all other cavities, including the ears, nostrils, and mouth. Be liberal with your salt. It costs only 25¢ a pound and will not harm the hide or head whatsoever but actually will help preserve it.

I like fine-grained table salt (containing no iodine). Compared to coarser varieties of salt, the fine stuff has a much higher absorbency factor per square inch of application, and it more easily finds its way into every tiny crack and crevice. To thoroughly salt a head and cape you'll need two to three pounds. Then place the head and cape in a cool, shaded location until you can deliver it to your taxidermist.

Other Taxidermy Ideas

Suppose that the buck you harvest is not spectacular enough to mount but you'd still like to somehow display the antlers. Do not saw the antlers off individually. Simply use your knife to carefully remove the hide on top of the skull and surrounding the antler bases. Now, use a saw to cut out a wedge-shaped chunk of skullplate to which both antlers are still securely attached. With the antlers so removed, trim away remaining tissue and other unwanted matter, thoroughly salt the skullplate, then set the affair aside for several weeks to completely dry before beginning the mounting procedure.

There are numerous types of antler-mounting kits on the market; these contain wooden plaques, paint, leather or velvet skullcap coverings, and complete instructions that allow even beginners to do first-rate jobs. The price range for such kits is $15 to $20, and they are available in most sporting-goods stores.

Another option that finds favor with many hunters is using a jig saw or coping saw to cut out a wooden plaque of their own creative design or in the design of the particular state in which the deer was harvested. It's then an easy matter to either paint or stain the plaque. Mounting the antlers is equally easy. Merely center them on the front of the plaque, then tightly secure them with screws coming in from the back of the plaque into the skullplate. Next, mold a glob of plaster of Paris over the irregular skullplate; when it dries you can shape its contours to your liking with a file and sandpaper, then cover it with leather or decorative cloth.

One advantage to mounting the antlers alone, as described above, is that you are left with a full-sized deer skin, which can be tanned. (See Chapter 8 for details on how to skin a deer.)

To prepare a hide for tanning, first lay it out flat, preferably on a hard

There are many types of antler-mounting kits on the market for do-it-yourself craftsmen. Or you can design your own, as this hunter did, by making a plaque outlining the state of Ohio where the deer was taken.

surface such as a picnic table or sheet of plywood. Now, use your knife to carefully—and thoroughly—trim away all tissue, fat globules, skin remnants, and other unwanted matter. Pay special attention to trimming away bloodied matter in the vicinity of the bullet or arrow hole and those areas around the outside edges of the hide. All of this is very important because if fat and fleshy debris is not completely trimmed away it serves as a breeding ground for bacteria, which in little time will cause the hair on the hide to begin to slip and fall out; once the hair has begun to slip, there is no way to curtail the process, so it's best to nip the possibility of this misfortune right in the beginning.

When the hide is "clean" to your satisfaction, salt it down. You'll probably need about five pounds of salt to do an average-sized deer hide.

Many hunters make the mistake of pouring the salt in the middle of the hide and then spreading it around with their hands. Too often, however, the outer edges of the hide don't get enough salt. Since any rotting that

There are many uses for deer hides, if they've been cared for properly. First, lay the hide flat and trim away tissue, fat, and other unwanted matter.

takes place always begins around the outside edges, you should do it the opposite way; pour salt liberally all around the outside edges, then gradually work excess salt toward the middle of the hide, rubbing it in with your fingers.

The purpose of salt is to draw out moisture and residual body fluids from the skin, which are the harbingers of spoilage. Naturally, therefore, once the salting process is completed you'll want to somehow tilt the hide up very slightly so various fluids are free to drain away. Simply raising one end of the picnic table a foot is usually sufficient, or prop up your plywood cutting board with a melon-sized rock.

After a day or two, inspect your hide and resalt any areas that still appear overly damp. Next, turn the edges of the hide inward, then *roll* the hide itself into a cylinder, with the skin-side in and the hair on the outside. Never fold the hide as this may cause damaging creases; always roll it, just as you would a painting or valuable document.

Then store the hide in a cool, dry location not exposed to direct sunlight.

Next, rub an ample quantity of salt into the hide to draw out moisture.

Finally, roll the hide into a cylinder (never fold it!) before sending it to a tannery or a taxidermist.

If the average daily air temperature is less than 50 degrees, a salted hide will remain in good condition for several weeks. If the temperature is higher, transport the hide to your taxidermist at your earliest convenience. If this is not possible, your deer hide can be stored indefinitely by slipping it into a large plastic bag and then placing the works in your freezer.

Tanning a deer hide yourself is a somewhat tricky proposition because numerous chemicals are required and each step must be very carefully executed. The best advice is to consult a good taxidermy book and, after studying the many different tanning methods, to decide which one suits you best.

Another possibility of course is having your taxidermist tan your hide. The cost is nominal, almost always less than $20.

Yet another intriguing idea is placing your hide in a plastic bag, then in a cardboard box, then mailing it to a commercial tannery. They'll either tan your hide (with the hair on, or off, as you request) and return it to you to use as you see fit. Or they'll fashion garments of your choice, which you can enjoy using for many years.

These companies advertise regularly in the leading sportsmen's magazines but perhaps the largest concern is the W. B. Place Company, 368 West Sumner Street, Hartford, Wisconsin 53207. The brochure describes more than a hundred garments and accessory items that hunters can have made from their deer hides at reasonable prices.

For many garments, such as full-length coats, it's necessary to supply more than one deer hide. In these cases, the standard procedure is to send in this hunting season's deer hide to be tanned and saved by the company until additional hides are sent in during following seasons.

However, there also are numerous items that can be made from single deer hides. From one deer hide you can have made two women's handbags, for example, or two pair of moccasins, or three pair of buckskin gloves. The gloves are my favorite as they are stylish, incredibly soft, durable, and yet cost less then $10 per pair. But you can also have made wallets, storage pouches for gear, vests, gun cases, or any number of other useful items.

What could be more uniquely exciting than giving such things—professionally made from your own deer—as gifts at Christmas!

CHAPTER 7

Transporting Deer Home

Y OU MAY HAVE some anxiety about getting your deer home in good condition. So far you've done everything right, but now unforeseen pitfalls seem to be awaiting you, threatening to rob you of a year's supply of venison.

Invariably, the scenario begins unfolding a good distance from home, usually in a hunting camp far from familiar surroundings, facilities, and services. You're at an elevation of 8,000 feet where the weather is cool during midday and frigid at night, optimum conditions under which your carcass is aging as it hangs from the camp meatpole.

Sure, everything is perfect right now in the high country, but in a day or two you and your partners plan to break camp, bring your four-wheel-drive trucks down out of the mountains, and begin the long cross-country trek home. You'll have to travel 1,800 miles, and according to a radio report the entire Midwest is presently besieged by an unseasonable warm spell. Temperatures are in the high eighties, not exactly the conditions you'd like your venison subjected to.

Or maybe you're hunting in an altogether different location, such as the desert Southwest, or you're in the deep South, partaking of an early-season hunt. Whatever the location, it's just plain *hot*. If you lived there, of course, you could dismiss the matter with a wave of the hand because in mere hours you could secure your cache of venison in a cold-storage locker. But you don't live there. You're far from your home turf and the more you think about it, the more your belly begins to knot.

As noted outdoor writer Larry Mueller believes, regarding the tender loving care any hunter should give his deer, "Transportation is the weak link between a field kill and a taste thrill." In other words, whether venison becomes a treat to the palate or a threat to the stomach depends almost entirely upon what happens from the time the animal falls until it is reduced to neatly wrapped packages that are solidly frozen.

Transporting Deer Short Distances

Obviously, when nature is providing the refrigeration, there is little risk of spoilage by heat. Nevertheless, using recommended transportation techniques is important, because no one wants to pull into his driveway with a disheveled looking deer covered from hoof to head with dust and road grime.

If the hide was removed from the animal in camp, you'll not want to expose a naked carcass to highway filth. So leave your deer in its protective gamebag. If the material of the gamebag is rather porous, it's even a good idea to double-bag your deer. I've mentioned the use of gamebags before, but they are so invaluable to deer hunters that it's worth lauding them again. Initially, high-quality gamebags do cost a good bit of money, but they can be washed and reused for many, many years. Every serious hunter should invest in several such bags, preferably those made of tightly woven muslin with drawstring closures.

If your deer still possesses its hide, however, it will serve amply to protect your venison until you arrive home, provided the deer rides as high as possible on your vehicle. Ideally, this means tying the deer onto the roof of the car or truck; if the vehicle has a roof rack of sorts, all the better. A roof rack serves to lift the carcass somewhat, so it is not resting directly on the roof. Therefore, the carcass is not exposed to much of the heat radiated by the vehicle, and what little heat there is, is quickly dissipated by flowing air that circulates beneath and around the carcass.

If your car or truck does not have a permanent, factory-installed roof rack, consider buying an inexpensive model that attaches by means of suction cups and hold-down straps that clamp onto the rain gutters. Then, once a year, you can use this apparatus for deer hunting or other vacationing. By the way, never drape your deer carcass over a front fender, as this practice will subject it to both engine heat and road grime thrown into the air by other vehicles immediately ahead of you.

Another idea, with conventional automobiles, is to drape the deer carcass on top of the rear trunk lid, then push it forward so it is directly against the back window (you'll still be able to see out). Rope ties can next go around

When transporting deer in hot weather, keep the meat cool and protect it from road grime. These hunters wrapped the carcass, which was already cool from hanging in the high-country night air, in a tarp and got it home in good condition.

When using a conventional automobile to transport deer, try to expose the carcass to chilling breezes by putting it on a roof rack, or tying it across the back of the trunk deck.

the haunch region on one side, around the neck on the other, then under the trunk lid hinges.

If the driving distance is very short, and the weather amenable, simply laying the deer on the lowered tailgate of a pickup, then tying it down, is adequate. However, under dirty driving conditions you'll not want to take this approach because the rearmost area of any vehicle receives the brunt of road grime thrown up by the wheels. If these conditions exist, merely push your deer carcass inside the pickup bed and raise the tailgate.

It's also possible to place the deer inside the trunk of an automobile. Just be sure the body cavity of the animal is propped open with sticks and the trunk lid left ajar a foot or so to facilitate the circulation of breezes around the carcass.

With larger camping rigs—pickup campers, van conversions, motorhomes, and the like—certain problems arise. These vehicles don't have tailgates, and their roofs are typically so high off the ground that it's difficult to lift deer up onto them. This tempts many hunters to transport their deer inside on the floor, which isn't wise because the passenger area of any vehicle always is quite warm. One way to get a deer onto the roof is by backing the vehicle close to the camp meatpole, where the deer already is hanging high, and swinging it sideways onto the roof. Later, at home, back up close to the overhead garage rafters or tree limb where you'll begin butchering operations to easily transfer the deer to the hanging device.

In all of these situations just described, the major concern is not so much keeping the venison cold (Mother Nature is attending to that) but rather keeping it clean.

When the Weather is Hot

I'll never forget the time Lenny Morris and I were deer hunting in central Tennessee during a record-breaking heat wave. We didn't plan it that way and neither of us can recall having before or since pursued deer under such sauna-like conditions. Lenny's buck, in fact, was first spotted in a deep valley lying down in a bubbling stream with only its head out of the water. Mine was taken in a shaded glen where it was bedded under the low-hanging branches of a maple tree.

How we got those whole deer carcasses home—about a 12-hour drive—without losing an ounce of venison, was a lesson in ingenuity. First, we were not too hasty to break camp the next morning because we knew, come mid-day, we'd be greeted with another scorcher. So we alternately napped and played cards until eight o'clock that evening, leaving our deer hanging in the shade during midday. Then we headed for home, driving throughout the night hours. The air temperature that night was close to 80 degrees, but that was cool compared to the 105-degree temperatures that prevailed in the afternoon!

One other trick we employed was undoubtedly even more responsible for doing a fine job of preserving our venison. After laying our deer on the roof rack of my truck and hitting the road, we immediately stopped at the first gas station and purchased several bags of ice, which we pushed inside the body cavities of the deer and laid between the hams. With the ice on the

In hot weather, one neat trick is filling the body cavity of your deer with ice bags. Then wrap the carcass with canvas soaked in cold water.

inside, and the insulating hide outside to help retain the cold, any chance of spoilage was virtually eliminated.

If the driving distance is so great that you must log many hours on the road during midday, use the same ice-bag trick but also employ one other measure. Once the ice bags are secured inside the body cavities of the deer, wrap the deer carcasses in an old piece of tarpaulin tied down securely. Then, thoroughly soak the canvas with water. Slosh it down liberally with buckets carried from a stream. On the road, the wet canvas on the outside will quickly become quite cool even in sweltering hot temperatures, due to the cooling effect of evaporation. In addition, you've also got the ice cooling the carcass from the inside—a double-whammy, so to speak, that does an excellent job of safeguarding your precious cargo.

Of course, in extremely hot weather, you'll have to replace the ice bags periodically or they'll melt down to water within two to three hours. Carefully remove the bags, replace them with fresh bags of ice, then use the icy cold meltwater from the former bags to soak down your tarp covering again. Admittedly, all of this takes a good deal of effort, and frequent stops, but the final reward makes it all worthwhile.

When the Weather is Cold and Hot

For those faraway hunting camps where hunters find themselves in frigid high country one week, then on the road in hot weather during the trek home, my hunting partners and I found several solutions that work very nicely.

Take what happened during our 1983 Colorado hunt. Luckily enough, by the end of our third day in the White River National Forest, we had six handsome bucks hanging from a spruce pole near our tent. The average day-time temperature was 40 degrees, but each night the mercury plummeted to 10 degrees.

As each buck was brought into camp it was duly stripped of its hide and then reduced to primal cuts. That is, initial butchering operations were begun to reduce the deer to front legs, hind legs, saddles, necks, and other major pieces (we planned to reserve our final meatcutting until we reached home).

We then fabricated a table consisting of a large sheet of plywood we'd brought along in the bed of one of the pickups, with legs fashioned from trunk sections sawed from a dead birch tree. A sheet of plastic was next laid on the makeshift table. Then the primal venison cuts were placed on top of the plastic and covered with a second sheet held down with rocks around the edges. The end result was marvelous. The meat was fully protected from marauding whiskeyjacks and ground squirrels, but more important the venison was allowed over a period of days to become extremely cold but not quite frozen.

When we broke camp, we placed the primal cuts in plastic-coated, double-walled cardboard boxes, with each hunter's name on the box containing the deer that belonged to him. These insulated boxes are quite sturdy (when filled, you can stack other gear on top of them) and they're usually available for free from fast-food chicken restaurants and stores that specialize in selling poultry. When we go hunting we fill the boxes with groceries and after con-suming the grub during the week have empty, unsurpassed containers for transporting venison home.

Anyway, with approximately six large, almost frozen primal cuts of meat in each box, each piece helps to keep the others quite cold for several days. In fact, when we arrive home, we usually find the meat still so cold we have to let it warm up just a bit before it's comfortable to handle with bare hands.

One important note, however. We've learned *never* to place the meat in plastic bags as they stick unmercifully to the meat and sometimes impart a bad flavor. Just place the glazed primal cuts in the box as is, or if they have not yet cased, wrap them with plastic-coated freezer wrapping paper. Then carefully seal each box with duct tape to help keep coldness in and dust out.

If you cannot conveniently obtain insulated poultry boxes, use lightweight wooden boxes you can fabricate yourself from scrap materials. Or use camping coolers.

Why Not Butcher Your Deer in Camp?

There are still other options available to the hunter far from home who wants to ensure his venison undergoes safe transportation. When you're deer hunting in the various western states, for example, and particularly when you're hiring an outfitter or working out of some type of big-game hunting ranch, it's highly likely that butchering facilities will be available to guests.

Sometimes, the rancher's hired help tends to all the butchering; you bring in a deer, turn it over to a several-man crew, they butcher the deer to your specifications, wrap the meat, then place it in their storage freezer. Just before you leave for home, the meat packages are packed in some type of adequate container. If you're a paying client at the ranch, this additional service of butchering your deer generally carries a nominal charge. Sometimes the cost is as low as $25, which is a deal beyond compare if you've priced plastic-coated freezer paper lately.

Other times, the rancher or outfitter in question will simply make available a work space where hunters can butcher their deer themselves, which is a good way to kill time while waiting for your partners to fill their tags.

It should go without saying that all of these possibilities should be ascertained well in advance of your hunting trip because if you decide to butcher your deer on location you'll want to have planned ahead and brought wrapping supplies, tape, knives, and other essentials not provided by the ranch.

In nearly all cases, however—whether you do the butchering or have the rancher's hired hands do it—you'll leave the ranch with frozen packages of meat, which brings up still other concerns.

As most hunters probably already know, once meat is solidly frozen it should *never* be allowed to completely defrost and then be refrozen again. This means the hunter will have to evaluate his own particular travel situation and take whatever measures are needed to ensure his frozen venison remains frozen through the duration of the drive home.

An insulated container packed tightly with wrapped packages of frozen venison will remain completely frozen for up to 30 hours, depending upon the air temperature and the type of container being used. In many instances, this 30-hour period will be more than sufficient to drive all the way home, where the still-frozen packages can merely be transferred to one's own freezer.

But if the driving distance is somewhat longer, or if the air temperature is unseasonably warm, other measures must be instituted to preserve the venison.

The first idea that comes to mind is buying ice along the way and placing it in the camping cooler or other container with the frozen venison packages. *Don't!* The only time ice should be used is for the purpose of keeping unfrozen venison very cold. Otherwise, ice actually has an adverse effect, which involves simple principles of physics. Ice is a liquid (water) that freezes at 32°F. Meat, however, is a solid commonly frozen at temperatures of 0° to 10°F. It stands to reason, then, that ice, although very cold, is nevertheless *warmer* than frozen venison and will therefore cause the venison to more quickly begin defrosting than if no ice is used! Consequently, what you want to use instead of conventional frozen-water ice is dry ice, which is frozen carbon dioxide.

Dry ice is available across the country in all major cities and is most commonly sold to private individuals by meat-packing plants, dairies, and ice cream factories. Upon leaving the ranch you've been working out of, or any other camp, simply stop in the first large city you come to, find a pay telephone and look in the Yellow Pages under the listings "ice" or "refrigeration" for the nearest facility that will sell you dry ice.

If hot weather is anticipated when you leave colder climes, it may be wise to partially butcher your deer in camp. Here, Al Wolter carries a skinned carcass to a work table.

The deer is then reduced to primal cuts and allowed to chill overnight.

For the trip home, store the primal cuts in boxes made of wood or plastic-insulated cardboard. The meat, nearly frozen, will remain cold for several days. Note how elastic cord is used to secure top.

As already noted, dry ice is carbon dioxide (CO_2) that has been frozen to $-109°F$, and it remains at this temperature as it gradually dissipates over a period of time. Unlike frozen-water ice, which melts and thereby changes into a liquid, dry ice gradually breaks down by "sublimating," or going from a solid state back to a gas with no resulting formation of liquid. As a result, it is neat, clean, and convenient to use. And since dry ice is capable of freezing meat five times faster than even a conventional freezer, it's an unsurpassed method of keeping frozen venison frozen during a long drive home.

Typically, dry ice is manufactured for distributors in 10-inch-square blocks, each weighing 54 pounds, which must be stored in pressurized vaults. The standard procedure is to have a workman saw, from a large block, as many inch-thick slabs as you calculate you'll need, each of which will weigh about five pounds. As of mid-1983, the going price for dry ice was about 75¢ per pound.

To offer an illustration of the mind-boggling capabilities of dry ice, consider this: A four-pound package of unfrozen venison that is sandwiched between two inch-thick slabs of dry ice will be frozen rock solid in only six minutes! As a result, when dry ice is placed in the middle of a box of already frozen venison packages they'll stay that way for as long as the ice lasts (until it completely sublimates), whereupon the ice must be replenished.

How long dry ice lasts before it reverts back to the gaseous state depends, as in the case of how long frozen-water ice lasts, upon the air temperature and the type of storage container being used. However, while tightly enclosed containers are recommended when using conventional ice, when using dry ice some provision must be made to allow the continually created carbon dioxide gas to escape.

Now, plastic-coated poultry boxes, while adequate, are not really the best choice when using dry ice. Inexpensive styrofoam camping coolers are better because they possess great insulating qualities and are porous enough to allow the gas to escape when the lid is tightly taped in place. Other popular storage containers are non-insulated, heavy-duty cardboard boxes or wooden crates in which the sidewall slats are not tightly joined together.

The recommended amount of dry ice to use at any given time is a ratio of one pound of dry ice for every 15 pounds of venison. In other words, if you've taken an average-sized deer, which has provided you with 75 pounds of wrapped packages of boneless venison, you'll need five pounds of dry ice to keep the packages completely frozen. Further, if the air temperature is 80 degrees, your five pounds of dry ice will last for about 15 hours before it entirely sublimates and has to be replaced.

Regarding the use of dry ice, a few words of precaution also are in order. First, never touch or handle dry ice with your bare hands as it is so cold it

Dry ice is superb for preserving and transporting venison, but care must be exercised in using it. Styrofoam containers are ideal. Place the ice in the middle of each cooler, then surround it with wrapped venison packages and plenty of excelsior or shredded newspaper. Never touch dry ice with your bare hands.

can actually "burn" you. Use heavy leather gloves, or a thick piece of towel.

By the same token, dry ice should never be allowed to come in direct contact with your wrapped packages of venison or instantaneous "freezer burn" will result. So be sure to wrap the dry ice in several layers of newspaper. Then, when arranging your ice and wrapped meat packages in the container of your choice, make liberal use of filler materials such as wood shavings, excelsior, or styrofoam crumbles. In many instances these materials are given away free at the facility that sells dry ice; if not, go to a newsstand and ask for free, day-old newspapers, which you can shred or tear into strips for packing materials.

Other Transportation Methods

There are still other ways to transport your cache of venison with little risk of spoilage, no matter what the weather conditions or air temperature. One idea that seems to be gaining in popularity is submitting your deer to a big-game processing plant. These operations have long flourished in most western states but of late have been popping up as well throughout the Midwest and even up into New England.

The procedure is relatively simple. You leave your deer at a processing plant and they attend to all butchering operations, including grinding meat trimmings into burger and stuffing sausage into casing links. They then wrap the individual cuts, flash-freeze them, and ship the venison packages (in an appropriate container) to a terminal in your hometown. The cost of the service averages $75 for a mule deer or whitetail, plus shipping charges.

I suppose all of this is an attractive alternative to otherwise time-consuming home butchering for some people, particularly those who are not such serious deer hunters as to insist upon handling all of their own meatcutting. But there are many disadvantages most hunters are not aware of.

First, there unfortunately exists across the nation an illegal black market involving the sale of venison and the problem seems to grow larger and larger every year. Consequently, when many hunters receive their shipment of venison packages, they are "shorted" a number of prime steaks and roasts. A beginning hunter seldom notices the shortage but an expert, veteran hunter quickly does, and there's not a thing he can do about it. Not all processing plants engage in such illicit activity, but so many do that it's impossible to determine which facility is honest and which is not.

Aside from this, I've also seen more than a few processing houses where hundreds of deer were hanging in coolers waiting their turn at the butchering table, many of the animals not possessing proper tags clearly identifying their owners. The result of this is that you may very well receive a shipment of wrapped packages of venison not from the deer you actually harvested! And if the hunter who did harvest that particular deer was not at all knowledgeable or meticulous in his field-care and transportation techniques, you end up the beneficiary of venison that tasts like turpentine while some stranger dines upon your delectable fare.

Also, when you leave all the butchering up to a processing plant, there's a good chance the venison will not be cut to your desired preferences: Some meat portions may be too large for your family, others too small, and still others not exactly the way you'd like them in other regards.

On the other hand, if you butcher your deer yourself, you know for certain it's your deer, that you've taken home the entire deer, and that the individual cuts are tailored to your family's exact needs and preferences. Sure, this means additional work. But you save a gob of money, and most hunters look at the so-called "work" as a labor of love, anyway.

Now, let's shift gears for a moment and look at several other alternatives for transporting your venison home.

Suppose you've flown by commercial carrier to some particular ranch or other location for your deer hunting and will be returning home by plane. It's quite easy and a very common practice to take your venison with you, submitting it to the ticketing agent along with your other baggage. Here's how to handle the matter.

Have your deer butchered at the ranch you're working out of, or do the butchering yourself, whichever you prefer. Then have the wrapped packages solidly frozen and secured in an appropriate box that is taped securely closed and plainly labeled with your name and home address.

Without dry ice, the venison packages will remain frozen for up to 30 hours. With an appropriate quantity of dry ice in the middle of the container, you've got at least 48 hours.

If the flight home will exceed either of these lengths of time, due to various plane transfers and one or more overnight layovers, check with the airport information center to find out if on-location freezer facilities are available. Many major airports make this service available to traveling hunters and fishermen for a nominal price. If no such facilities are available at the airport, talk with the desk manager at the hotel where you'll be staying overnight and he'll undoubtedly allow you to stow your box of venison in the hotel's restaurant freezer. In either case, the following morning when you are ready to continue your journey, your venison, which has been sitting in a freezer overnight, will be frozen as solidly as possible.

Still another tack, if you're already overburdened with luggage and hunting gear, is to have the outfitter at your base camp freeze your venison packages, properly box them, then two or three days after your departure ship the box to your hometown via air-freight express. Boxes clearly labeled "Food . . . Perishable!" receive top priority and will arrive in your hometown within 24 hours, but the price for this service varies enormously among commercial carriers, so make a few investigative phone calls if possible. I've found rates as low as 20¢ per pound to as high as 80¢ per pound. But even at the higher rates, getting 75 pounds of boneless venison safely home costs only 60 bucks or thereabouts, which is not terribly unreasonable.

One important note: If at all possible, when having your venison shipped home (venison that is not accompanying you and your other baggage), specify that you want the package to leave early in the week. If the package is not shipped until Thursday or Friday, there's a remote chance, but nevertheless a chance indeed, that it will end up sitting in a terminal on some loading platform where it is sure to spoil over the weekend.

Still another option to consider—but a last resort—is shipping your venison by commercial bus. Many carriers maintain what they refer to as "next bus out" service, which is reserved exclusively for perishable foods, medical supplies, and the like. They guarantee, or so they claim, overnight delivery to any other terminal within 100 miles. Obviously, however, if you're much farther than that from home, the service isn't worth a hill of beans.

In summary, the best way of getting your venison home is via your own vehicle, using dry ice if necessary. Second best is submitting your packaged venison as luggage when traveling by commercial airlines. Beyond this, every hunter will have to evaluate the circumstances and logistics involved in his own particular hunt—and make appropriate plans well in advance of his departure—so that he gets his venison safely into his home freezer.

CHAPTER 8 ———

Home Care of Venison

THERE'S AN undeniably warm, smug, secure feeling about finally being home after a long, hard, cold hunt and having a handsome deer hanging out back.

Harvest time is now completely over and the root cellar is almost bursting at the seams with burlap sacks filled with potatoes, onions, and carrots. On nearby shelves there are dozens of jars of canned vegetables from the garden. In the freezer there is a good quantity of fish, upland gamebirds, small game, and wildfowl. And there's more than just a little comfort in peering through the kitchen window at several nearby cords of split and neatly stacked oak and hickory.

But more than anything else, it's that hefty buck that highlights all the other bounties of the land and the preparations for winter's long and bitter onslaught. Even in pioneer times no garden crop, catch of fish, or successful trapline-run drew as much applause, joy, and happy attention as a hunter arriving home with a winter's supply of venison. So sit back and savor your prideful accomplishment, for these are among life's precious moments and the very things memories are made of. But don't dawdle with your thoughts too long for there are still other deer-care measures that must be attended to . . . things that will weigh heavily upon those final taste treats you're looking forward to in coming months.

Essentially, what the hunter has to do now is hang his deer, age it, remove the hide, clean the carcass again, and otherwise prepare it for butchering operations (these are discussed in Chapter 9). However, the exact sequence in which these tasks are done is far from cut and dried because many variables, including the unique circumstances of any specific hunt, enter the picture. For example, the deer may already be minus its hide, this particular step having been taken care of in camp. Perhaps the deer is even partially butchered and now is in the form of primal cuts stowed in meatbags. Then too, the existing air temperature will play a role in determining which tasks should be given priority.

Therefore, the only way for me to handle the presentation of material in this chapter is by taking the so-called "shotgun" approach. In other words, I'll cover all pertinent techniques and advice regarding the home care of venison. But then, it's up to you to perform these procedures in the particular sequence that seems best given the present condition of your deer and other variables such as existing weather.

How to Hang Your Deer

Compared to merely laying your deer somewhere on the ground or on your garage floor, which I've actually seen some hunters do, hanging the carcass is much wiser. The venison stays much cleaner this way, air circulation around the carcass is facilitated, and most insects are kept at bay. It's also much easier to work on a deer when it's suspended from some overhead hanging device.

There is always great debate among hunters as to whether a deer should be hung by the head, with a rope around the antlers or neck, or whether the deer should be hung upside-down with a gambrel between the gambrel-tendons of the rear legs. If you'll recall, I recommended hanging a deer by the hind legs when it is first brought into camp, for two reasons. First, body heat can more easily rise and escape from the chest region of the animal to more quickly cool the meat; simultaneously, any remaining blood and residual body fluids can more quickly exit from the head-neck-thorax region without draining down and through the prime cuts of venison.

But with your deer already thoroughly chilled, drained of all fluids, and transported home, it can now be rehung in any manner that suits you. I've personally found it much easier to begin work on the forequarter region of a hanging deer and gradually work my way down to the hindquarters. If you prefer to do it the opposite way, fine and dandy!

However, one thing you may wish to consider once again is the possibility of having a head mount made by a taxidermist, in which case strangling the deer with a rope noose around the neck or antlers is guaranteed to damage the hide.

As in camp, deer should be hung once they reach home. A stout tree limb in your backyard, the rafters in your garage, or the roof joists in an open-air shed are all ideal.

But aside from this, far more important than deciding whether to hang the deer by the head or rear legs is deciding *where* to hang the deer in the first place. Using a stout tree limb in the backyard is a very common practice but one I cannot recommend unless no other choice is available. A deer hanging from a tree limb is outside a protected enclosure and may be exposed to inclement weather. In addition, since the tree's leaves are gone, your venison will be subjected to bright sunlight and perhaps even very warm temperatures, particularly if you live in the South or took your deer early in the fall during the bowhunting season.

Ideally, the place for hanging your deer should be shady, a bit breezy, and protected from neighborhood pets roaming at large. Consequently, a garage or shed possessing a door you can close is perfect, but even an open-air shed or carport may work fine if your neighbors don't have free-ranging dogs and cats.

Hoist the deer so its head, or hind legs, are approximately two feet off the ground. This will reduce any risk of rodents and other four-legged varmints from sampling your venison. If someone is around to lend a hand, it's relatively easy for one man to bear-hug the carcass and lift while the other simultaneously pulls on a rope that has been thrown over an overhead beam. However, it's virtually impossible for one man to do this alone, as beams and roof joists are squared off along their dimensions and a rope defies being pulled over such acute edges.

This is why I always recommend that a hunter invest in a lightweight block and tackle utilizing two or more opposing pulleys. Sportsmen's models, which are specifically intended for lifting big-game animals, are inexpensive and allow one to easily winch his deer aloft.

If you plan to lift your deer carcass by the hind legs you'll additionally need some type of gambrel. If you have a home workshop you can make one yourself from half-inch reinforcing rod. Measurements are not critical but try to stay with something about two feet wide, with upturned sharpened points at each end and in the top-center a means of attaching the lower hook of your block and tackle. Factory-made models also are available.

Also be sure to exercise extreme care in slitting the thin skin of the hocks, through which the gambrel is to be inserted, because if you inadvertently cut the Achilles tendon that particular leg will flop free and be useless for hanging the deer. The only alternative then is to hang the deer by the head.

Aging Venison

The reasons for aging venison are manyfold. Of course, there is the gratifying opportunity of being able to admire the game a while longer. But from a strict meat-care standpoint, aging imparts tenderness and enhances the flavor of the venison. It does this by allowing the slow, controlled growth of natural bacterial organisms to break down tissue cells. Once a deer has been properly aged, butchering and quick freezing then brings an immediate halt to any further bacterial action, which preserves the meat.

The act of aging venison carries an almost romantic quality, but some hunters go to extremes and age their deer far longer than necessary; they risk going beyond the point of merely tenderizing the meat and having spoilage begin to set in.

This is a shameful waste of precious venison. And it's one of the very reasons why some deer meat often tastes overly strong, pungent, and gamey, despite other explanations that are sure to gush forth from various sources. One hunter will claim this year's deer tastes absolutely awful because the buck was in rut. Another will say the meat tastes bad because the musk glands were not removed from the hind legs. And still another will attribute the terrible tasting venison to the deer being too old. In actuality, all of these and still other myths are merely excuses for the hunter's own poor handling of the meat during field-dressing operations, in camp, on the road, or at home in allowing the meat to age to the point of spoilage.

Perfect aging is accomplished under these conditions: The deer should be hanging, with its hide on, for a length of time ranging from four to eight days, at a temperature consistently between 38 and 40 degrees, at a relative humidity of 75 to 80 percent.

However, this is the ideal and it is not often that these conditions can be met exactly. Take the matter of air temperature. If the mercury climbs to 50 or 60 degrees during the day, but then dips down into the twenties at night, no problem; the temperature of the meat itself will still remain in the desirable 38- to 40-degree range. Just remember never to allow the meat to freeze while aging; nor should the temperature of the meat ever climb above 50 degrees or bacterial growth will be vastly accelerated. One way to monitor the temperature of your aging carcass—a tip I've never seen printed elsewhere—is to use an ice pick to pierce a hole into the neck meat of the carcass and then insert a thermometer.

As to the recommended length of time venison should be allowed to age, again a bit of flexibility is permissible. Although the ideal time is four to eight days, ten days will do no harm if optimum air temperatures prevail. Similarly, if the deer you harvest is in prime condition, as described in Chapter 1, you may commence butchering operations after only one or two day's hanging time with the full assurance that the venison will be tender and flavorful.

The best way to monitor the humidity is by simply listening to a daily weather report. A relatively high humidity is desired, to ensure moisture retention by the meat. Venison, which already is quite "dry" and lean, may actually become less tender if the humidity drops to exceedingly low levels. This is why it's always recommended that hunters living in the far North and desert Southwest not age their wild game; in such consistently dry areas of the continent aging actually has an adverse effect. Conversely, if the humidity is too high—85 percent or higher—which often is characteristic of the southeastern states, the added moisture in the air not only spurs bacteria growth but also encourages the formation of mold on the outside of the meat. All of these things have an important bearing upon the successful aging of venison and how long a hunter should allow his deer to hang.

Ideally, a deer should age with the hide on because the hide helps the carcass to retain moisture. This not only prevents it from drying out too much but also eliminates excessive glazing that must later be trimmed away, at the sacrifice of a good deal of prime meat. However, if the hide has already been removed in camp, due to overly warm weather or some other reason, there is no alternative but aging the meat without its overcoat. To offer a bit of protection, slip a gamebag over the animal.

In momentarily going back to the subject of hanging a deer, I'd like to reveal some new savvy you may eventually find use for. It's a third hanging method you've never seen mentioned in any other book or magazine article. Quite different from hanging a deer by the hind legs, or by the head, this method involves hanging the deer by a single hook or rope that is passed through the boney channel through the pelvis just beneath the aitch bone, which formerly was the home of the bladder.

I call this technique the *tender-stretch* hanging method. It's specifically designed for those deer a hunter may suspect are not likely to be tender. Compared to hanging a deer by the head or hind legs, both of which see the brunt of the carcass weight borne by the hanging device, tender-stretch hanging strains and pushes the weight of the meat against itself to good advantage. That is, when the deer is hanging by the pelvic arch, the heavy weight of the unsupported hindquarters is allowed to exert downward pressure upon the remainder of the carcass. This has the effect of stretching the longitudinal muscle fibers (which always are the toughest) and thereby somewhat breaking down the integrity of their cellular structure, which in turn makes them more tender.

In order to gain maximum advantage from this technique, two other steps are necessary. First, in addition to hanging the deer by the pelvic arch, tie a concrete block to a short length of rope tied around the neck, which further pulls and stretches downward upon the carcass to make the neck meat and upper regions of the front shoulders tender beyond belief. Then, after a couple of days of hanging and aging in such a manner, turn the deer around so it is now hanging by the head, with the concrete block tied between the knees of both rear legs. This stretches the deer in the opposite direction and thereby further tenderizes both hindquarters and the saddle.

To repeat, in most cases the tender-stretch procedure is not necessary. Rather, it is a refinement of traditional aging techniques, designed to tenderize those occasional animals that upon close inspection appear not to be as tender as desired, but which the hunter doesn't want to relegate entirely to the meat grinder.

There are still other aspects of aging that warrant careful thought. If it is terribly hot outside and even a brief aging period might cause spoilage, here's what I recommend. Strip the hide off your deer if you haven't already done so and immediately butcher the animal. Wrap all the meat cuts, but instead of placing them in your freezer place them in your refrigerator.

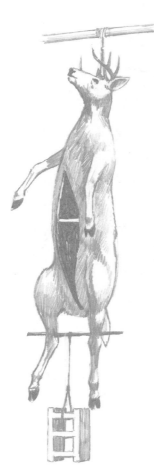

The tender-stretch method of aging venison. Carcass first is stretched in one direction by means of a concrete block, then reversed and stretched again in the opposite direction.

The inside of your refrigerator has an average temperature of 38 degrees, which will allow for a week of perfect aging. One important thing to understand, however, is that the inside of your refrigerator has a quite low humidity level, which will cause your venison to become overly dry as it ages if special precautions are not taken. So remember to set inside the refrigerator an uncovered bowl of water to add moisture to the air.

Since you'll have so many wrapped packages of venison, they will take up nearly all the room inside your refrigerator and you'll have to contend with the problem of what to do with your milk, eggs, vegetables, and other foods. But usually, if you plan a bit in advance, many of these foods can be consumed and not immediately replaced. The remaining staples you need on a daily basis can be temporarily stored in iced-down camping coolers while your venison ages.

If outside weather conditions do not permit proper aging, you can butcher the venison and age it in your refrigerator for several days before freezing the packages. Or you can quarter the deer and hang the venison in a cool cellar near an open window, with a fan turned on to circulate breezes.
Photo by Kenn Oberrecht.

Now let's look at conditions that are just the opposite. Suppose that instead of being overly warm outside, it's bitter cold and a deer allowed to hang outside will quickly freeze. If you have a garage or similar storage building, close all the doors and windows and turn on a small space heater in a far corner. It won't be terribly expensive to operate because you only have to maintain a 38-degree temperature.

Another alternative is transferring your deer to your basement and hanging it from a hook or beam on the ceiling. If the temperature of your basement generally is higher than 40 degrees during the winter, hang the deer near a window that can be left ajar and turn on a small fan to keep cold air circulating around the carcass.

Finally, it may not be necessary to age your venison at home at all. If you've been hunting far away from home and your deer has already undergone three or four days aging as it hung in camp, then was subjected to another two or three days aging while you were on the road traveling home, additional home aging is not necessary or recommended.

Removing the Hide

Several times I've mentioned skinning deer and this is a good place to examine the subject in greater detail. The hunter himself, however, will have to decide exactly when to remove his deer's hide, depending upon a wide range of factors such as the existing temperature and weather conditions, how the deer is to be transported home, and in what manner the deer is to be aged. All of which presents something of a dilemma.

What I mean is, if you can skin the deer immediately after it is killed, or within a few hours, while the hide is still fresh and warm, it will peel off more quickly and easily compared to the tough work involved in trying to remove a hide days later when it is cold and much drier. But, as already noted, leaving the hide on, if the weather permits, is beneficial because it protects the carcass during transport and helps the venison retain moisture during aging. What to do?

Well, only you can answer that. But my opinion regarding any decision that must be made about deer care is that the quality of the venison should always be given priority consideration above everything else. So I have mentally trained myself to tolerate the more difficult work that delayed hide removal entails, knowing the venison will be all the better.

Begin by hanging the deer by either the head or hind legs, whichever you prefer. It makes no difference whatever. Next, slit the skin on the inside of each leg, just above the knee, being sure to make the cut very shallow so as to not damage any meat, and continue those slits up to the body cavity. Assuming you're not planning to have a head mount made, next make a cut through the hide encircling the neck, just below the chin. Now, extend the abdominal cut you made when field dressing by going right down the centerline of the chest, brisket, and neck to the neck cut you just completed. In making all of these cuts, use just the tip of your knife with the blade edge facing up. The same knife you use for field dressing is adequate for this chore.

Now reach for your skinning knife, the one with the wide, flat blade designed to be worked beneath animal hides without damaging meat. Grab a flap of the hide at the neck and begin pulling it down and away with your hand, using the knife to help free the hide wherever it is securely attached. Or, if the deer is hanging by the legs, free the hide from around the legs first, being careful not to cut through the Achilles tendons, then around the tail.

The remainder of the hide-removal procedure is accomplished mostly with the hands alone. Grab the hide, roll it just a bit to get a secure handhold, then with the weight of your body begin pushing downward with your fists. As the hide begins to come away from the carcass it can be rolled even more

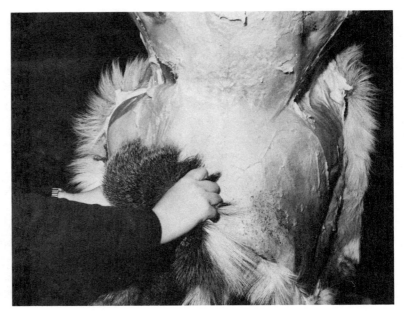

Removing the hide is easiest when it is still fresh. Use your knife minimally; instead, push and pull the hide away to avoid damaging the venison.

for a firmer grasp and therefore additional leverage. The advantage of this method is that it eliminates the chance of accidental slices into the meat or hide that even an expert might make if he used a knife continually.

Another method of hide removal is rapidly gaining in popularity because it is faster and easier than the traditional method of using the "knife and knuckle" approach. Furthermore, it provides no chance whatever of accidental cutting into the venison.

With the deer hanging, make your preliminary knife cuts as described earlier—down the insides of the legs to the body cavity, down the centerline of the chest and neck, then encircling the neck. Now, lower the deer to the ground so it is lying upon a clean sheet of plastic, cardboard, or plywood. One end of a short length of chain is then wrapped around the animal's head just beneath the chin. The other end of the chain is attached to some immovable object such as a tree, stump, or utility pole.

Next, with your knife, cut and pull away a flap of skin at the back of the neck, as though you were beginning to remove the hide in the usual manner, but go no farther. Then, on top of this loosened flap of hide lay a golfball-sized rock, then pull the hide flap back on top of it. With a stout rope make a small noose, slip it over the lump of neck hide with the stone inside, snug the noose up tightly, then tie the opposite end of the rope to the rear bumper of a vehicle. As the driver begins very slowly pulling away, the hide quickly strips from the animal just like peeling the skin from a banana.

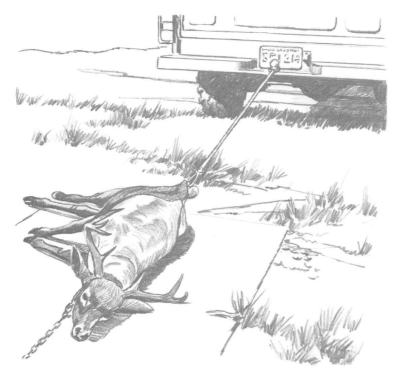

A unique method of hide removal that is very fast is pulling the hide off with a vehicle. Try it once and you may never again use any other.

After the hide has been removed, the final task is to cut off the lower legs at the knee with a saw.

This procedure may sound complicated but after doing it one time you'll see that it is much faster and easier than skinning a deer any other way.

After removing the hide, you may wish to saw off each lower hind leg just below the knees, especially if you plan to enclose the carcass in a gamebag. Otherwise the lower legs may be removed during butchering.

It's now a good idea to closely inspect the carcass for damaged or bloodshot areas that should be carefully trimmed away. Pay particular attention to the region of the gunshot or arrow wound, entirely encircling it with your knife blade and cutting it out, in addition to any surrounding tissue that is severely bloodshot.

If a shoulder or any other part of the deer has been damaged by the bullet or arrow, it may be salvagable. Simply place the meat overnight in a bowl of saltwater. Nine times in ten bloodshot meat looks worse than it really is, and this overnight soaking in saltwater does an impressive job of cleaning it up and restoring it to an acceptable state for use in burger or sausage. If the bloodshot area is too severely damaged, or appears riddled with digestive or fecal matter, discard it.

Finally, use a clean cloth dampened with very warm water to wipe down your deer carcass. As careful as anyone may try to be in skinning a deer, it is inevitable that numerous hairs from the hide will be found clinging to the carcass and a warm, dampened cloth is the fastest way to remove them.

CHAPTER 9

Getting Ready for Butchering

BUTCHERING A DEER requires many advance preparations so that an assemblage of knives and other tools can be used to reduce big pieces of venison quickly and efficiently into numerous smaller ones ready for the freezer. In accomplishing all of this there is no substitute for plenty of firsthand, trial-and-error experience to find out what works best for you. And those unique routines, methods, and equipment preferences you eventually come to rely upon may well differ from the likes of another expert.

Ideally, these building blocks of experience are gained through your success over the years in regularly bringing home enough venison so that you will have continual practice. A good illustration of this happened during the 1982–83 deer season when I was lucky enough to collect three splendid bucks: a handsome whitetail on my farm in Ohio, another whitetail in northern Minnesota, and a mule deer in western Colorado. With such a quantity of venison at hand, this was the season that I finally perfected my previously dubious "skills" in preparing rolled shoulder and rump roasts. Yet something else became patently clear as I worked on that bonanza of venison: One never learns everything there is to know about the art of meatcutting. That's why I always jump at the opportunity to watch other professional butchers and expert deer hunters at work; invariably you receive a college education of little-known tips and techniques that can be adapted to your own meat-cutting efforts.

So allow me to begin this chapter by introducing my friend Charlie Hause, who many years ago took me under his wing and who I've always looked upon as a "professor emeritus" of the chopping-block table. Hailing from St. Paul, Minnesota, Charlie is not only a skilled deer hunter with bow and gun but also by trade a professional meatcutter, a combination of attributes that right off gives you the utmost confidence he knows what he's doing. In addition to every year cutting up hundreds of carcasses from beef steers, hogs, and other livestock, as well as the deer he harvests himself, he moonlights during the hunting season by doing custom-butchering for local sportsmen.

I wouldn't want to guess how many deer Charlie has cut up in his life, but there was a particular day that stands out in his memory when he was so swamped with orders he just couldn't handle everything himself. So he bought a couple of cases of premium beer, which always is a good persuader, and then called three fellow meatcutters and asked them to come over and help him out of a jam. Beginning at three o'clock in the afternoon, the foursome set to the task and continued working through the late night hours until four o'clock in the morning. During that time Charlie and his pals completely butchered a total of 40 deer. Not only that, they also made 1,200 pounds of burger and sausage from all the trimmings and, yes, even managed to polish off both cases of beer.

It must have been a wild and woolly night, but everything was completed to perfection and several hours later hundreds of wrapped, labeled, and frozen packages of venison were waiting for their respective owners to pick up. I remember Charlie saying that about the time he finished cleaning up his home butchershop from this marathon meatcutting session he had just enough time to grab a quick shower before having to open his grocery store downtown and put in a long day cutting up several beef steers. A pro's pro, indeed!

Preparing Your Work Area

A common thread that runs through my many memories of watching Charlie Hause and other professional butchers is that, just before beginning work on their venison, they invest prodigious amounts of time readying their work sites.

This is crucially important to success, speed, and happiness because you don't want to be so physically uncomfortable that the butchering operation becomes a miserable ordeal. Nor do you want to take 12 hours to complete a 6-hour task, and perhaps even do a sloppy job at that. And with several venison quarters lying before you, now is certainly *not* the time to launch a search for your knives and other paraphernalia, as all of these aspects of poor planning doom the effort right from the start.

First decide upon the best place to do your butchering. Likely as not the weather and outside air temperature will play a major role in this decision, dictating that the job be accomplished indoors. A garage is a perfect location, provided that it is clean, well lighted, and warm enough that you can work in shirtsleeves. Another ideal location, if the same prerequisites can be met, is your basement.

In many instances, the *least* favorable place is your kitchen, and with good reason. The kitchens of most homes are high-traffic areas where meals must be prepared three times a day and hunting dogs must be fed and kids are always looking for snacks or wanting a drink. Also, in most kitchens, available counterspace isn't really large enough for major butchering operations.

What you need is ample time to complete your meatcutting without hassles and interruptions. You need a large work surface and plenty of elbow room. And you need the assurance—not the constant worry—that some errant speck of blood or scrap of meat that perchance falls to the floor is not going to draw the wrath of other family members. All of which, again, brings us back to either the garage or basement as the recommended location for butchering your deer.

A large table is fine as your work surface. This can be an old table in your basement, or it can be a picnic table carried into your garage. It can also mean something as spartan, and yet efficient, as a large sheet of plywood resting upon sawhorses. Just make sure it's as clean as possible and situated in such a manner that you will be cutting at comfortable waist level.

To guarantee cleanliness, cover your work table with protective paper. I've found conventional white, plastic-coated freezer wrapping paper is ideal. Lay it down in several long, overlapping sheets with the shiny, plastic side up; secure the edges in place around the perimeter of the table with masking tape.

The purpose of this tabletop covering is to have a neat, clean place to set various cuts of meat before and after working on them. However, you'll not want to do actual cutting on this surface because your knife blade would quickly reduce the paper to shreds.

For cutting work, you need some type of cutting board. This can be a standard kitchen model made of strips of laminated wood, a professional meatcutting board made of pressed styrene and thermoplastic resin, or merely a clean square of plywood. Whatever your choice, make sure it is large enough to provide you with ample working space. Something in the neighborhood of 24 inches wide by 48 inches long by 1 inch thick is just right.

Various types and sizes of chopping-block tables, of course, are the best bet of all. They're worthwhile investments on the part of serious hunters who take deer every year because in addition to splendidly accommodating

Preparing your work area is essential to speedy, professional-quality meatcutting. A well-lighted garage and some type of work surface is ideal. Here, meatcutter Charlie Hause cleans the top of a chopping-block table.

venison, they have numerous other food-preparation uses throughout the remainder of the year.

Just be sure you carefully follow the manufacturer's instructions before and after each use of the table because wood is a very porous material that may harbor bacteria if not properly cleaned and maintained. Some chopping-block tables, such as the one I'm presently using, have special polyurethane coatings that require no maintenance whatever, other than occasionally wiping down the cutting top with a damp rag. Others, however, require periodic "scraping" with a stiff-bristle wire brush, application of a disinfectant, and annual treatments with rubbing oil.

Tools of the Trade

"A meatcutter is no better than the knives he uses," Jim Borg, a professional butcher from Nashville, Tennessee, remarked as we began working on two deer. With that, he opened his special briefcase, a hallmark that distinguishes such tradesmen, and gave me a peek at a gleaming array of knives of every conceivable design, all assigned to their own protective slots in styrofoam.

Borg's opening comment was right, of course, because proper tools always enable their users to do far more commendable work than otherwise. And like a master mechanic given only one type of wrench, a deer hunter who has only one poorly chosen knife can expect to do little more than an amateurish, hacked-up job on his deer.

Admittedly, every skilled meatcutter has certain preferences regarding his selection of knives depending on the particular way he likes to reduce a deer carcass to various cuts of meat. So it's impossible here to recommend a specific assortment of tools as better than any other. Yet we can talk in generalities.

First, some type of conventional butcher's knife with a blade at least 10 inches in length is needed to reduce large chunks of meat to smaller ones in one fell swoop; otherwise, several smaller cuts will have to be made instead of a single slice, and those cuts will seldom meet, leaving a ragged, irregular appearance.

A boning knife also is imperative. As the reader will soon discover, I am a strong proponent of boning out meat whenever possible, for two important reasons. Bone-cutting with a saw is eliminated, so distasteful marrow "dust" cannot sprinkle the meat. Second, you save on freezer space when you don't have to store bones along with your meat.

Most boning knives have a long, slender blade that culminates in an upswept tip. They also are quite thin, which gives the blade flexibility to allow a cutter to carefully guide the blade around irregular bone curvatures like a blind man using a cane.

A butcher is no better than the tools he uses. An assortment of quality knives ranging from a boning knife (bottom) to a cleaver will enable any hunter to do superior work.

This is the author's custom-made boning knife, perfect for getting into tight places and following the irregular curvature of a deer's anatomy.

In addition to a conventional boning knife, I use a miniature version made in my workshop by taking an old steak knife and submitting it to a grinding wheel. This little beauty is invaluable when it comes to working in tiny, tight places where a full-sized boning knife would be awkward and inefficient.

If you don't have a boning knife, or can't afford one just yet, a good alternative is a common fish fillet knife. These possess the very same attributes—narrow, sharp tip, long blade, and thin, flexible steel—that will allow you to easily follow the contours of bones hidden from view within meat.

A second, smaller, all-purpose or utility knife may also come in handy for final trimming operations and other close work calling for a meticulous touch. And you might also from time to time find use for a heavy meat cleaver, especially when working on ribs and steaks prepared bone-in.

Some type of meat saw is also sure to be periodically needed in the processing of venison. As already mentioned, I firmly believe minimal bone-cutting produces the most flavorful venison, but since some cutting is inevitable, a quality saw comes in handy. Such a saw is chiefly used to cut off the lower legs and separate the head from the carcass by cutting through the neckbone. Then, during actual butchering operations you may desire to cut sections from the rib cage for broiling, and preparing certain types of roasts, such as blade roasts, also may require a bit of bone-cutting. There's even one technique to be described later that involves halving the carcass by cutting down the centerline of the backbone.

Several types of special meat saws may come in handy, beginning with this small model that's ideal for both camp and home use.

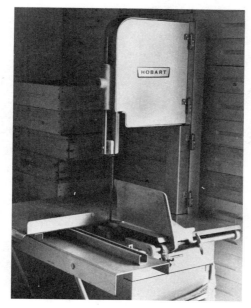

In hunting clubs where numerous deer are butchered every week, a good investment shared by all might be a professional band saw especially designed for meatcutting.

There are many models of saws to choose from, depending upon your needs and how much you can afford to spend. The smallest meat and bone saw I'm aware of is the Wyoming Saw, which is designed primarily for field use or in camp.

The largest and most expensive saw is an electric, table-mounted bandsaw of the type found in professional butchershops. These can make quick work of deer and do extremely high-quality work, but their staggering prices generally limit their use to those who do custom-butchering of deer for others, and hunting clubs where numerous members can share the cost.

A good compromise is the traditional butcher's saw. A quality model such as this will last your lifetime.

In between these two extremes are moderately priced, professional meat saws that resemble giant hacksaws but are specifically intended for cutting meat and bone.

In a pinch you can even improvise by using a common hacksaw fitted with a new blade having no more than 10 teeth per inch (typical blades intended for cutting metal have up to 26 teeth per inch; since the teeth are so small and close together they quickly clog with bone and meat residue, which renders them inoperative). If you decide to go the hacksaw route, be sure the new blade you install is first cleaned with hot, soapy water to remove any oily film that may be on the blade.

Some means of keeping your knives scalpel-sharp through the duration of your meatcutting also is imperative. A quality whetstone such as an Arkansas or Ouachita is a good choice. And there are ceramic rods, diamond-dust impregnated steel rods, and numerous other gadgets to choose from. However, using any of these properly can involve a lot of time. This is why professional butchers, at the outset, sharpen their knives on a stone but then during the course of meatcutting operations make periodic use of a "steel."

A sharpening steel looks like a large rat-tail file in that a long, tapered, rough-surfaced rod is inserted into a wooden handle. The purpose of a steel is not to sharpen a knife in the conventional sense by removing metal and forming an edge, as with a stone, but rather to temporarily restore a bit of the knife's sharpness by removing the wavy edge all knives take after considerable use. This stopgap measure therefore allows a meatcutter to continue his work and finish the job without a lengthy absence at the stone.

Sharpening steels (in fact, even meat saws and other tools) are best obtained from restaurant supply companies located in every major city. At first, using a steel may seem somewhat awkward, but with a bit of practice it will become second nature. Basically, the knife is held in one hand, tip pointing up, and the steel is held in the other, tip pointing up. The knife is then gently sandpapered against the steel in rapid up and down fashion with each pass seeing the knife alternate across the front of the steel and then the back, to work both sides of the blade edge. If you find great difficulty mastering the use of a steel, ask your local butcher to give you a firsthand demonstration.

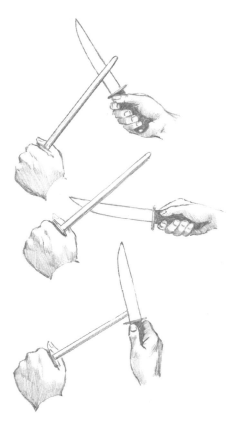

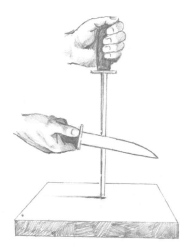

A sharpening steel doesn't really sharpen a knife blade but realigns the wavy edge of the blade to keep it continually sharp during the course of cutting chores. There are two ways to use a steel. One is by lapping the blade back and forth with the steel held in the left hand (left). The other is by standing the steel on end on a tabletop, then making vertical passes up and down the steel.

Tricks of the Trade

Among the little tips and techniques you can pick up by watching other experts and one of the first that Charlie Hause passed onto me is making sure the meat is very, very cold. The shoulders, haunches, and other primal cuts should be almost but not quite frozen. The reason for this is that when it is warm, any kind of meat is loose, floppy, soft, and uncontrollable and in this condition it is virtually impossible to make neat, precision cuts.

Furthermore, a large quantity of relatively warm meat from any kind of animal, domestic or wild, has a distinct odor. It is not at all an unpleasant aroma but after six or eight hours of continually breathing it in you may begin feeling a bit nauseous.

Very cold meat, on the other hand, has almost no odor whatever. And since it is so firm, you can handle it with ease, propping it up just so to make certain cuts, turning it this way or that to perform all manner of surgical operations cleanly and neatly without the meat sagging, separating, and seemingly having a mind of its own.

Another characteristic of very cold meat is that it is not sticky, which is something no one can really appreciate until he's had the experience of working with warm meat, particularly small pieces being trimmed for burger. Like flypaper, the stuff sticks to your hands, your worktable, your knife blade and everything else it touches, which generates so much frustration you want to knash your teeth and growl.

So make a point of always ensuring that your venison is quite cold. You'll find your butchering takes far less time and the finished work will appear far more professional looking.

Another thing Charlie Hause emphasizes is the importance of working with clean meat. It is inevitable when working with deer that countless, tiny hairs from the hide will adhere to the venison. These are all sources of contamination if not removed, but picking them away one by one can test the patience of Job.

That's why Charlie thoroughly cleans all surfaces of the meat before the first knife cut ever is made. He does this by using a small piece of terrycloth towel soaked in very warm water and then thoroughly wrung out. Amazingly, several swipes in one direction and then another removes every stray hair easily and quickly. Although this step is also done just before hanging the carcass and letting it age, it's necessary to do it a second time when each primal cut is removed from the carcass and set upon the meatcutting table to be worked upon.

Still another tip Charlie Hause taught me long ago has to do with testing the tenderness of various meat cuts. Merely pinch a small piece of each major meat cut between the fingernails of your thumb and forefinger. Meat that is not so tender will offer resistance at first and then upon exertion of more fingertip pressure will begin to slightly dimple or compress itself. Conversely, tender meat will readily be cut by your fingernails and almost begin to "mush" between your fingertips.

There are several advantages in knowing how tender various parts of the anatomy are likely to be. First, you know how the meat should be cut. Should it be sliced into steaks to be panfried, made into roasts to be baked, or cut into cubes for stew meat? In producing roasts and such, you know whether you should go to the extra trouble to lard or bard particular ones (both of these techniques are discussed later). You even know whether certain cuts should be tenderized more just before cooking by sprinkling with a commercial meat-tenderizing salt or soaking them in some type of marinade.

Finally, I should emphasize, as in the previous chapter, that in addition to many different ways to cut up your deer, there also are many different sequences in which various procedures can be rightfully enacted. So don't worry at all about whether the neck meat should be removed from the carcass first or last, or whether you should begin butchering the front legs before the hind legs, or vice versa. Tackle the various meatcutting operations in any order you prefer. In time, after you've acquired a bit of experience, you'll settle down into a particular routine you like best.

CHAPTER 10

Easy Meatcutting Methods

BUTCHERING A DEER is both easy and difficult. The easy part merely has to do with using knives and assorted other tools to cut big pieces of meat into numerous smaller ones. The entire procedure is basically a manual chore not unlike changing a flat tire in that once you've learned which steps have to be performed and then acquire some practice you can do a professional job almost blindfolded.

The sometimes difficult aspect of butchering a deer is deciding which of many meatcutting methods to use, depending upon the size of the deer, the amount of time you have available, and the types of meals your family prefers. Understandably, a very large deer is going to have anatomical features more conducive to certain uses than a small deer. And some of us are going to want to go to the extra trouble to make rolled roasts from the rumps, for example, instead of merely slicing off round steaks, because past experience has shown that everyone in our particular family likes roasts so much.

It is not even unusual for many hunters to relegate their entire deer— front legs, hams, tenderloins . . . everything—to the meat grinder in the making of various types of sausage. Venison sausage, to them, is positively ambrosia and that is therefore the ultimate destiny of their entire deer. Period.

But maybe the greatest hurdle of all that most hunters face at the outset is feeling absolutely overwhelmed by the enormous size of that deer carcass hanging in the shed. I mean, several weeks before the deer season we bagged two plump rabbits and in a matter of minutes had them ready for the frying pan. But now, the beast hanging before us is of such ponderous dimensions we feel more than just a little intimidated. Where in the world does one possibly begin?

My recommendation has always been to approach the job piecemeal. In other words, remove from the carcass one piece of meat that is relatively easy to handle, such as a front leg, take it to the cutting table in your garage or basement and, following the step-by-step instructions I'll give in a moment, thoroughly reduce that leg to wrapped cuts of meat ready for the freezer. Then go back and get the other front leg and proceed as before, momentarily forgetting about all the rest. Since you've already just finished a front leg and learned something in the process, the second front leg should be a snap. Then butcher a hind leg, and so on. By following this suggested routine, the carcass will steadily become smaller and smaller in size and yet all the while not pose such a formidable challenge.

Here, venison expert Charlie Hause looks over one-half of a large mule deer he has just finished butchering. To some, achieving such professional results may seem like a formidable undertaking. But follow the step-by-step guidelines in this chapter and the job will be easy, even for first-timers.

Keep in mind as well a key thought expressed in the last chapter. You need not follow any specific butchering sequence, such as front legs before hind legs, or whatever. Feel entirely free to tackle any of the following meat-cutting procedures in any order you like.

Front Legs and Shoulders

Removing a front leg and shoulder assembly from the carcass is quite easy because there is no ball-and-socket attachment as there is with the hind legs. Instead, the wide, flat shoulder bone, known as the scapula, is free-floating and independent of any other bone connection with the body, the attachment merely consisting of a series of thin muscle segments covered by thin skin tissue.

Therefore, all that's necessary is to grab the lower leg near the knee and pull it away from the carcass while simultaneously using a long-bladed butcher knife to cut the connective muscle tissue on the backside of the scapula adjoining the rib cage. Keep the blade flat and close to the rib cage as you continue to lift and pull away the shoulder scapula and cut it free. In this manner, you should be able to remove the entire front leg and shoulder assembly in less than one minute.

With the front leg and shoulder now lying on your cutting table, wipe it down with a warm, dampened cloth to remove any stray hairs or other debris. Then, with a thin-bladed knife, begin carefully trimming the meat of unwanted tallow and the very thin, protective, skinlike glazing crust the meat acquired during aging.

At this point, let's take a break from the butchering because it is very important to briefly discuss the trimming away of fat from various parts of a deer's anatomy. Other books and magazine articles dealing with deer hunting and the handling of deer meat have historically preached the dire necessity of trimming away every speck of fat you find, claiming it is so distasteful that if left intact no one will enjoy eating your venison. But I've never been one to simply parrot that which has been written before, so read on.

Actually, deer possess three types of fat, and according to studies at Utah State University, not all of them are sources of disagreeable flavor. First there is *cod fat,* which is found only on the brisket. Then there is *tallow fat,* which is found mainly on the back, covering the rump, and to a lesser extent around the perimeter of the neck and on the rearmost areas of the front shoulders. Finally, there is *marbling fat,* which is found throughout the body but concentrated in muscle tissue and between series of opposing muscle structures.

Cod fat and tallow fat are both designed to keep the animal warm in cold weather, so they are located on the exterior surfaces of the anatomy just

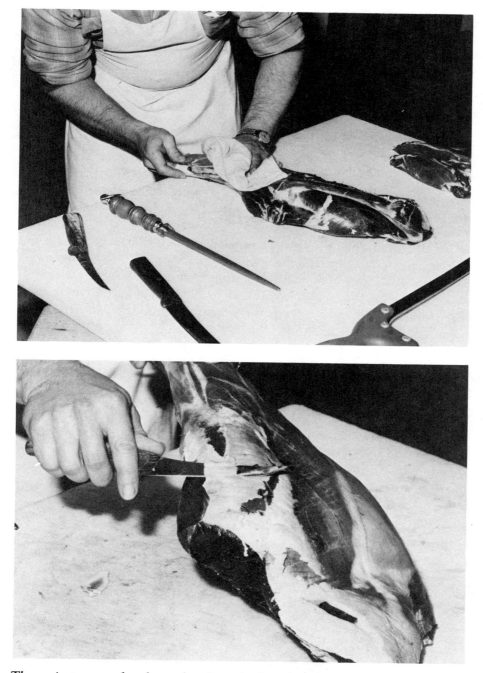

The easiest way to butcher a deer is to do the job piecemeal. Begin with a front leg (top), which is easily removed from the carcass by running your knife blade beneath the flat scapula. Now wipe the leg down with a damp cloth to remove hairs. Next, use your knife to trim away dried flesh, thick layers of tallow fat, and other unwanted matter.

beneath the hide. Cod fat and tallow fat have flavors not terribly disagreeable but indeed noticeable and upon occasion a bit strong. So good advice is to try and remove as much cod fat and tallow fat as possible. But there's no need to be so meticulous about this that you end up spending twice the amount of time it should ordinarily take to butcher a deer.

Marbling fat, on the other hand, is deep fat woven interstitially through and between muscle fibers, muscle segments, and connective tissue. It looks like thin, elongated white streaks and as much of this fat as possible should be allowed to remain! Not only is marbling fat virtually tasteless but the Utah State studies proved its presence significantly increased the tenderness of cooked venison compared to other cuts of meat that had much of their marbling removed.

Consequently, when you first lay each large chunk of meat on the cutting table, no matter what part of the anatomy it came from, turn the meat this way and that and as you do so carefully trim away as much surface fat as you see on all sides of the meat. However, after this is accomplished and as you begin to reduce the meat to various freezer-ready cuts, leave intact the remaining fat found deeper inside.

Now that the front leg and shoulder is ready to be butchered there are

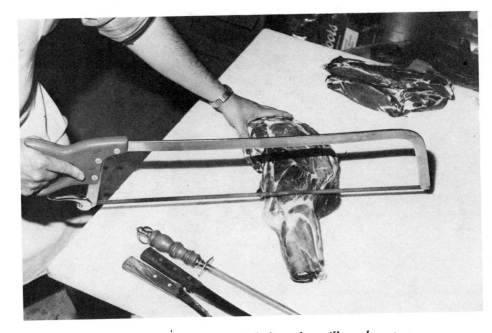

Some prefer bone-in shoulder roasts. Each front leg will produce two.

three meatcutting methods you may wish to consider, depending upon your intended preferences for later utilizing the meat.

The first and easiest method is to quickly cut the meat from the bone into irregular chunks to be used in stews, casseroles, or in the grinding of burger and sausage.

The second method, a bit more time-consuming but not at all difficult, involves laying the leg and shoulder assembly before you with the inside of the leg down and the lower leg facing to the right, in order to produce two bone-in roasts as shown in the accompanying diagram. The first cut removes the lower leg just above the knee; since this lower leg is thoroughly laced with sinew and ligaments, about the only value it has for human consumption is as fodder for the meat grinder. In creating the two bone-in roasts, the one nearest the lower leg is called an *arm roast* and the second cut of meat, located beyond this and still higher up, is called a *blade roast*.

When engaging in these two operations, make them as neat and professional looking as possible by trying to avoid cutting the meat itself with your saw. Cut down through the meat with your knife, using the saw only when you come to bone.

The third meatcutting method, still a bit more time-consuming involves boning out the meat to produce sumptuous, rolled shoulder roasts. Begin by laying the meat with the inside of the shoulder and leg down and the lower leg pointing away from you. You'll immediately see a very distinct white line vertically separating the right one-third of the shoulder from the left two-thirds. This is actually the top edge of a boney ridge standing upright on one

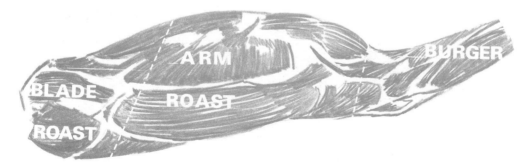

Here are the saw cuts needed to produce two bone-in shoulder roasts from each front leg. The upper cut of meat, at left, is called a blade roast, the middle portion an arm roast. The lower portion of the leg, at right, is not at all tender and goes into the scrap pile for burger.

side of the scapula. Butchers commonly refer to the oblong meat on the right side of the boney ridge as *scotch roll* meat, and that to the left as the *clod* meat.

Run your knife blade close to the left side of the vertical bone ridge and down through the clod meat until the knife edge stops on the flat scapula, then turn the blade flat and continue slicing toward the left until you almost reach the edge of that side of the shoulder. Now cut down on the right side of the vertical bone ridge through the scotch roll meat until the knife blade stops on that side of the scapula and continue slicing all the way to the right (a distance of about two inches). Use just the tip of your knife blade in carrying out these two steps. And be careful, as you approach the far left and far right edges to *not* cut the two pieces of meat free from the bone just yet because you want to next turn the works over and continue separating the meat from the entirely flat surface of the scapula on the back side.

The end product is one large, flat slab of shoulder meat with a smaller, almost detached segment constituting the lower leg meat which, again, should be cut free and reserved for the meat grinder if you haven't already done so.

It is now necessary to momentarily set aside this large slab of meat and remove the opposite foreleg and shoulder from the carcass in order to obtain a comparable slab of shoulder meat from that side of the deer.

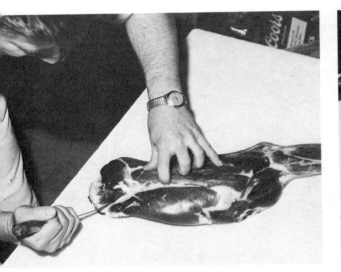

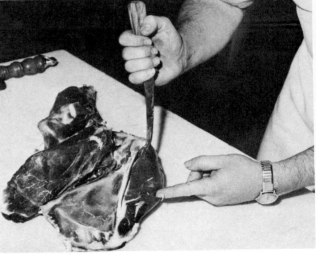

Other hunters prefer boneless shoulder roasts that are rolled and tied. With the shoulder lying on its side, begin the boning-out process by locating the standing ridge. To the left of this is the clod meat. Run your knife blade very carefully beneath the clod meat to separate it from the scapula, but do not cut it entirely free.

On the other side of the elevated boney ridge is the scotch roll meat. Carefully separate it from the bone as well, then turn the leg upside-down and continue cutting close to the bone to remove the meat on the other side.

Now take the two slabs of identical shoulder meat and, insides facing each other, lay one on top of the other. Shape them somewhat with your hands to form a nice-looking, football-sized roast.

Tying the roast is the next step and a few tricks of the trade will make it quite easy. Use cotton string and the so-called "surgeon's knot," that is a triple-overhand tie followed by a conventional double-overhand tie. The triple-overhand, when snugged up against the meat, will grab it tightly and therefore not begin to come loose when you release tension on the string to next make the double-overhand tie to complete the knot.

Another tip is to make your first two string ties at opposite ends of the roast. This will serve to hold the two slabs of shoulder meat firmly together in the shape you've formed; you can then make subsequent string ties moving progressively closer to the middle of the roast. Conversely, if you were to make the first string tie in the middle of the roast, it would tend to compress the two meat slabs in such a way as to force them far out to each opposite side, which would result in a long, slender, weird-looking roast instead of a more desirable thick, plump one.

When all of your string ties are completed (about ten should be sufficient), trim the ends of the roast so they look nice and toss the remaining meat scraps into the burger pile.

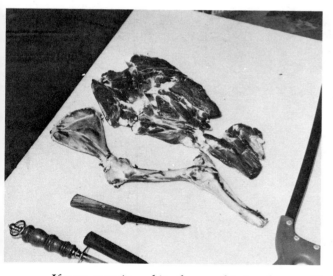

If you exercise a bit of care, this is what you'll have: a large piece of intact front shoulder meat and beside it a naked leg bone with nothing attached to it.

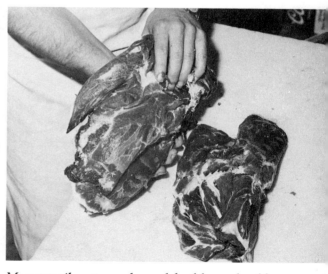

Momentarily set your large slab of front shoulder meat aside and repeat the same procedure with the other front leg. Then take the two equal portions of front shoulder meat and lay one on top of the other (continued next page).

You now have a professional-looking rolled shoulder roast of venison. If you have a very large family, this roast can be wrapped in one piece for a future meal. Or you can slice it in half right down the middle, between two of the string ties, to give two medium-sized roasts.

Never make a very small shoulder roast, or a small rump roast for that matter, or try to reduce a large one to smaller ones less than two pounds in weight. This is a common mistake made by hunters when there are only two or three people in the family. The result is a roast that, in cooking, becomes very dried out and tough. You need a somewhat large or medium-sized roast whose very bulk will help the meat retain moisture and therefore tenderness.

With a small family, this obviously means there will be a good quantity of meat left over when the meal is finished. But this certainly does not mean the venison will be wasted because whatever is remaining can be cubed and added to soups and stews. Or you can slice it very thin and the following day make positively delicious hot or cold sandwiches.

The last step in removing the shoulder and leg is to merely go back over the bones with a small knife to remove any additional meat remnants, salvaging these tender tidbits on behalf of the meat grinder.

See how easy it is to become an expert meatcutter? In fact, it's worth mentioning that my friend Charlie Hause, who wielded the knife while I

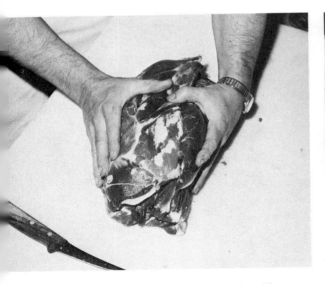

Form and shape the two portions of shoulder meat into a very large roast.

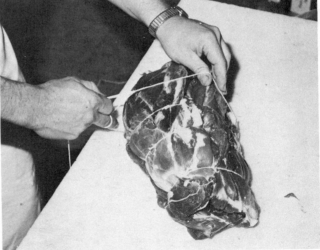

Tie the two roasts securely with cotton string, beginning at each end and working toward the middle.

operated a camera, produced the shoulder roasts shown in this chapter in less time than it took you to read this particular section!

Butchering the Hind Legs

Removing the rear legs from the carcass is a little more difficult than the front legs because the haunches are attached to the pelvic girdle by means of a ball and socket. Moreover, the pelvic itself presents many irregularly shaped contours that must be blindly followed with the knife blade to separate muscle from bone.

Some hunters prefer to use their saw to cut the spine in the region of the small of the back, just before the hams, whereupon both rear legs, still joined by the pelvis, are allowed to fall free. Then they carry the awkward, two-legged hunk to the butcher table and saw down vertically between the two, through the aitch bone and spine, to separate the legs.

Of course, feel free to use this method if you like. But know in advance you're making far more work for yourself than necessary because once you have each hind leg on the cutting table, you still have to bone it out and remove the meat from that half-side of the pelvis. So why not simply eliminate

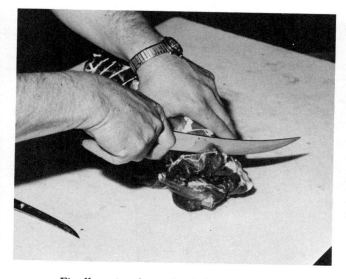

Finally, trim the ends of the roast and throw the scraps into the burger pile.

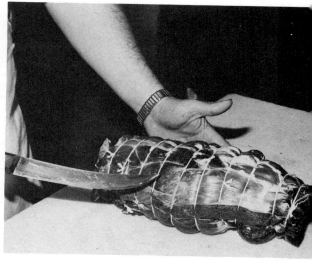

This roast, from an average-sized deer, will weigh about eight pounds.

a lot of the aforementioned effort and, right from the start, cut the leg from its attachment, leaving the pelvis attached to the skeleton.

Start at the root of the tail and with your knife begin cutting down through the meat on the left side of the spine to initiate removal of the left leg. Always use just the tip of your boning knife and try to keep the flat blade as close to bone as possible to minimize lost meat. You may wish to occasionally use your hands to pull the leg away from the body to somewhat enlarge your work area and better see what you're doing.

As you continue to cut down and around the ham, allow your knife blade to gently travel over the irregular surfaces of the pelvic girdle. In time, you'll come to the ball and socket but there is no need to do any bone-cutting here. The ball sits loosely in the socket, attached only by a small piece of cartilage. If you slip just the tip of your knife blade down into and between the ball and socket, you can easily cut the cartilage and the leg will begin to fall almost entirely free at this point, requiring just a bit more meatcutting in the vicinity of the aitch bone.

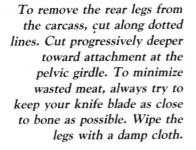

To remove the rear legs from the carcass, cut along dotted lines. Cut progressively deeper toward attachment at the pelvic girdle. To minimize wasted meat, always try to keep your knife blade as close to bone as possible. Wipe the legs with a damp cloth.

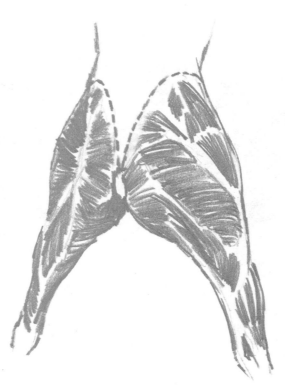

Do not fume and fuss if, upon removing this rear leg, you discover a moderate amount of prime-looking rump meat still clinging to various parts of the pelvic region. Even an expert misses some of this meat, because of all the blind cutting that is required. By no means is the meat lost, however, because later you'll clean the carcass of all these little remnants and they'll go into burger to make it especially tender.

With the left leg now lying on the butcher table, once again spend a few minutes getting the meat ready for cutting as you did with the front shoulder. Trim away the majority of the surface tallow fat you see, most of which will be high on the leg where it was previously attached to the spine/pelvic region. Then trim off the thin, protective "rind" or dark-colored casing, which the surface of the venison acquired during aging. After this is accomplished, go over the entire leg with a damp rag to remove any stray hairs or other debris clinging to the meat.

If you wish, you can now use your knife and saw to cut away the lower leg, just above the knee. As with the front legs, the lower sections of the rear legs are laced with sinew and ligaments and therefore have no use other than for burger.

Now let's get down to the nitty-gritty. The rear leg is composed of three muscles lying side by side. Due to their odd shapes the tissue fibers run in somewhat different directions, but there is a thin membrane covering that unites the three into a whole. Consequently, there are two ways to butcher the rear leg, depending upon the types of meat cuts you'd like to obtain: You can remove the thin membrane covering the entire haunch and separate the three exposed muscles to produce three roasts (two rump roasts and a sirloin tip roast); or, you can remove only that part of the membrane covering the sirloin tip in order to remove it (which you can then use as a roast or slice vertically into sirloin tip steaks), but leave the membrane intact on the remaining two muscles and slice them into round steaks.

To remove the sirloin tip, which is the first and easiest step, take the entire leg and prop it up on its edge with the lower leg bone facing away from you. You'll easily see the tip of the hard white knuckle bone and this is your starting point. Cut down through the meat just above the knuckle at a slight angle as shown in the accompanying photo. After going only a short distance, your knife blade will come to an abrupt halt against the leg bone. Now turn the blade flat and bring the knife cut toward you, keeping the blade continually against the bone, until the sirloin tip is cut entirely free.

You now have an oblong chunk of solid, boneless meat called the sirloin tip. Easy, huh? You can do either of two things with this glob of meat. You can leave it whole, to be later cooked as a sirloin tip roast, in which case it's a good idea to tie the roast with cotton string as described for roasts from the front shoulder. Since this is very tender meat, it will tend to fall apart during cooking if it's not tied.

Or, you can vertically slice the meat into six or eight sirloin tip steaks, which are fine for broiling over coals or can be made into Swiss steaks. Since this meat is football-shaped and hence thick in the middle and small at both ends, you'll want to somehow make sure all the steaks are roughly of uniform size. The best way is to *butterfly* the two ends of the sirloin tip. In other words, cut down through the meat about two-thirds of the way but not completely through. Then make a second cut, this time going all the way through. You can now flop the twin pieces of meat open, yet they'll remain intact due to their connective hinge. Then go ahead and slice the remaining steaks in the usual manner—about one-inch thick—until you begin reaching the opposite, narrow end of the sirloin tip, which you can make into another butterfly steak.

In continuing with butchering of the haunch, the next step is the same, regardless of whether you want to use the remainder of the rump for roasts or round steaks. Lay the remaining leg portion with the inside down and the lower leg bone facing you. You'll now be able to clearly see the white line

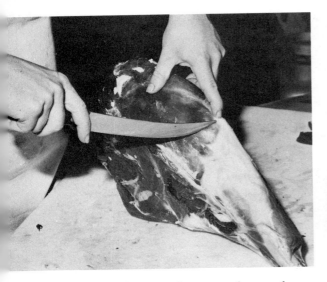

To remove sirloin tip, first prop the rear leg up on edge so the tip of the white knuckle bone is clearly visible.

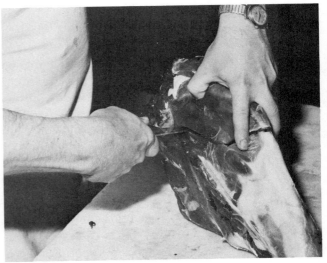

Just above the knuckle, cut straight down with your knife for about two inches until the blade stops against the leg bone. Then turn the blade flat and continue your knife cut all the way to the end of the leg.

of the top of the leg bone still buried in the meat; this is the bone that became partially exposed when the sirloin tip was removed.

What you want to do is remove this entire bone without damaging the meat wrapped around it. Begin by using just the tip of your boning knife to work along the topside of the bone and very slowly go all the way around its perimeter, gently pulling away the created slab of meat as you proceed. Eventually, you'll have gone all the way around the bone and will reach the other side and the meat will fall free in one large, boneless slab.

This meat can now be returned to its former shape by molding it with your hands so it looks exactly as it did a minute ago, with the exception that ·it is now boneless. You can then use your long-bladed butcher knife to slice thick round steaks.

Another way of producing these round steaks is by merely skipping the boning-out procedure just described and, instead, using your saw. In this manner your round steaks will be the same size and shape but each will have a disclike piece of round leg bone in the center.

It's nothing more than personal opinion, but I distinctly like the boning-out method because you avoid tiny bone chips and marrow dust on your round steaks. They also look nicer and far more professional when sliced

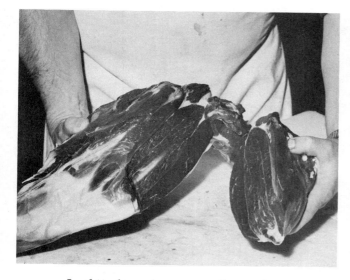

In this photo, you can easily see the top of the leg bone, buried in the meat, that your knife blade followed. The oblong chunk of meat that has been removed is the sirloin tip. If you like, you can tie it with cotton string for a sirloin tip roast.

Or, you can slice the meat into inch-thick sirloin tip steaks.

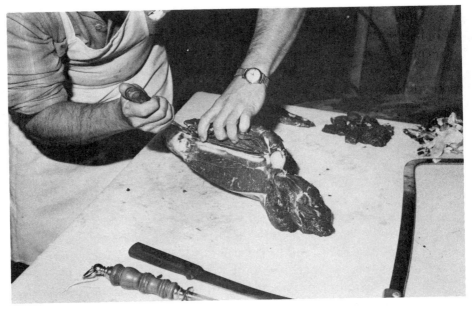

To bone out the remainder of the rear leg, simply use the tip of the knife blade to encircle the exposed leg bone and remove the meat intact in one large piece.

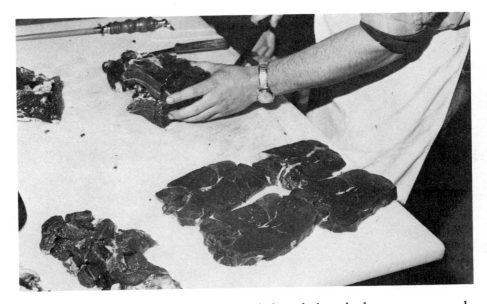

Form the large slab of meat into its original shape before the bone was removed. Then, beginning at one end, slice the meat into round steaks. Or, if you prefer, tie the large slab of meat to produce a very large rolled rump roast. Follow the same procedure as for making a rolled shoulder roast.

with a sharp knife as compared to the sometimes ragged appearance produced by a sawblade's teeth. But the choice is yours.

If, instead of round steaks, you'd like roasts, that is a splendid decision because in coming from the rump they'll be as tender as the deer has to offer. Rolled rump roasts are produced in essentially the same way as are shoulder roasts.

With your hands, shape and form the meat back together so it looks the same as before the leg bone was removed. Now use cotton string to tie the roast in ten or twelve places, beginning at opposite ends and working gradually toward the middle. Once secured with string, you can leave the roast whole for a sumptuous repast that will serve eight, or you can slice it in half to serve four. Just remember that roasts that are too small may become dry and tough during cooking.

Despite his most valiant efforts, any hunter is likely to occasionally end up with several rather smallish pieces of rump meat for one reason or another. The excuse I use is that my knife blade had a mind of its own. In any event, these pieces of meat will predictably be so irregularly shaped it seems there is no way to tie them together into a roast and one is therefore tempted to reserve them for the meat grinder. That's fine, because you'll have the tenderest burger imaginable. But you can make roasts from those odd-shaped pieces of meat by using cotton string meat "socks."

You can probably get your local butcher to give you a few of these socks for free; otherwise, they should cost no more than 25¢ apiece. They are woven, meshlike affairs that come in different sizes depending upon your needs. Some are pouchlike in design with a drawstring closure at one end, while others are tubelike with drawstring closures at both ends.

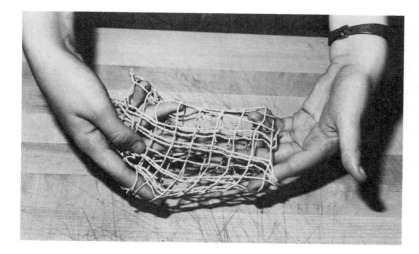

Occasionally, even the most careful hunter may goof and end up with several irregularly shaped pieces of meat left over. To make pot roasts from these, stuff a string "sock" of the type shown here with your meat chunks and securely tie off the ends.

In either case, their intended purposes are the same. You stuff into them your irregular-shaped pieces of rump meat, trying to keep as many pieces as possible situated lengthwise within the sock. Then you shape the roast with your hands and tightly close the drawstrings and tie them off. Walla! You now have another tender rump roast or two which can be cooked in any manner recommended for such cuts. The cotton sock keeps the meat intact throughout the cooking and is cut away just before serving.

Now that you've finished butchering the left rear leg, and gained a little practice, the right leg should go even faster. You can butcher it exactly the same way if you like, or you may decide to do it just a little differently in order to acquire a wide variety of meat cuts. For example, if you left the sirloin tip of the left leg intact to have a sirloin tip roast, you may wish to use the other one, sliced vertically, for numerous sirloin tip steaks. Similarly, if you sliced the rump meat of the left leg into round steaks, you may wish to use the rump meat of the right leg for rolled rump roasts. To each his own pleasure!

Larding and Barding

Before proceeding to other butchering procedures, let's take a few moments to discuss two techniques for tenderizing venison that you may wish to incorporate into meatcutting operations dealing with either the front shoulder roasts or the rump roasts produced from the rear legs. Although these cuts may already be tender in their own right, they can be made even more so. Also, an occasional deer may not be as tender as we'd like unless special measures are instituted.

To understand the two techniques I'm about to describe, several characteristics of meats derived from domestic livestock as compared to wild-game animals must be mentioned.

Livestock—beef steers, for example—spend lives of leisure lazing around pastures and feedlots and seldom utilize their muscles to the fullest extent of their physical capabilities. And, all the while, they dine complacently upon assorted high-fat and high-carbohydrate foods, which in turn makes them quite fatty in their muscular structure. Additionally, about a month before they are to be slaughtered, they are subjected to a "finishing" process whereby they are force-fed milk, corn, and similar rations to even further increase the fat content of their musculature.

The result of this modern animal husbandry is that domestic livestock meat contains a very high level of "marbling" throughout its flesh. This marbling fat is found in striations between and through the tissue fibers of the meat, and during cooking it melts and subsequently helps to break down the tissue's cellular structure. What you have, then, is *very* tender meat.

Exactly the opposite sequence of events occurs during the lives of deer and other wild animals. Although they may often launch a raid upon some farmer's cornfield or beanfield, a majority of the year sees deer dining upon whatever native foods they can find, and often they do not find all that much, particularly during the winter. Further, deer spend much of their time "on the run," so to speak, and this continual exercise, as with a human athlete, builds strong (and tough) muscles. You just don't see fat, flabby deer, no matter where you live. And, of course, deer do not undergo a "finishing" process shortly before their demise; indeed, they may even be somewhat "stressed" due to the nature of the hunt.

Consequently, unlike domestic livestock, venison does not possess a high level of marbling. Instead, it is a "dry," very lean meat with very little in the way of tissue fat to internally lubricate and baste the meat as it cooks.

There are several ways to remedy this state of affairs and make your venison just as tender as the finest beef. Some of these ways entail certain cooking techniques that I'll discuss in coming chapters, but others entail tricks you can employ during meatcutting operations.

First, as emphasized previously, trim away as much tallow fat as time and convenience allow, but leave whatever marbling fat you find woven between the muscle and tissue fibers. Marbling fat is easily identified because unlike tallow fat, which is formed in thick layers, marbling fat appears as long, thin streaks and flecks.

Second, you can *bard* the meat in any of several ways. Barding involves artificially adding to the venison the fat it otherwise lacks. One method, when you have a large slab of meat you are preparing to assemble into a roast, is to first lay in the folds of the meat several slices of bacon before forming it into a roast and tying it with cotton string. This will do a good job of tenderizing the meat, and will also impart a very subtle, yet pleasing, bacon flavor. Or, instead of using bacon, you can use thinly cut strips of beef suet or salt pork, each of which will impart their own slightly unique flavors as well.

Another barding method is to drape the exterior of the roast with bacon strips just before tying it securely with string. Whatever the method chosen, dictated more by personal preference than anything else, barding accomplishes the desirable result of basting, lubricating, and thereby tenderizing the meat as it cooks.

The one slight disadvantage to barding is that any kind of pork or beef fat does not keep very long in your freezer, which means roasts that have exterior bacon drapes or interior barding in the form of bacon, beef suet, or salt pork must be used within several months.

Barding helps to tenderize meat through the addition of fat that it lacks. One easy way is to lay bacon strips on the meat prior to rolling and tying it as a shoulder or rump roast.

If you desire to conserve your cache of deer meat and make it last as long as possible, so your family can enjoy venison dinners all year right up until the next hunting season comes along, you'll not want to use barding as a meat-tenderizing technique. So go ahead and produce your rolled, tied roasts as described earlier, and place them in the freezer where they'll remain in good condition for up to a year or slightly longer.

Then, each time you remove a roast from the freezer, and just before cooking, use another technique called *larding,* which accomplishes the very same tenderizing as barding but without the drawback of limited storage time in the freezer. Larding means injecting fat and similar lubricants into the meat, and there are several neat tools on the market that make the job quite easy.

One is a larding gun. It looks like a pistol but instead of a barrel it has a long needle full of holes and at the base of the handle there is a four-ounce reservoir. You fill the reservoir with melted bacon fat or rendered beef suet or salt pork, jab the needle into the meat in various locations, squeeze the trigger and the fluid permeates the tissue spaces to provide the internal basting and cellular breakdown otherwise accomplished by barding or natural marbling fat.

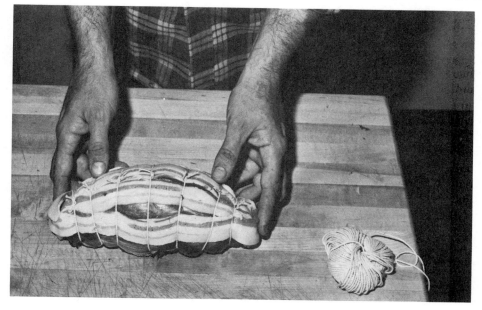

Another barding method is to lay the bacon strips along the outside of a roast before cooking and hold them in place with string.

As before, the bacon, suet, or salt pork will impart subtle flavors of their own. If you'd prefer to retain the exclusive flavor of the venison, with nothing to detract from it, use some other type of tasteless larding fluid. Sometimes I use melted butter, sometimes I use cooking oil, and sometimes I use half of each mixed together.

Another type of larding tool does the very same job but is of a different design. It looks somewhat like a siphon in that a rubber squeeze bulb is fitted to one end of a stainless steel tube, and at the other end is a long, hollow needle. Simply insert the needle in random locations, squeeze the bulb and the larding fluid will saturate the inside of the roast.

Every serious hunter should also have a basting bulb. This looks almost identical to the larding needle described above except that instead of a needle at one end it has an open spout. The purpose of this tool is to periodically dribble basting fluids and juices over the exterior surfaces of various cuts of venison in accordance with certain recipes.

All three of the tools just discussed cost less than $10 apiece and all can be quickly disassembled for easy cleaning.

Finally, if you find yourself about to prepare a roast in circumstances where no larding gun or larding needle is available, such as in camp, you can improvise with an ice pick. Simply punch holes in the roast in random locations and insert long slivers of bacon or beef suet.

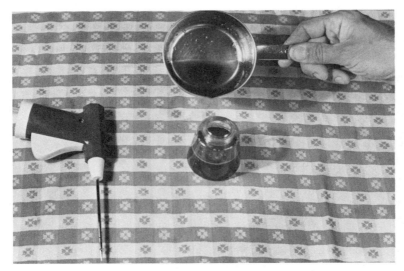

Larding is similar to barding in that some type of fat is added to the venison. The traditional method is to use a larding gun or needle. First, fill the reservoir of the gun with bacon drippings, cooking oil, rendered suet, or melted butter.

Then inject the fat into a roast or other large cut of meat in random locations. In cooking, the fat will help to break down the meat fibers and make them tender.

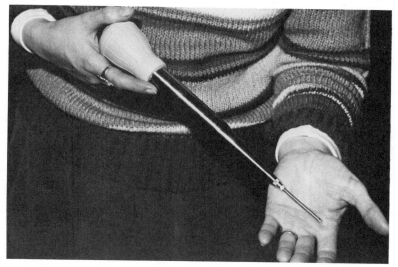

This is a larding needle, which accomplishes the same end as a larding gun. It's made of stainless steel, with a durable squeeze bulb. All components are quickly disassembled for easy cleaning.

Another kitchen implement every serious venison cook should have on hand is an inexpensive basting bulb for dribbling juices and drippings over meats in accordance with certain recipes.

The Tenderloins

You can refer to them as loins, tenderloins, steaks, backstraps, or other common names, but by any description they are the tenderest cuts of venison a deer possesses. They are located along both sides of the backbone and their counterparts, on beef steers, are the filet mignons and popular steaks such as the T-bone and porterhouse.

There are several ways to remove these delectable cuts of venison, depending upon whether you like pure meat, as with filet mignon, or whether you like bone-in steaks. I prefer to bone out backstraps to avoid bone chips and marrow dust from contacting the meat. Also, as noted in Chapter 5, I like to remove the mini-tenderloins, located along either side of the spine on the inside of the body cavity, in camp. This avoids having them age to the extent that trimming away glazing is necessary at the expense of a good deal of prime meat. However, in the interest of personal preferences that may vary among hunters, I'll describe both methods.

The backstrap, on the exterior of the skeletal system, lies adjacent to the backbone, running from just behind the front shoulder back to where the front of the rear legs begin, and is situated in a type of triangular-shaped pocket created by the offset vertebrae of the backbone.

Removing both backstraps intact, in long strips, is accomplished by using a fillet knife or boning knife with a flexible tip that will easily bend to conform to the curvature of the bones. Insert the tip of your blade just behind the front shoulder and with the blade flat against the backbone, carefully guide it all the way along the length of the spine to just above the pelvic girdle. It will feel at times like the blade is traveling over a rippled surface (these are the vertebrae), so proceed slowly and work the blade slightly in and out as you go to retain as much meat as possible.

Now, back at that point where you began the shoulder cut, make another cut, this time perpendicular, about four inches in length. Then it is quite simple to cut and lift, cut and lift, gently filleting the backstrap right out of its spinal cavity until its entire length is removed.

At this time, if you haven't already done so, you'll want to remove the mini-tenderloins from inside the body cavity. They are so tender they will almost fall apart in your hands so exercise great care. They, too, lie in a shallow pocket and once you cut one end or the other away, you can almost pull them the remainder of the way out with your fingertips.

At the butcher table, let's work on one of the long backstraps. First, you'll notice a thin, silvery-colored membrane-like sheath covering the exterior of the tenderloin. You can carefully trim this away with your knife, if you wish, by starting at one end and alternately lifting the membrane while running

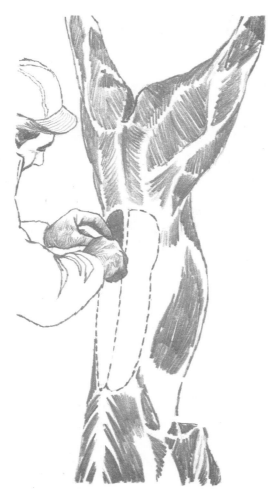

Dotted lines show locations of tenderloins or backstraps along both sides of the backbone. They sit in a triangular pocket created by the offset vertebrae of the backbone and peel right out with a bit of judicious cutting.

the flat blade of your fillet knife between it and the tenderloin. However, this operation is merely for the sake of appearance; it is not at all necessary as the membrane will "cook out" very tender.

Next, you'll want to slice the backstrap horizontally into numerous steaks. On a very large deer, which in turn will have large backstraps, you can simply begin slicing tenderloin steaks any thickness you prefer (I recommend one inch thick).

Once backstraps are on the butcher table, you may wish to remove the thin, silvery membrane covering the exterior of the tenderloin, but this is entirely optional.

However, when the deer is only average size, this technique results in the sliced steaks being rather small, and so I use the *butterfly* method of cutting them. In this procedure, you begin slicing a one-inch-thick steak but do not cut all the way down through the meat. Now, make a second cut another inch away and this time do slice all the way through. What you'll have, then, are a pair of inch-thick steaks side by side, connected to each other by a type of hinge that, when the steaks are opened and laid out flat, produces a tenderloin steak double the usual size and weighing about eight to ten ounces.

As you approach either end of the long backstrap it will become progressively smaller and smaller in size, so begin making your cuts just a bit thicker. Then use a wooden mallet to gently pound them out flat. This will spread out their surface areas somewhat, so that all the steaks from the backstrap are of uniform size, rather than some large and some small.

The mini-tenderloins are handled in a slightly different manner. Sometimes I freeze them whole because my family like to broil them over charcoal and then slice them very thinly, diagonal to the grain, to make the most delicious steak sandwiches you've ever sunk your chompers into. Other times we slice these tenderloins horizontally into steaks. However, since these tenderloins

Backstraps can be sliced vertically into numerous tenderloin steaks. To make them extra large, butterfly the cuts as shown here and described in the text.

are so small, make extra-thick cuts. Then stand each on end and mash it down flat with your fist or a wooden mallet, to make petite filet mignons weighing four to six ounces apiece.

The other meatcutting method, which produces bone-in steaks (some hunters call them "chops"), requires considerably more work, but the procedure is easily described.

You begin by cutting the neck off just above the front shoulders, then cutting off the pelvis to which the rear legs were attached. You then saw the carcass in half, lengthwise, down the centerline of the backbone to produce two "sides." Each side is laid upon the cutting table and steaks are vertically sawed to whatever thickness you prefer, then the rib-ends are removed.

If you harbor doubts as to which method you might like best, here's a good suggestion. Why not try both? Fillet out the entire backstrap from one side of the animal and butterfly it into boneless steaks. Then saw the remainder of the carcass down the middle of the backbone and with a side lying on your work table, cut bone-in steaks from that half of the deer.

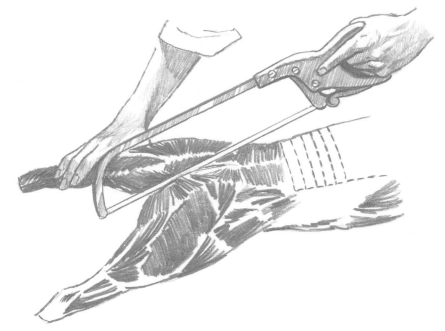

If you prefer bone-in steaks, lay the rearmost portion of the carcass belly-down on your work surface. Use a meatcutting saw to cut the carcass into two equal halves down the exact centerline of the backbone. You can then cut inch-thick bone-in steaks from each half.

Final Meatcutting Tasks

All that should now remain on your deer carcass is the meat on the neck, between the ribs, and in random other places such as along the flanks and on the brisket.

On very large deer, you may wish to use your saw to cut out a rib-plate section from each side of the carcass. Saw the upper rib cage region horizontally to the backbone, just below the vertebral pocket that held the backstraps, and then make another horizontal saw cut just above the sternum. These ribs can be charcoal broiled or cooked very slowly in barbecue sauce in your oven. Some hunters claim they don't especially care for venison ribs, yet others love them. I won't take sides. Try them and see for yourself.

On smaller deer, there is so little lean meat on the rib cage that most hunters simply forget about cutting them out with a saw. Instead, using their

A rib plate removed from a large deer looks like this. You can freeze it whole, or reduce it to smaller two-rib sections.

knife, they salvage what meat they are able to find between the ribs and reserve it for burger or sausage.

The meat on the brisket has many uses, and it is especially well suited for stews. It is flavorful but also slightly tough, which, as strange as it may seem, is actually to its advantage. You want stew meat to hold together well during long hours of cooking but eventually become tender. Brisket meat does this very well. Conversely, trying to make stew from already tender cuts such as rump meat or shoulder blade meat often is a futile endeavor. By the time they've simmered several hours over low heat—as all stews should be cooked— the meat no longer is firm and something you can sink your teeth into but mushy and fallen apart.

I like to cut off the brisket meat in one large slab. Then at the cutting table I carefully remove as much fat as possible before slicing the meat into thick cubes.

The neck meat also has many uses. Remove it from the carcass by boning it out. The easiest method is to begin at the back of the neck with a lengthwise cut down the centerline on one side of the neckbone or the other. Make it a deep cut as this will produce a large flap of neck meat and simultaneously expose the neck bone, allowing you to continue working around its perimeter.

With the slab of neck meat on your cutting table, remove as much surface tallow as possible, but retain the more deeply imbedded marbling fat. This large slab of meat can now be rolled into a roast and tied with string, then halved or even cut into thirds for very slow cooking over low heat. Or you can cube the neck meat for use in stews. Or you can reserve the entire thing for burger and sausage.

The last step in butchering your deer is to go over the entire carcass with a small utility knife to remove every little bit of remaining meat you can find. Pay particular attention to the pelvic region and the vertebral pockets that held the backstraps because this meat is incredibly tender and adds immensely to the quality of your burger and sausage. Then go over the flanks, neckbone, and elsewhere. All in all, you'll be surprised how many pounds of meat this will amount to.

Now, all that should remain of your deer is a skeleton picked clean. Undoubtedly, however, as you've been carrying out your butchering you'll have accumulated a hefty scrap pile of skin remnants, junk meats, and other body parts that are too fatty or too sinewy to be used for human consumption. Instead of throwing them away, they make splendid dog food!

In fact, whenever we first begin butchering a deer we always place a five-gallon pot on the stove, half filled with water and turned on low heat. Then we toss in undesirable meat scraps as we go along. The "stew" slowly simmers for many hours, to the point that even the gristle is tender. Sometimes we even throw in a bit of dry cereal or cornmeal.

We usually end up with as much as 40 pounds of nutritious, high-protein food our dogs absolutely love. After the food has cooked, allow it to cool, then ladle it into half-quart plastic containers and freeze them. Every few days, defrost one container and mix it with Fido's usual dry kibbles and watch him attack the meal like there's no tomorrow.

Not only do you save a lot of money making this dog food, but you gain the additional satisfaction of knowing you utilized the entire deer, throwing nothing away but the bones. If you don't own a dog, the favor is sure to be appreciated by a friend or neighbor who does have pets.

CHAPTER 11

Grinding Deerburger

A LONG TIME AGO I maintained a strong prejudice against those hunters who pushed their entire deer through the tiny spout of a meat grinder. I thought they were ignorant clods who never took the time to learn the proper way to butcher their deer in order to acquire steaks, roasts, and other desirable cuts. Consequently, they always copped out by simply whacking off the carcass meat in chunks and shreds, not caring how pitiful it appeared because it would all soon be reduced to an indistinguishable, ground-up substance anyway. Gad, what a criminal way to treat venison!

It was Harvey Wilks who made me see the light and changed all my preconceived notions about these burger and sausage fanatics. An avid hunter from Cleveland, Ohio, Wilks has *sometimes* been known to filch the backstraps and rump roasts from his deer because he recognizes them as so good in their own rights, but generally the whole deer goes through the cutting blade of his grinder.

"Before I took up the sport of deer hunting many years ago," Wilks explained, "all of our burger and sausages came from a grocery store and we always thought they were delicious. But then we started paying close attention to our diets and became concerned about all the chemicals, additives, preservatives, and artificial coloring agents being added to foods. There were so many of these, especially on the labels of sausage packages, we wondered where they found the room to put the meat! So I started making venison burger and sausage. We found them even more scrumptious than their store-bought counterparts and just as important we knew exactly which ingredients went in and which did not."

As to the propriety—or impropriety, depending upon how you look at it—of using the *whole* deer in such a manner, Harvey Wilks describes his philosophy this way:

"There are various grades of quality in burger and sausage. And naturally, that which includes all the hams and tenderloins is going to be far superior to that which is made only from meat scraps, trimmings, and otherwise tough cuts taken from the lower legs, neck, brisket, ribs, and flanks."

Understandably, therefore, each hunter will have to decide for himself how much of his deer to turn into burger and sausage, depending upon not only the quality grade he wants to strive for but also how much his family likes burger and sausage compared to other meat cuts.

Another thing that is sure to influence the amount of meat that eventually goes through the grinder will be the size of the deer itself. This can even result in somewhat of a shock, especially when a hunter vividly recalls the hard work of dragging his trophy out of the hinterland, because most deer are not really all that big. I often grin with amusement when disbelieving hunters gawk at the weigh scales, shake them a bit to see if they are working properly or jammed, continue to look very puzzled, and never really do accept the fact that the buck they thought easily field-dressed at least 200 pounds really comes in at only half that.

It's true that whitetails, and particularly mule deer, can weigh quite a bit upon occasion, but biologists say an average deer, on the hoof, tips the balance at only about 145 pounds. Subtract from this about 35 pounds as the weight of the offal removed during field dressing. Then subtract the weight of the antlers, head, hide, lower legs, and all the bones comprising the skeleton and you'll end up with only 75 pounds of edible meat.

If you've butchered the deer in the traditional way—as we described in the last chapter—and therefore have only the trimmings and tougher cuts left over to submit to the meat grinder, you'll end up with around 25 pounds of burger or sausage. That's not much at all because when its usage is spread out over the entire year it amounts to your being able to enjoy only one pound of burger or sausage *every other week*.

Incidentally, you can easily calculate weights and meat-yield figures for any deer you take by purchasing a scale specifically designed for butchers. The one I have, made by the Sportsman's Guide Company in Hopkins, Min-

Every hunter should have a sportsman's scale for calculating meat-yield figures and numerous other uses.

nesota, is of exceptional quality and will handle animal weights up to 300 pounds. The cost (as of 1983) is about $27, and on its faceplate there is a reference chart that gives an accurate idea of how much meat to expect from a field-dressed animal.

This brings us back, again, to the personal dilemma each hunter will have to resolve on his own in accordance with how much his family likes burger and sausage, how many different varieties of the two he might therefore like to make, and hence, how much of the deer to use toward this end.

Harvey Wilks, for example, makes quite a lot of burger, some of which will be used for hamburger sandwiches, some for meatloaf and meatballs, and the rest to be incorporated into chili or sauces to go along with spaghetti, lasagna, marzetti, and various types of casseroles.

In the sausage department he begins by making bulk sausage to be used for sandwiches, pizza toppings, or patties to serve with breakfast. But he doesn't stop there. Next he makes link sausage such as kielbasa, polish sausage, summer sausage, and sometimes even potato sausage, salami, bologna, and pepperoni. No wonder he needs to use the whole deer!

What, then, is one to do if he wants to go the entire route? How can one possibly stash in his freezer a year's worth of good eating in the form of steaks and roasts *plus* several varieties of burger and sausage? Well, you can't, unless you bring home at least two nice bucks every year. Or get your wife interested in deer hunting and hope she occasionally scores as well.

Meat-Grinding Equipment

Meat grinders are available these days in a wide variety of brand names, sizes, prices, and quality. The least expensive and, ironically enough, one of the most durable, is a cast-iron, hand-crank model that costs less than $25 and is available in any houseware's department.

By means of a thumb-screw, you clamp it onto the edge of a table or work counter. Meat trimmings are then fed into the top mouth of the grinder and the handle turned. The front of the grinder has a removable faceplate, underneath which can be installed interchangeable disks with holes of various sizes. There also is a three- or four-bladed cutting "knife." This arrangement allows a hunter to coarse-grind the meat first, then feed it through the grinder a second or even third time to produce burger or bulk sausage of various textures. To make link sausage, as I'll describe in detail in the next chapter, a long spout is attached to the front of the grinder and the meat stuffed into casings.

The one drawback to this hand-crank grinder is that it can take an in-

The most inexpensive meat grinder is this hand-crank model (left) with interchangeable blades. Commercial grade grinder used by cafes and restaurants will process three pounds of meat per minute.

ordinate length of time and muscle power to process an entire deer. In short, it's just plain hard work.

The next category of meat grinders includes intermediate-sized electric models produced by the major appliance makers. I have both good words and bad words about them. Their prices range from $65 to $125, and they operate under the same basic principles as the hand-crank models with the exception that a 110-volt motor does the work instead of you and in far less time. For hunters who like to savor steaks and roasts from their deer and therefore plan to make only modest quantities of burger and sausage (less than 25 pounds per year), these grinders are very worthwhile investments.

Realize, however, these grinders are not intended for, or built to withstand, heavy-duty use. They are kitchen appliances designed with the housewife in mind who might occasionally find need to grind small quantities of meat. If you instead try to cram an entire deer through one of these machines, it will moan and groan, and then there will be a table-rocking shudder and it will screech to an immediate halt. I was given one of these grinders as a gift several years ago and it succeeded in chewing up a grand total of only two deer before finally self-destructing. Considering the price of the grinder, we dined on *very* expensive burger that year.

Then there are still larger, table-model electric grinders made by those companies that manufacture "commercial grade" equipment. Instead of being

164

Countertop electric grinders are moderately priced and favored by many, but they are not intended for heavy duty and have an exasperating way of self-destructing when put to large tasks.

rated by voltage, their motors fall into the category of horsepower ratings. Their prices range from $500 to $800 and the most popular motor sizes are ⅓, ½, and ¾ horsepower.

I can't praise these heavy-duty, table-model grinders enough. They're ruggedly built because they are intended for use by farmers who occasionally slaughter a beef steer, as well as by restaurants and small grocery stores, so you know they will serve admirably in the processing of as many deer per year as you may harvest. To give an idea as to how efficient these grinders are, those with rated ½-horsepower motors will process an average of three pounds of meat per minute. And they will continue working hour after hour, even day after day if need be, without showing any signs of fatigue whatever.

I know, I know, asking a deer hunter to drop $500 or more for a meat grinder is likely to be greeted with as much enthusiasm as asking an Arab sheik to lower the price of his oil. But you can rationalize such an expenditure if you consider this. First of all, such a grinder will easily last the rest of your life. No kidding. These grinders are designed to work hard for 30 years with little or no maintenance; at that time, after paying for an overhaul, you can expect still another 30 years of service. They simply live on and on. Moreover, the machines are a real pleasure to use, not only in the processing of venison but in many other types of food preparation as well. In this light, their per-year-use-cost is quite low.

However, don't expect to find these quality grinders sitting on the shelves with the El Cheapo models in the houseware's section of the local department store. You have to go to the manufacturer's retail outlet or to a restaurant supply company (there's at least one in every major city).

Another possibility for those on a tight budget is picking up a used, commercial-grade meat grinder. Restaurants and Mom and Pop grocery stores periodically trade in their meat grinders for new ones that are larger or have more features. Many such establishments even go out of business from time to time, at which time they either advertise their equipment for sale or have it disposed of at a public auction. Sometimes you can pick up a used grinder in mint condition for a mere song. The best way to learn of their availability is by regularly checking the classified-ad section of your local newspaper.

Whatever meat grinder you decide upon, it will require a bit of special care. The heart of any meat grinder, be it a hand-crank or electric model, is its three- or four-bladed cutting knife. A continually sharp knife cuts the meat quickly and cleanly, while a dull blade only mashes it.

It's easy to detect any deterioration in your grinder's cutting knife. First, you'll begin noticing that the ground meat has a pulpy and mushy, rather than a sheared, appearance. And you'll begin seeing a lot of juice dripping from the exit flange of the grinder as a result of the meat being squashed rather than sliced. Remove the blade and undoubtedly its beveled cutting blades will reveal dulled edges.

These cutting blades can be sharpened but the procedure requires a special machine possessed only by service outlets that recondition meat grinders. Since new blades cost less than $5 apiece, most people just replace them every few years. In fact, it's a good idea to keep a spare on hand, which can be immediately installed if the need arises.

After each use, always disassemble the grinder's hopper, feed screw, and other parts that can be washed and thoroughly clean them with hot soapy water, using a toothbrush to get into places that are hard to reach. Then rinse the component parts with scalding water to both kill germs and facilitate evaporative drying of moisture in tiny places. Of course, never submerge the grinder's motor housing in water; just wipe down the outside of the housing with a damp cloth.

Before putting the grinder away, you have to ensure that the metal meat-cutting parts do not rust, which means giving them a light coating of vegetable cooking oil. In the event that you retrieve your grinder from its storage place after several months of nonuse and discover light scale rust on the inner surfaces of many parts, the recommended way of cleaning the grinder before use is to run a handful or two of saltine crackers through the grinder. The abrasive nature of the salt, and the absorptive nature of the soda crackers themselves, will restore the grinder's metal surfaces to a bright shine in a jiffy.

In addition to your meat grinder, you'll need one or two knives for trimming your intended burger meat of ligaments and sinew. Because of their radically upswept tips, boning knives don't fare too well in this work. Much better are paring knives, utility knives, or those variations of fish fillet knives with "shorty" blades about five inches in length.

Finally, you'll need a workspace—the same area prepared for butchering your deer is fine—and several large tubs, trays, bowls, or other containers for holding the bulk quantities of meat you'll be processing.

Making Burger

Producing your own deerburger is enjoyable work and anyone should be able to do a professional job on the very first attempt.

But before actually grinding the meat, it's necessary to acquire a quantity of beef suet or beef fat. How much you need depends upon how much burger you plan to manufacture. The recommended ratio is three parts of venison to one part suet or fat. So before the deer season even opens, begin thinking about how much burger you'd like to later make and then place your suet or fat order with your local butcher. If the whole deer is going to be used for burger, you'll need about 25 pounds of fat or suet; with that in mind, you should be able to estimate proportionately smaller amounts.

Beef suet is comparable to the tallow found on deer and consists of the thick, hard, white, lardy fat found in layers around the kidneys, down both sides of the back and across the rump. The going price of suet is around 25¢ per pound but if you are a regular customer, your butcher may give the stuff to you for free.

Beef fat, on the other hand, lies closer to the carcass meat, beneath the suet, and therefore is not quite so thick and lardy; it's the excess fat butchers remove when doing their final trimming around steaks and other loin cuts. If there is any cost at all for beef fat trimmings, the price will be about the same as for suet.

Since beef fat is more tender than suet, it makes better burger in my opinion, although the actual difference may be more imagined than real. So try to get beef fat trimmings, but if you can't, suet will be fine.

It's quite important to place your order before the deer season opens because very shortly there will be a sudden drain on the amount of suet and fat available, due to other hunters wanting to do their own meat grinding as well. So reserve in advance the quantity of suet or fat you think you'll need. If something goes amiss and you don't collect your deer after all and have to cancel your order, the butcher will easily be able to find another buyer.

Prior to beginning your meat grinding, you'll want to make sure your venison is *very* cold so that the blade in your grinder can cut the meat crisply and cleanly. If the meat is at room temperature, it will have a tendency to mush even under the cutting action of a new, sharp blade. I usually take care of major butchering operations one day, then allow my accumulated meat scraps to sit overnight in a covered bowl in my refrigerator and commence grinding the following day. However, if you want to process the entire deer in one day, spread your intended burger meat out on trays or cookie sheets and place them in your freezer for 15 minutes or until they are thoroughly chilled.

Meanwhile, as your burger meat is chilling, begin cutting up your suet or beef fat into thumb-sized chunks. These will go through the grinder much faster and easier than big globs of suet, which will only serve to clog the grinder's internal workings. If the feed screw and other parts do become clogged with a thick, pasty layer that is beginning to retard the operation of the machine (this is more common with hand-crank rather than electric

In making burger, begin by cutting up beef suet into chunks that will conveniently fit into the hopper of the grinder you're using.

Now trim the venison of sinew, ligaments, fat, and other unwanted matter; then cut it into chunks that can be handled by your grinder.

models), simply remove those parts and with a pair of tongs hold them briefly under a stream of very hot tap water; all the fat residue will dissolve and wash away almost instantly, whereupon you can reassemble the parts and pick up where you left off.

The suet, or beef fat, after passing through the coarse grinding plate, will come out of the grinder's exit flange looking somewhat like "crumbles," for want of a better term to describe their appearance. Just accumulate them in a large tray or bowl and then set them aside.

Now, feed your chilled venison through the same coarse plate, remembering again to feed small pieces through the grinder rather than large chunks.

You can use a small baby scale or produce scale to obtain the desired three-to-one-ratio of venison to suet with unerring accuracy. But the truth of the matter is, being precisely accurate isn't really imperative. In fact, after making burger several times you'll probably discover, as I did long ago, that you can dispense with the time and trouble involved in weighing the meat. Since venison and suet have about the same density, with practice you'll find you can merely make a visual estimate of three parts venison to one part suet or beef fat and come mighty close to the desired proportions.

After the suet and venison have been ground separately through your coarse

After grinding the suet and venison separately, using the coarse plate, spread the two on a work surface and knead them together with your hands.

After the suet and venison are well mixed, run them through your grinder again, this time using the medium or fine grinding plate.

grinding plate, the next step is to spread the venison out on a large flat work surface. On top of it, sprinkle your beef fat or suet "crumbles." Then thoroughly knead the two together with your hands until they are well mixed. This accomplished, remove the coarse grinding plate and insert the medium grinding plate and run your burger through the mill again. It may now be of exactly the consistency you like, but if not it can be run through the grinder a third or even fourth time to produce increasingly finer textures.

Favorite Deerburger Recipes

The burger just produced is splendid for making sandwiches (call them deerburgers, buckburgers, hamburgers, or whatever you like), but a few tricks of the trade will make them turn out even better.

First, due to the fat content in the meat, it is not necessary to add any cooking oil to your skillet or griddle before frying the burgers. It is wise, though, to sprinkle just a bit of salt onto your cooking surface, as this will prevent the meat from sticking and scorching until the fat in the meat has had a chance to render out slightly for the remainder of the frying.

Due to the fat content in deerburger, it's not necessary to grease your skillet or griddle, but sprinkling a bit of salt on the cooking surface is beneficial.

Second, if you've included in your burger the prime meat of the tenderloins and rumps, the burger will be so tender it may begin to fall apart in the pan. This poses no problem if you're merely browning the meat before adding it to spaghetti sauce or chili, but it's quite annoying when you're trying to fry hamburgers for sandwiches.

The solution is to add some type of flavorless "binder" to the burger just before forming the burger patties with your hands. The best binder-combination I've come across is one slice of fresh, crumbled bread, an egg, and just a bit of cold water for every one pound of burger. Add the burger and binding ingredients to a bowl and knead them together with your hands. Then make each individual burger patty in the usual way.

If your family begins to tire of hamburger sandwiches prepared in the customary manner, try adding a little flare to your burgers. Before forming them into patties ready for the skillet, add a splash or two of Worcestershire Sauce, A-1 Steak Sauce, or barbecue sauce, kneading it thoroughly into the meat. For still different variations, knead into the burger a bit of finely chopped onion and garlic powder, or a combination of sweet basil and thyme. One of the simplest and yet most delectable ways to enjoy your burgers is to sprinkle them with nutmeg while they're frying for a unique nutty flavor.

You'll also want to use your burger to prepare these special treats from time to time.

Since deerburger is so tender, some type of "binder" is necessary to make a meatloaf that doesn't fall apart in the pan. Usually, breadcrumbs or crackercrumbs help to hold the works together.

Venison Meatloaf #1

1½	pounds deerburger	2	tablespoons chopped green pepper
1	cup crackercrumbs, crushed	1½	teaspoons salt
2	eggs, beaten	1	medium bay leaf, crumbled
1	8-ounce can tomato sauce		dash thyme
½	cup chopped onion		dash marjoram

In a bowl, combine all ingredients and knead together well with your hands. Shape into a loaf and place in a bread pan. Bake at 350° for 1 hour. Serves 6.

Venison Meatloaf #2

1½	pounds deerburger	¼	teaspoon black pepper
1	cup milk	½	teaspoon sage
⅔	cup dry breadcrumbs	½	teaspoon thyme
2	eggs, beaten	½	teaspoon rosemary
¼	cup chopped onion		catsup or tomato sauce
1	teaspoon salt		

First soak the breadcrumbs in the milk, then add the remaining ingredients and knead with your hands. Form into a loaf and place in a bread pan. Pour about ½ cup catsup or tomato sauce over the top of the loaf, then bake at 350° for 1 hour. Serves 6.

Venison Meatloaf #3

1½ pounds deerburger
2 eggs, beaten
¾ cup milk
3 slices fresh bread, crumbled
1¼ tablespoons prepared mustard
5 tablespoons catsup
1 tablespoon mixed Italian herbs
1 medium onion, chopped
1 green pepper, chopped
1 tablespoon salt

In a bowl, first blend together the eggs and milk, then add the remaining ingredients and thoroughly knead with your hands. Form into a loaf and place in an ungreased bread pan. Place this pan in a shallow, flat-cake pan holding about 1 inch of boiling water and bake at 375° for 1½ hours. Serves 6.

Deerburger Chili

2 pounds deerburger
1 green pepper, chopped
2 16-ounce cans red kidney beans with liquid
2 12-ounce cans whole tomatoes with liquid
1 tablespoon red cayenne pepper
2 tablespoons garlic powder
1 teaspoon ground cumin powder
4 tablespoons chili powder
2 bay leaves, crumbled

Brown the deerburger in a skillet. When the meat is cooked, spoon off and discard grease. Then add the burger and remaining ingredients to a deep pot along with 2 quarts of cold water. Slowly simmer on low heat for 2 hours. Serves 8.

1. To make Venison Pepper Supreme, begin by blanching pepper halves in boiling water. Meanwhile, in another pan, heat chili until it is piping hot.

2. Blend chili with cooked macaroni, spices, and one-half of the cheddar cheese. Spoon the mixture into the blanched pepper halves.

3. Sprinkle tops of peppers with the remaining cheddar cheese, then sprinkle on Parmesan cheese.

4. Arrange the filled peppers on a pan. Slip under broiler until the tops are lightly browned. Superb!

Venison Pepper Supreme

1	7-ounce package macaroni	½	teaspoon salt
8	green peppers, sliced lengthwise into halves	¼	teaspoon black pepper
		½	teaspoon oregano
1½	quarts Deerburger Chili (see previous recipe)	½	cup grated Parmesan cheese
1	cup grated cheddar cheese		

Cook the macaroni according to the package instructions, then drain. Place the sliced peppers in a second large pot of salted boiling water and blanch them for 2 minutes, then quickly remove the peppers while they are still crisp and place on a paper towel to drain. Heat the chili, then stir in the cooked macaroni, one-half of the cheddar cheese and the salt, pepper, and oregano. Stuff the pepper halves with the chili-macaroni mix. Sprinkle on top of the filled peppers the remaining cheddar cheese, then the Parmesan cheese. Arrange the stuffed peppers on a large cookie sheet and slip the works under your oven's broiler for several minutes or until they are lightly browned on top. Be careful not to allow them to burn. Serves 6.

Venison Meatballs, Noodles, and Gravy

1½	pounds deerburger	⅔	cup chopped onion
3	slices fresh white bread	¼	cup butter
2	teaspoons salt	1	10-ounce package wide noodles
¼	teaspoon black pepper		
⅛	teaspoon basil	1	cup milk
⅛	teaspoon oregano	1	tablespoon flour

Crumble the bread and knead it into the deerburger with the salt, pepper, basil, oregano, and onion. Now form one-inch-diameter meatballs with your fingers. Place the meatballs on a cookie sheet and chill in your refrigerator for one-half hour, then brown the meatballs in a skillet containing the butter, turning them frequently. Reduce the heat under the skillet to as low as possible, cover with a lid, and let the meatballs continue to cook very slowly for another 15 minutes. Meanwhile, cook the noodles in a large pot of salted, boiling water according to the instructions on the package, then drain. Transfer the meatballs from the skillet to a plate set in your oven to keep them hot. Add to the drippings in the skillet the milk and just a pinch of flour at a time, constantly stirring on medium high heat until it turns into the consistency of gravy. Add the meatballs to the gravy, stir gently, then ladle over the top of the bed of noodles on a hot platter. Serves 6.

Polynesian Meatballs

1½	pounds deerburger	2	tablespoons cornstarch
⅔	cup cracker crumbs	½	cup brown sugar
⅓	cup minced onion	1	13-ounce can pineapple tidbits
1	egg, beaten		
1½	teaspoons salt	⅓	cup vinegar
¼	cup milk	1	tablespoon soy sauce
¼	teaspoon ground ginger	1	green pepper, chopped
1	tablespoon cooking oil		

In a bowl, add the deerburger, cracker crumbs, onion, beaten egg, salt, ginger and milk, then thoroughly knead with your hands. Take tablespoons of the meat mixture and mold into meatballs with your hands. Brown the meatballs in a skillet containing the cooking oil, remove to a hot plate where they will stay warm, then spoon off any grease remaining in the skillet. Now blend the cornstarch and brown sugar. Stir in the syrup the pineapple was packed in, then stir in the vinegar and soy sauce. Pour this mixture into the skillet and cook over medium heat until the mixture thickens and begins to bubble. Now add the meatballs, pineapple tidbits and green pepper. When everything is piping hot, serve on a hot platter. Serves 6.

Venison Goulash

1 4-ounce package noodles
1 pound deerburger
1 onion, chopped
½ cup catsup
3 stalks celery, chopped

1 4-ounce can sliced
   mushrooms
1 14-ounce can tomatoes
2 teaspoons salt
½ teaspoon black pepper

Cook the noodles in a pot of salted, boiling water according to the instructions on the package. Meanwhile, brown the deerburger in a skillet. Drain off the grease, then add the onions and continue cooking until they are clear. Stir in the cooked, drained noodles, catsup, celery, mushrooms, tomatoes, salt, and pepper. Cover the skillet with a lid and simmer on very low heat for one-half hour. Serves 4.

Creamed Deerburger with Potatoes

1 pound deerburger
2 tablespoons milk
1½ teaspoons flour
1 medium can condensed
   cream of mushroom
   soup

1 4-ounce can mushrooms
1 can beef broth
4 medium potatoes, cut into
   chunks
½ teaspoon salt
¼ teaspoon black pepper

Make deerburger patties of the usual size, then dip each in the milk and then in the flour. Brown both sides in a skillet containing a bit of cooking oil until the burgers are almost done. Now add the mushroom soup, mushrooms, beef broth, potatoes, salt, and pepper. Cover the skillet and cook slowly over low heat until the potatoes are done. Serves 4.

Stuffed Cabbage Rolls

1 head of cabbage
1 cup uncooked Minute Rice
1 pound deerburger
1 teaspoon salt
¼ teaspoon black pepper
½ teaspoon cinnamon
⅛ teaspoon allspice
⅛ teaspoon ground cloves
3 tablespoons melted butter
1 12-ounce can tomatoes
¼ cup lemon juice

With a long knife, remove the pithy core from the center of the cabbage, then soak the cabbage in very hot water for five minutes to wilt it. After momentarily draining the cabbage, carefully separate and remove the leaves. Use your knife to carefully trim out any ribs that are hard and wide. Cook the rice as directed on the package, then stir in the deerburger, spices, and butter. Lay several tablespoons (more or less) of the deerburger-rice mixture in the center of each cabbage leaf and carefully roll them up. In the bottom of your cooking pot, lay a steamer rack to support the cabbage rolls so they are not directly lying on the bottom of the pot. Add enough water to barely cover the cabbage rolls, then cover and cook over low heat for one-half hour. Now add the tomatoes and cook an additional 5 minutes. Finally, dribble the lemon juice over the cabbage rolls, cover the pot and allow to simmer another 2 minutes. Very carefully transfer the cabbage rolls to a hot platter, then spoon over the tops of them the sauce in the bottom of the pot. Serves 4.

Undoubtedly, you also have many favorite recipes of your own that call for "hamburger" or other forms of ground meat. For example, there are probably hundreds of variations of spaghetti sauce alone. But no matter, for your deerburger can easily be substituted for any recipe that calls for ground beef, pork, or veal. I'm sure you'll be pleased with the results.

CHAPTER 12

Making Bulk Sausage and Links

THE ART AND CRAFT of making sausage has always held a mysterious, enchanting attraction in which one harbors visions of Old World recipes, closely guarded family secrets, and a padlock on the smoke-house door. All of these things scare away many hunters, discouraging them from making their own venison sausage, but it needn't be that way.

You've already made burger from much of your deer and saw how quickly and easily you did a professional job the first time. Making sausage is essentially the same, with two exceptions. In addition to grinding together a mixture of venison and beef fat, you often add a third ingredient in the form of lean pork, depending upon the specific recipe being followed. Then, between the first and second grinding operations, you sprinkle the meat with seasonings.

Let's begin, then, by first looking at the equipment you'll need. Likely as not, the meat grinder you previously used in making burger will also do a fine job producing sausage, particularly if you're going to make bulk sausage. If you're going to make link sausage or ring sausage you'll need an inexpensive casing stuffer. This is nothing more than a long plastic spout that fits on the front of your grinder. If one wasn't included as an accessory when you purchased your grinder, check the owner's manual and undoubtedly you can order one. If not, go to a restaurant equipment supply company and obtain a "universal" casing link stuffer that is designed to fit most brands of meat grinders (the price shouldn't be more than $4).

There also are special sausage link stuffers on the market that look like huge hypodermic syringes; you simply fill the tube with meat, insert the casing over the spout, then push a plunger to fill the casing and create links. These gadgets are generally priced around $15.

Another type of casing stuffer is a cast-iron, shoelike affair that mounts on a board. Again, you fill a meat reservoir, slip a casing over the stuffing spout, then work a pump handle plunger to push meat into the casing. These do an extremely professional job, they're built to last a lifetime, and they cost around $60.

Do not try to improvise, as I've seen recommended in some sportsmen's magazines, by using a funnel, the spout of an angel food cake pan, or the neck region of a cut-off plastic bottle. Such crude contraptions produce very poor results and the only thing you'll accomplish is working yourself up into a knot of frustration.

In making sausage, depending upon the recipe, you may need a quantity of suet or beef fat trimmings and what was said about these in the last chapter apply here as well. You may also need to obtain pork and I suggest lean pork such as pork butt or pork shoulder. Trim off the rind and the major chunks of fat around the outside, but don't worry about being too meticulous. You can even allow the entire pork fat to remain if you wish, but in this case you should proportionately reduce the amount of suet or beef fat the particular recipe you're using may call for.

Same equipment used for grinding burger often can be adapted to making sausage. All you need is a stuffing spout that fits onto the front of the machine.

Begin with Bulk Sausage

Okay, for starters, let's produce a simple bulk sausage. Keep in mind the ratio three-to-one-to-one. In other words, three pounds of venison will be mixed with one pound of beef fat and one pound of lean pork. Remember also, if you use very "fatty" pork to cut down the quantity of beef fat or even eliminate it altogether.

As in making the burger, grind your quantity of venison first and set it aside. Then grind the suet, and then the pork. The meats should be quite cold before submitting them to the grinder, and small chunks of meat will go through the cutting blade much faster than big, unwieldy globs.

After running these meats through the coarse grinding plate the first time, thoroughly knead them together with your hands and then run the mixture through the grinder a second time, now using the medium grinding plate.

You now have basic bulk sausage. It's almost too simple, hey? But wait! Now we have to season the meat. Spread the sausage over a large work area such as a chopping-block table or a countertop covered with protective paper.

The characteristic flavors of different types of sausage are obtained by blending various seasonings, spices, and aromatic seeds. Later I'll describe several sausage seasoning recipes intended specifically for venison that you can make yourself by assembling individual ingredients.

But this first time in your sausage-making endeavor, I highly recommend you try a commercially prepared sausage-seasoning mix. These come in paper

1. Making bulk sausage is quite easy and begins with cutting pork, suet, and venison into chunks. Use the ratio specified in the recipe you're following.

2. Feed each of the three meats once through the coarse plate of your grinder (continued next page).

envelopes and are available in most grocery stores and meat markets. They are customarily packaged in 4-ounce and 8-ounce quantities; 4 ounces costs about 79¢ and is sufficient to season 12 pounds of sausage, while 8 ounces will season 25 pounds.

These sausage seasonings vary enormously in their component ingredients. Even the same company may have several specific variations they distribute to stores in certain ethnic neighborhoods. For example, in a predominantly Italian community, the sausage-seasoning packets available in meat markets are sure to have fennel spice and garlic as two main ingredients (among many others). Yet in Polish communities you'll find fennel and coriander. In Scandinavian regions you'll find fennel and sage, and in Spanish and Mexican-American regions you'll find red cayenne pepper, sage, and cumin seed. There is not a Hungarian or Slovakian sausage recipe that does not possess paprika, and popular German sausages invariably have heavy dosages of black pepper, allspice, cloves, and nutmeg. In each case, uniquely different flavors are achieved and over several centuries have served as tasty hallmarks distinguishing different nationalities.

Still other spices, herbs, and aromatic seeds commonly found in sausage include salt, white pepper, sugar, mustard, thyme, rosemary, marjoram, bay leaves, ginger, and mace.

So my hearty advice, as mentioned earlier, is to try two or three prepared seasoning mixes, making at first only small quantities of sausage using each. Then decide which particular ones you like a lot and which you do not especially care for. This is really the only logical way to season sausage because we all come from different backgrounds and therefore have acquired taste preferences.

3. *Then knead the three meats together with your hands and grind a second time through a medium or fine plate.*

4. *Use a prepared seasoning the first time you make sausage. There are numerous variations to choose from.*

Going back to your tabletop covered with sausage mix and your packet of prepared seasoning in hand, here's one word of caution. Don't simply dump the seasoning onto the sausage mix. Scrounge around your cupboard for a seldom used saltshaker and fill it with the seasoning mix. Then sprinkle it over the sausage to ensure an even distribution rather than spotty places of oversaturation. With the seasoning applied, now knead the meat thoroughly with your hands.

At this point, many people like to place their sausage mix in the refrigerator overnight, believing this "grace period" allows the spices and herbs to completely meld with each other and permeate the meat before it is pushed through the grinder a final time. I've tried both ways—letting the sausage "age" overnight, or immediately going onto the next step—and honestly can't tell the difference in the final product.

In any case, the last step is to run the sausage mixture through the medium-coarse plate of your grinder, and then to wrap individual packages of your bulk sausage for the freezer.

Stuffing Sausage Links and Rings

Many hunters, after they've produced bulk sausage, like to practice the more refined art of next stuffing it into casings.

You can obtain either synthetic or natural casings, depending upon your preferences. Synthetic casings have an indefinite storage life, they cook out quite tender, and they look quite pleasing, just like you had a custom butcher

5. An old salt shaker evenly distributes the seasonings on top of the sausage mix.

6. With the seasoning applied, knead the sausage with your hands, then run it through your grinder a third time. You can now form individual patties for freezing, or freeze the sausage in bulk.

make your sausages. The drawback is that they're quite expensive and in some regions may be very difficult to find.

Natural casings, on the other hand, don't cook out nearly so tender and yield a definite skinlike covering on the sausages. They also are limited in their storage life and the final appearance of your sausages will often take on a distinct "homemade" look. Yet natural casings are readily available and very inexpensive, which is exactly the reason why I prefer them.

Natural casings, of course, are the intestines of sheep, hogs, or beef steers. In a packinghouse they are removed from the animal, turned inside out, thoroughly cleaned, and then packed in either coarse dry salt or a brine solution.

The smallest casings come from sheep and are primarily used in the making of breakfast sausages, wieners, and pepperoni; these are the most tender casings you can buy. Slightly larger in size, and the most commonly used, are hog casings, which typically are stuffed as polish sausage, kielbasa, and the like. The looped sections of beef steer intestines are the largest casings and they are used in making potato sausage, ring bologna, and salami. The middle sections of beef steer intestines—also called "straights"—are used in making summer sausage. Since beef steer intestines are quite tough, they are generally peeled away and not eaten.

In this chapter I'll describe the use of hog casings, merely because that's what a majority of all deer-hunting sausage makers seem to prefer most. The techniques that apply to the use of sheep and beef casings are the same; only their sizes differ, and therefore the sizes of the stuffing spouts required of them.

Hog casings can be purchased through most grocery stores that have large meat departments that make their own sausage. If your local store doesn't have them, and can't order them, go to a small family-owned meat market, which probably makes its own sausage, or to a delicatessen. Still no luck? Check the Yellow Pages of your phone book for the nearest meatpacking plant and I guarantee they'll have them!

As of 1983, hog casings fetched about $4 per pound, but one pound of hog casings is sufficient to stuff 100 pounds of venison sausage! In most instances, you'll require only four or six ounces of casings. The trouble is, many suppliers of casings just don't want to bother with selling such small quantities at a time and therefore have them put up in sealed packages weighing two pounds. That's enough to turn three entire deer into sausage! If you don't have an immediate need for that many casings, you can store them in your refrigerator for up to a year as long as they are packed in an adequate amount of dry salt or brine. Another possibility is to share them with deer-hunting friends or members of your local gun club.

Before using hog casings to make link sausage, flush out their insides with water to remove all traces of their salt preservatives.

When preparing to make sausage links or rings, don't try to handle long lengths of the casings at one time. With scissors or a knife, snip off several sections about four feet long.

Before using the casings, you have to first rinse them with running water to remove all traces of their salt preservative. Pay particular attention to flushing out the insides of the casings by simply taking one end and slipping it over the mouth of your sink faucet. Be careful! At first the casings are slippery and if your stopper or plug is not in place, and you drop the casings, they'll slide right down the drain. In fact, we like to lay a terrycloth towel in the bottom of the sink to eliminate any chance of this happening.

After washing the casings, allow them to soak in a bowl of lukewarm water for about 20 minutes. They were very cold from being stored in your refrigerator and now it's necessary to make them soft and pliable. After they're soaked, shake the casings so excess water falls off, then place them momentarily on some paper toweling to drain.

Meanwhile, you can remove the cutting knife and grinding plates from your meat grinder and attach the casing stuffer spout. Also, fetch several yards of heavy-duty sewing thread or lightweight cotton string, which will be used to tie off the casings in various locations.

The most common mistake committed by first-time sausage makers is slipping one end of a casing over the end of the stuffing spout and then trying to fill the entire casing as it lays draped in coils on the tabletop. It just doesn't work because several big globs of sausage will clog the casing and go no farther.

The prescribed method of stuffing sausage is to take one end of the casing and slip it over the mouth of the stuffer spout and push it as far back as possible. Then continue pushing the remainder of the casing onto the spout until the entire casing is all scrunched up in accordion-like fashion. When you reach the other end of the casing, tie it closed with a bit of your string or thread.

You're now ready to begin stuffing the casing. One person can do it all by himself but asking your spouse or one of your kids to help makes the job proceed far more quickly. One person turns the crank handle, or operates the on-off switch if it's an electric grinder, and simultaneously feeds the bulk sausage into the mouth or overhead hopper-tray of the grinder. The helpmate works with the casings.

The first bulk sausage to come out of the grinder will fill up the little loose end of casing hanging from the stuffer spout. As the casing continues to fill and balloon out, additional casing material is slowly pulled off the spout and allowed to duly fill.

At this point, you've got two choices. You can slowly fill a two-foot-long segment of casing to make a so-called "ring," or you can make shorter, six-inch-long sausage links. If you plan to later smoke the sausage, you'll want to make rings as they are much easier to hang in a smokehouse or small electric smoker. If you'll merely be freezing the sausage with intentions of later frying or baking it, you'll find links are easier to work with.

The way to segment your individual links is to first let six inches of casing fill, then momentarily turn off the grinder or cease turning the crank handle. Next, turn the sausage link two or three times to make a twist in the casing. It's very important to remember to make successive twists always in the same direction. Otherwise, if you were to make a right-hand twist in the first

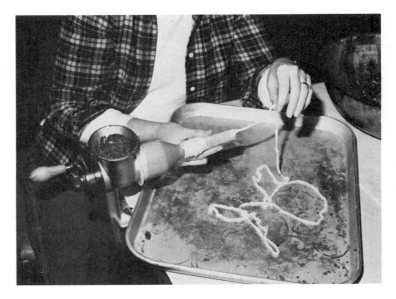

After attaching the stuffing spout to your grinder, slide a length of casing all the way onto it so it is accordioned. When you reach the opposite end, tie the casing closed.

casing link, then a left-hand twist in the second casing link, the second twisting, going in the opposite direction, will have a tendency to untwist the first.

When you finally reach the opposite end of the casing, of course, you have no choice but to close the opening with a string tie as a twist would not hold the sausage contents inside that casing; this means you'll always have two string ties, one at each end of the string of casing links or at the two ends of a long ring sausage.

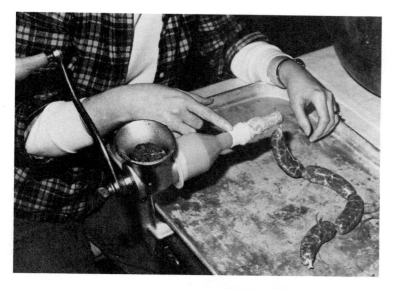

As the casing begins to fill with sausage, occasionally twist the casing to form links, then pull a bit more casing off the end of the stuffing spout.

When you've completed as many links as you want on a series of sausages, tie string after the last link, cut the chain of sausages free, and then begin making another chain as before.

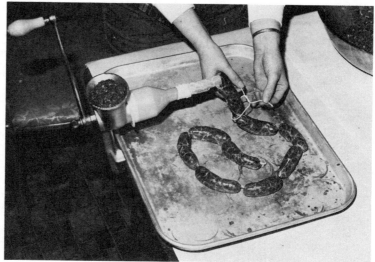

One other little trick should be mentioned and it's something that can be gained only through hands-on experience. You want to make sure your casing is stuffed quite tightly and that small spaces or air pockets between clumps of sausage are eliminated. Otherwise, during later cooking, these will become tiny pressure cookers that will allow steam build-up to split the sausages. The trick, therefore, is to keep enough finger tension on the accordioned casing so it doesn't slide off the stuffing spout too easily as this will invariably result in slack-filled links or rings. Yet at the same time you don't want to stuff your sausages so tightly that you risk rupturing the rather fragile casings and subsequently having sausage mixture spilling on your table. To obtain just the right shape and degree of compactness, using your fingertips to squeeze, mold, and shape the sausage links seems to be the most popular way of getting everything just right.

All of this may sound terribly complicated but after only ten minutes of trial and error you'll be producing sausages that look like they were created by an artist.

Here, Marianne Weiss checks the progress of her sausages in a portable smoker. This method of smoking merely enhances the flavor of the sausages; after coming out of the smokehouse, they must be refrigerated or frozen.

Finally, I should say a few words about smoking your finished sausage rings. A small, inexpensive smoker of the type designed for use by sportsmen for smoking fish and game is perfect. But realize you will not be achieving an internal sausage temperature sufficient to either eliminate the possibility of trichinosis from the pork or achieve necessary preservation attributes in order that the finished sausage does not need refrigeration.

Consequently, submitting sausage to the smokehouse for several hours should only be looked upon as a method of enhancing the flavor of the sausage, and it still needs to be cooked before being eaten. It also needs to be stored in your refrigerator, if it will be eaten within one week, or in your freezer if it's to be stored longer.

Authentic smoked sausage, which requires no refrigeration, such as some types of pepperoni and summer sausage, is treated in an entirely different manner. These are fully cooked, in bulk form, in vats of boiling water (or, sometimes they are allowed to soak and cure in a brine solution), then they are stuffed into casings, and after that smoked until an internal temperature of at least 110° is achieved. Since there are so many techniques and fine points dealing with this aspect of sausage making, I suggest the reader, if he is so inclined, obtain a book specifically on the subject of smoking meats.

Sausage Recipes

After testing any number of commercially prepared sausage seasonings, you may wish to try making your own. In all cases, remember that the spices, herbs, and seasonings must be thoroughly blended to ensure their even distribution when sprinkled on the meat. The best way to accomplish this, if you're making only a small quantity of sausage, is using a discarded saltshaker. If you're making more than 20 pounds or so, take a widemouthed pint-size jar and punch holes in the screw-cap lid to fashion an adequate shaker. Here are the venison sausage recipes my family like most. The majority are suitable for producing either bulk sausage or stuffing into casings for links or rings.

Venison Sausage #1

9 pounds venison, trimmed and cubed
3 pounds lean pork, cubed
3 pounds beef fat or suet, cubed
3 teaspoons garlic powder

1 teaspoon red cayenne pepper
3 teaspoons black pepper
1 teaspoon thyme
1 teaspoon sage
1 bay leaf, crumbled
3 teaspoons salt

Thoroughly grind the three meats separately, knead together with your hands, then grind again. Shake seasonings in a jar until they are blended well, then sprinkle evenly over the sausage mix, knead with your hands, then grind again. Freeze the sausage in bulk form or make links or rings from hog casings.

Venison Sausage #2

5 pounds venison, trimmed and cubed
1 pound lean pork, cubed
1 pound beef fat or suet, cubed
2 tablespoons salt

3 tablespoons sage
2 teaspoons black pepper
1 teaspoon red cayenne pepper
2 tablespoons molasses

Grind the three meats separately. Knead together, then grind a second time. Mix the dry ingredients and sprinkle over the sausage, then knead thoroughly with your hands. Place the sausage mix in a bowl, then thoroughly knead in the molasses. Wrap and freeze in bulk form.

Venison Sausage #3

6 pounds venison, trimmed and
   cubed
3 pounds beef fat trimmings or
   suet, cubed
2 tablespoons salt
2 teaspoons black pepper
4 teaspoons dried fennel
   powder

3 teaspoons garlic powder
4 teaspoons sage
4 tablespoons sugar
3 tablespoons finely minced
   parsley

Grind the meats separately, knead together with your hands, then grind a second time. Shake seasonings in a jar until well blended, then sprinkle over the sausage. Knead with your hands, then grind a third time. Freeze the sausage in bulk or make casing links.

Venison Sausage #4

8 pounds venison, trimmed
   and cubed
2 pounds beef fat or very fatty
   pork, cubed
4 teaspoons salt

2 teaspoons black pepper
½ teaspoon red cayenne pepper
4 teaspoons sage
1 teaspoon allspice

Grind the venison and beef fat (or pork) separately, then knead with your hands and grind a second time. After mixing the dry ingredients, sprinkle over the sausage, knead with your hands, then grind again. Freeze the sausage in bulk or stuff into casing links or rings.

Venison Sausage #5

5   pounds venison, trimmed
    and cubed
2   pounds lean pork, trimmed
    and cubed
1   pound beef fat or suet,
    cubed
4   teaspoons black pepper

7   teaspoons salt
1½   teaspoons thyme
2½   teaspoons sage
¾   teaspoon nutmeg
¼   teaspoon red cayenne
    pepper

Grind the three meats separately, then knead together and grind a second time. Sprinkle the seasonings on the meat, then knead again with your hands. Grind the sausage a third time. Freeze in bulk form or stuff into casings.

Venison Polish Sausage

3 pounds venison, trimmed and
    cubed
1 pound beef fat or suet, cubed
1 pound lean pork, cubed
5 teaspoons salt

2 teaspoons black pepper
4 teaspoons marjoram
3 teaspoons garlic powder
1 teaspoon red cayenne pepper

Grind the meats separately, knead together and grind again. Sprinkle seasonings on the meat, knead with your hands, then grind a third time. Stuff into casing links or rings. Place the sausage in a rectangular cake pan, cover the sausage with water, and bake in an oven at 350° until all the water has evaporated. Wrap and freeze.

Venison Pepperoni

5   pounds venison, trimmed and cubed
3½ pounds slightly fatty pork, cubed
2   teaspoons ginger
2   teaspoons fennel seed
1   teaspoon red cayenne pepper

1   teaspoon black pepper
1   teaspoon garlic powder
1   teaspoon oregano
¾ teaspoon white pepper
½ teaspoon allspice

Grind the two meats separately, knead together with your hands, then grind a second time. Sprinkle seasonings on the meat and knead with your hands, then grind a third time. Stuff into casing links or rings. Place in a rectangular cake pan, cover the sausage barely with water and bake at 350° until the water has evaporated. Then hang the sausage in your electric smoker for 3 hours. This pepperoni must be refrigerated and it is excellent when served as an appetizer with assorted cheeses and crackers.

The previous seven recipes are our favorites, and if you add to them the wide number of prepared sausage-seasoning mixes that are available, it may conceivably take you many years to try them all. Just remember that you've got every right to be both flexible and creative in satisfying your own particular tastes. If you like your sausages a bit hotter than most, add more red cayenne pepper or black pepper than any of the recipes call for. If you prefer mild sausages, cut the stated pepper amounts in half. Also, sage and garlic powder, if you especially like their flavors, are two ingredients that can be added to any sausage with good results even if they're not called for in a specific recipe.

Finally, if you want to be even more adventuresome and try your hand at making potato sausage, salami, summer sausage, bratwurst, knackwurst, or still others, using your venison as the prime ingredient, I heartily recommend obtaining the book *Homemade Sausage* by Lester Alton. The price of the book is $4.50 (postage paid) and it is available by writing to the publisher, Vera Allen, P.O. Box 7126, Duluth, Minnesota 55807. This book contains more than 100 sausage recipes, which should keep you busy until you're stroking your long white beard.

Favorite Ways to Cook Sausage

Venison sausage, whether in bulk form, links, or rings, can be cooked and served exactly the same as you would their beef or pork counterparts purchased at your local grocery store.

To make sausage sandwiches, form patties from bulk sausage and fry as you would burgers, then serve in sandwich rolls. As a pleasing variation of this, melt two tablespoons of butter in a skillet. Then knead into the equivalent of each intended sausage patty one egg, one teaspoon of water, and ¼ teaspoon parsley flakes. Form into patties and fry in the usual way. When the sausage patties are almost done, top each with a slice of mild cheddar cheese and cover the pan briefly. When the cheese is melted, quickly serve each sausage patty between two slices of buttered rye toast.

When using sausage links or ring sausage for sandwiches, I like to fry them very slowly on low heat and, when they are cooked all the way through, slice them lengthwise and serve in Italian buns.

You can also, of course, fry either bulk or link sausage in the usual way and serve it as a side meat dish with fried potatoes and sautéed vegetables such as onions, mushrooms, and green bell peppers. An unusually zesty way of perking up other familiar dishes is browning bulk sausage in a pan, then adding it to your favorite spaghetti sauce in place of deerburger. Or add it to marzetti, or lasagna. Considering the many, many sausage-seasoning mixes available, plus the ones given here that you can manufacture yourself, the many slight menu variations you can achieve are almost endless.

Be sure to do at least one other thing as well, particularly around holiday time when guests are visiting. Cook sausage links or rings, made from several different seasoning mixes if possible, then refrigerate the sausage overnight. The next day, slice it thinly and create an attractive dish of hors d'oeuvres for your friends to nibble upon. If there are any sausages left over, which, to tell the truth, isn't very likely, you can slice them a bit thicker than hors d'oeuvre slices and add them to your favorite vegetable soup for a new and tangy taste treat.

Following are still more recipe ideas for using your venison sausage.

Espanole

8	large sausage links	1	12-ounce can tomatoes
3	cups white rice, cooked	1½	teaspoons salt
¼	cup chopped onion	¼	teaspoon black pepper
¼	cup chopped green pepper		

Fry the sausage links in a skillet containing a bit of oil until they are thoroughly cooked. Meanwhile, cook the rice according to the instructions on the package. Remove the sausage links from the pan and slice them into half-inch thick "rounds." Add the onion and green pepper to the drippings in the skillet and cook until the onion is clear. Now stir in all the remaining ingredients and cook, uncovered, over low heat for 15 minutes. Serves 4.

Stacked Sausage Towers

1½	pounds bulk sausage	¼	cup minced onion
1	cup packaged herb-seasoned stuffing	2	tablespoons chili sauce
1	cup finely chopped tart apples	2	tablespoons parsley flakes
¼	cup chopped celery	¼	teaspoon black pepper
		6	spiced crabapples

Form 12 thin sausage patties with your hands. Prepare the stuffing according to the package directions, then with your hands knead in the apples, celery, onion, and seasonings. Place six of the patties in a lightly greased shallow pan. On top of each place ½ cup of the stuffing mix molded into a patty. Now top each of these with a second sausage patty, held in place with a toothpick down through the center. Bake at 375° for 45 minutes. Five minutes before the sausage towers are finished, top each with a spiced crabapple, skewered on top of each toothpick sticking out. Serves 6.

Sausage-Tomato-Pepper Ragout

8 large sausage links
1 cup chopped onion
½ teaspoon garlic powder
1 green pepper, cut into ½-inch-wide strips

2 tablespoons paprika
1 12-ounce can tomatoes
¼ teaspoon black pepper
½ teaspoon salt

Gently fry the sausage links until they are thoroughly cooked, then cut them into slices ½-inch thick. In the same pan, sauté the onions and garlic until the onions are clear. Add the green pepper, tomatoes, sausage pieces, and seasonings. Cover and simmer over low heat for 30 minutes. This dish can be served as is, or ladled over a bed of rice or noodles. Serves 4.

Easy Barbecued Sausage

8 large sausage links

1 bottle Open Pit Barbecue Sauce

Arrange the sausage links in the bottom of a shallow baking pan. Cover with the barbecue sauce, then bake at 350° for 1 hour, turning the sausages twice during the allotted baking time. Serves 4.

CHAPTER 13

Freezing and Defrosting Venison

MEAT IS A perishable foodstuff. Therefore, immediately after butchering your deer, you must wrap the packages of venison and sharply reduce their temperature. Both of these procedures can be satisfactorily accomplished in many ways that will be examined in this chapter.

Unfortunately, many deer hunters look upon the temporary refrigeration or freezing of venison as a relatively minor concern. Actually, it is just as important as proper field care, transportation, and aging of venison. However, refrigerating or freezing venison is no cure-all for improper handling of the meat. The quality of the venison you remove from the cold-storage locker can be no better than the quality and condition of the meat you put in.

To emphasize this point, I'm reminded of an incident that happened not long ago. I was rummaging around in my freezer, taking an inventory of my cache of venison, when I discovered a rump roast that was 18 months old. Apparently, the venison was from a deer taken the previous year, but somehow the package had gotten lost in the shuffle when this year's buck was taken and quickly placed in the freezer. Most recognized authorities recommend 12 months as the maximum length of time frozen meat should be stored before its consumption. But I just couldn't bring myself to throw that rump roast out, so I began looking through my card file for an appropriate recipe, figuring that if the meat proved inedible we could always go out to dinner on short notice. Surprisingly, the meat was delectable. It was just a bit on the dry side, which is understandable, and since I predicted this would be the case, I used a moist-cooking method. Nevertheless, the venison roast tasted very, very good.

Coincidentally enough, a week later I was recounting my experience with a friend who had been noticing, lately, that his own venison wasn't tasting very good, even though it had been in his freezer less than four months. I was shocked when I opened the door of his freezer and saw the disarray of packages. All were wrapped with only one layer of paper, some of the packages had part of the paper actually ripped away from rough handling, which allowed portions of the meat to be exposed, and many of the packages didn't even have any kind of label or other identification upon them!

It would be difficult for me to blame these atrocious storage methods for the venison tasting so badly—possibly, the deer was not cared for properly in the field, or was aged so long it reached the point of spoilage—but I'd bet a week's pay my friend's careless wrapping of his venison was at least *partly* responsible.

So let's look at the proper way of storing your venison. Much of this information comes from leading food experts associated with agricultural extension agencies and the nutrition departments of leading universities.

Refrigerator Storage of Venison

The vast majority of any hunter's meat packages will go into his freezer for future use. However, he's almost certain to be excited about taking this year's deer and will want to serve several sumptuous venison dinners to his family almost immediately. This meat can be stored, unfrozen, in his refrigerator for a very brief period of time. Refer to the following chart for safe storage times of particular cuts or types of meat.

How you store venison in your refrigerator is just as important as carefully heeding the length of its storage-time limitations. As strange as it sounds, fresh meat should be stored *unwrapped* because exposure to air facilitates a partial drying of the surface of the meat which, in turn, increases its keeping quality. The best bet, therefore, is to place the meat on a plate and cover it loosely with a small towel that has been dampened and then thoroughly wrung out. Or, wrap the meat rather loosely in brown or white butcher's paper. Although moisture-and vapor-proof materials such as freezer wrapping paper and clear plastic wraps are ideal for freezing and long-term storage of meat, they should not be used for limited refrigerator storage.

Incidentally, when you purchase meat at your local grocery store, be it beef, pork, lamb, or whatever, it is usually sitting on some type of cardboard or styrofoam tray and then wrapped tightly and heat-sealed with plastic. Meat purchased this way can go right into your freezer, but if you plan to eat it within several days, and therefore store it in your refrigerator, you should remove the tight plastic cling-wrap and then set it on a plate or wrap it loosely in butcher's paper as described above.

If your refrigerator has a special drawer or other compartment designed for the storage of fresh meat, by all means use it. This compartment is invariably situated at the very bottom of the inside of the refrigerator where the temperature averages several degrees colder. Also, since it is enclosed, you're able to discourage the possibility of flavor-transfers between your venison and other foodstuffs, or vice versa.

Freezer Wrapping Materials

Appropriate freezer wrapping materials accomplish several things simultaneously: They protect the venison from bumps and bruises as meat packages are stacked and arranged in the freezer; they lock in meat moisture and juices to ensure the venison remains tender; and, they block out dry, stale freezer air, which otherwise can cause rancidity and give meat a bad flavor. Considering the weighty responsibilities that must be borne by freezer wrapping materials, it's poor economy indeed to buy cheap materials or improperly wrap your venison.

Begin with some type of cling-wrap as your first means of protecting your venison. This might be a transparent plastic freezer wrap, Saran, heavy-duty cellophane, or aluminum foil. In any case they all serve as nonporous vapor barriers, which can be pressed and formed around the irregular surfaces of any meat to hug it tightly. This eliminates pockets of air trapped against the meat and at the same time prevents moisture from being drawn out or "sublimated," which is what gives it a dry, blah taste.

With a cling-wrap tightly in place around the meat, now cover the meat a second time with a quality-grade freezer wrapping paper that has a glossy plastic coating on one side; the glossy, plastic side always goes on the inside when you make your wrap.

This paper is quite heavy, which is what protects the meat when it occasionally contacts other items in the freezer. The plastic coating, on the other hand, serves as still another vapor barrier to prevent dry, cold freezer air from working its way into wrapped packages and doing its dastardly deed. It's this second wrap that is primarily responsible for preventing "freezer burn," in which the meat becomes entirely depleted of surface moisture, discolored, and then rancid.

Aside from the specific materials you may elect to use, there are two wrap-

DRUGSTORE WRAP

1. *Secure the meat in some type of cling-wrap. Then lay the cling-wrapped meat in the center of a piece of plastic-coated paper.*

2. *Bring up the two sides of the paper.*

3. *Crease and fold the paper as many times as necessary until it lies flat against the package.*

4. *Fold the corners inward.*

5. *Completed drugstore wrap, with tape sealing the edges on bottom and clearly labeled.*

ping methods I highly recommend. They're called the "drugstore wrap" and the "butcher's wrap."

The drugstore wrap works best when your venison cuts are relatively flat and rectangular shaped, as when wrapping tenderloin steaks, round steaks, stew meat, and bulk quantities of burger or sausage. First lay out a rectangular sheet of white freezer wrapping paper, with the glossy plastic side up, and place your venison (already tightly enclosed in a cling-wrap such as aluminum foil) in the center. Bring up the top and bottom edges and, holding them together in the middle, crease and fold them several times to bring them down snug and flat against the top of the meat. Then take the two tail ends, one at a time, and fold them inward, creating triangular flaps which can then be tucked under and taped in place. Accompanying photos show how to make this easy wrap.

For larger round, oval, or irregular-shaped cuts of venison, such as rolled shoulder roasts, neck roasts, and rump roasts, the butcher's wrap seems to work best. Lay out a square sheet of freezer wrapping paper, glossy side up. Place the cling-wrapped meat in one corner, then begin rolling it diagonally across the paper toward the opposite corner, folding over the right and left sides as you go, as shown in the photos.

When your freezer wrap is completed, use tape to seal any edges or seams. One word of caution. Don't use scotch tape or cellophane tape as both will loosen when subjected to the cold air of your freezer. So-called "freezer tape" is fine, but it is only common masking tape at double the usual price. I've been using regular masking tape for years and never have encountered any problems.

Labeling is a very important part of storing your venison in cold storage because you'll want to be able to identify the various cuts of meat, how large they are (how much they weigh), and when, exactly, they were frozen. I use a common laundry marking pen that contains indelible ink, which won't smear when frost particles begin forming.

You may even wish to have on hand felt-tipped pens containing several different ink colors. For example, all of our venison packages are labeled in black ink, our fish packages in red, our small game in blue, and waterfowl in green. This way, when you're rummaging around in your crowded freezer for a particular type of meat for a meal, you don't have to pick up and read the label on each and every package.

Here's another little neat trick we've been using for many years. We occasionally give a venison roast or some other cut to a relative, neighbor, or special friend. Since many of these people are not hunters, and therefore are not intimately familiar with the proper ways to cook venison, we want to make sure they don't inadvertently ruin their meal. So we take a favorite, failsafe recipe we're confident they'll enjoy, and with our felt-tipped pen write it right on the outside of the package. In this manner, there's no way for them to forget my cooking instructions or misplace a recipe; it's always right there, with the meat, even if that roast goes into their freezer for several months.

In addition to cling-wraps and plastic-coated freezer wrapping paper, a couple of other types of freezer-storage materials may also be warranted from time to time, particularly when you want to refreeze meals that have already been cooked.

Let's say, for example, you make a humongous quantity of venison stew and there's more than enough left over for a second meal sometime in coming weeks. You can refreeze the stew right in the same glass or ceramic casserole dish you cooked the meal in, if you wish, providing of course that it has a suitable lid. The only disadvantage to this practice is that such dishes are usually round or oval, which is not a good shape for economical use of freezer space. Much better would be to transfer your stew to square-cornered plastic freezer boxes with vacuum-seal snap-top lids because, after being appropriately labeled, they can easily be stacked and arranged in such a manner that no freezer space is wasted.

You can also transfer stews, casseroles, and the like to heavy-duty zip-lock poly bags, but there's a trick to removing all of the air, which if left inside reduces the food's freezer lifespan. After placing the food inside the bag, seal almost the entire length of the zip-lock closure except for one small corner. Then use your hands to squeeze out as much air as possible.

BUTCHER'S WRAP

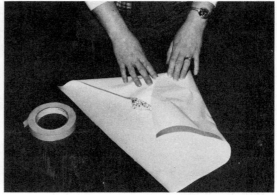

1. Secure venison in a cling-wrap. Then place the cut of meat in one corner of a sheet of plastic-coated paper.

2. Fold inward the right and left corners of the paper.

Next—and here is the trick—place your mouth over the tiny opening at the corner and suck the remaining air out of the bag. This will create a vacuum inside the bag, causing the plastic to actually collapse inward and tightly hug the irregularly shaped contents within the bag. Doing this will take a bit of practice because after the air has been sucked out of the bag you have to briefly continue sucking while simultaneously using your fingers to pinch the remainder of the zip-lock device closed.

Afterwards, write the nature of the contents and the date on a strip of masking tape and stick it onto the outside of the bag.

What Freezer Is Best?

There are presently five types of freezers on the market. Three are refrigerator-freezer combinations, in which the freezer, with its own separate door, is a compartment located on top or at the bottom of the refrigerator compartment, or stands vertically at the left side. The other two types of freezers are designed strictly for that purpose, one being an upright freezer with shelves and the other a chest-type freezer or "low boy."

Some of these freezers have distinct advantages over others. It's important to discuss them because, while you may not be in the market for a new freezer right now, you will be sometime in the future, and the information here may influence your choice at that time.

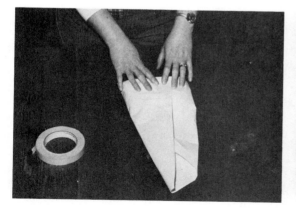

3. Make sure the paper is as tight as possible as you proceed to roll the meat diagonally toward the opposite corner.

4. This is the completed butcher's wrap. Again, use tape to seal the edges, then label the package as to contents, weight, and date frozen.

Those freezers built in combination with refrigerators are not really suitable for long-term storage of meats. This is especially the case with newer, energy-efficient models and those which have self-defrosting capabilities. In both instances, flash-freezing of large quantities of meat is virtually impossible, as is the prolonged storage of such meats.

Flash-freezing, to be discussed in detail in a moment, ideally requires a temperature of −10°F to −20°F. And according to the U.S. Department of Agriculture, long-term storage of frozen meat requires an internal freezer temperature that does not exceed 0°F. Now, here's the point to be made. *A majority of freezer units built in conjunction with refrigerators, and especially energy-efficient and self-defrosting models, are incapable of achieving or sustaining internal temperatures lower than 15°F.*

Consequently, these types of freezers are fine for storing vegetables, TV dinners, convenience foods, ice cubes, and, yes, even meats, provided the storage time of these foods is not allowed to exceed six weeks! If you instead stack one of these freezers to the brim with several dozen packages of venison, with the intention of leaving many of them there for six to nine months or even longer, I guarantee you'll be in store for a sad and very displeasing reunion with your deer.

That brings us to those freezer units — uprights and chest-type freezers—especially intended for long-term storage of meats and other foods. Both are capable of easily flash-freezing meats and then maintaining them for long periods at subzero temperatures. But even with these two models there are advantages and disadvantages.

I distinctly prefer the low-boys over the uprights, for several reasons. Uprights, because of their wire-rack shelves, do not allow one to make efficient use of their internal capacity. If you compare a 15-cubic-foot chest freezer with a 15-cubic-foot upright, for example, you'll find the chest freezer will actually hold 25 to 30 percent more food, simply because it does not have the significant amount of wasted space between the shelves that is typical of uprights.

Unquestionably, however, the main reason I don't care for upright freezers is that studies have shown they are far more expensive to operate than low-boy freezers with lift-up lids. What's involved here is the basic principle of physics having to do with cold air being heavier than warm air and therefore sinking to the lowest level it is capable of reaching.

Therefore, when you open the door of an upright freezer, the subzero air trapped inside quickly sinks and rushes out the bottom and in so doing is replaced by warm air from the room rushing in at the top. When you close the freezer door, the electricity must immediately kick on and the freezer must work hard for sometimes a half-hour or longer to return the internal temperature to its previous level.

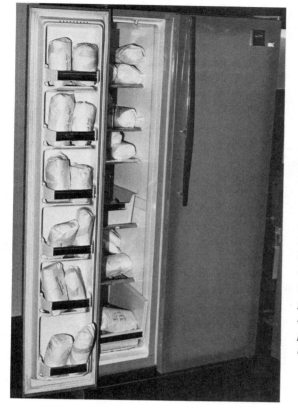

Both chest-type and upright freezers can flash-freeze meats and keep them in good condition for a year or more. The disadvantages of uprights include inefficient use of storage space, higher initial cost, and higher operating costs. Chest-type freezers, though less expensive to purchase and operate, take twice as much floor space, and packages stored at the very bottom are difficult to retrieve.

The situation is not nearly so serious when you lift the lid on a chest-type freezer. The bulk of cold air remains trapped inside because there is no wide opening at the bottom to allow it to escape. True, a bit of warm room air will come in through the top when you open the lid, but not nearly as much as with an upright freezer, and when the lid is quickly closed the freezer will have to turn on only momentarily to restore its internal temperature.

Still another disadvantage of upright freezers is that their initial cost averages 25 percent higher than a chest-type freezer of comparable capacity. The one very nice attribute of upright freezers is that they take up far less floor space than a low-boy. Also, it's much easier to organize your packages of frozen meats and other foods, and you can retrieve specific items with ease.

Chest-type freezers require double the floorspace of uprights, which might be a significant concern for those who live in apartments or small homes. And you have to pray that a particular package you want is not at the very bottom of the freezer because this will mean lifting out and setting aside a lot of stuff to retrieve it. One other disadvantage of chest-type freezers, in our household anyway, is their tabletop-like lids, which invite people to stack all kinds of things on top of them. When I want to cook a venison roast, I usually have to first remove an assortment of laundry baskets, school-books, BB guns, bags of dogfood, and everything else imaginable before I can even open the lid of the freezer.

Whatever your decision about buying an upright freezer or a chest-type freezer, another question you'll face is whether you should pay a slightly higher price for a frostfree model. Actually, the answer to this depends upon where you live more than anything else. If you live in a dry region of the country where the humidity characteristically is quite low, a frostfree model may be a waste of money, both in terms of the initial higher cost and also the increased electricity the unit will use. In this case, it might be wiser to purchase a less-expensive freezer and once a year manually defrost it. Conversely, if you live in a region known for its unrelenting, muggy humidity, a frostfree model can save you plenty of time; otherwise, you may have to manually defrost the freezer two or three times a year or more.

How to Freeze Venison

Flash-freezing, which simply involves freezing the meat as quickly as possible by using an extremely low freezer temperature, is essential to the prolonged storage of meats in prime condition.

All meat has a high water content. Naturally, when the meat freezes, the water in the meat also freezes and in so doing gives birth to ice crystals. The slower you freeze meat, the larger these ice crystals are and thus the greater the amount of cellular damage they are able to cause through expansion, which often results in the defrosted meat having a mushy texture. Conversely, the faster meat is frozen, the smaller the ice crystals and, hence, the minimum amount of tissue damage.

It stands to reason you can flash-freeze meat far more efficiently and effectively if you have very cold meat to start with instead of warm meat. So it's a good idea to place your wrapped packages of venison inside your refrigerator for several hours to thoroughly chill them before placing them in your freezer. If your available refrigerator space is limited and it's bitter cold outside, stack your venison packages in a cardboard box and set the works on your back porch for a few hours.

Meanwhile, turn the temperature dial of your freezer down to its coldest setting to properly "condition" the inside of the unit for flash-freezing. Depending upon the particular model of freezer, this conditioning period may take as long as four hours, or as little as 30 minutes. A small thermometer placed inside your freezer is a wise investment because it tells you exactly when the internal temperature of the freezer is at least −10°F and therefore conducive to flash-freezing.

You can now begin transferring your wrapped venison packages to the freezer, but don't place them all in the freezer at the same time because this will tend to raise its internal temperature and overload the freezer's flash-freezing capability. I like to place one-third of the venison packages in the freezer, wait two hours before adding the next one-third, then wait still another two hours before adding the final packages. To be more specific, a good rule of thumb for flash-freezing is to add no more than two pounds of meat per cubic foot of freezer capacity; in other words, if you have a 15-cubic-foot freezer, which is capable of holding approximately 350 pounds of food, you should nevertheless add no more than 30 pounds of meat at a time when flash-freezing your venison.

A few other tips also should be mentioned. First, when placing your meat packages in the freezer, position them as close as possible to the freezer's walls. This is where the coils are located. Also, make sure the packages do not come in direct contact with each other, as that would retard freezing air from circulating around and between them.

The following day, when all of the venison packages are frozen rock solid, you can then arrange or stack them any way you please. At that time, also be sure to return your freezer's temperature dial to its original setting, checking your thermometer a day later to ensure the freezer is maintaining an internal temperature no higher than 0°F.

If the freezer you now own is not capable of flash-freezing your venison or maintaining a 0°F temperature, there are several alternatives. Perhaps you have a friend or neighbor who possesses a freezer you can use overnight. If so, ply him with a succulent roast or two and he's sure to accommodate your needs. Or, if you are a regular customer of a local meat market or grocery store, your butcher may agree to flash-freeze your meat either free or for a nominal charge. Simply transport it to him in clearly labeled cardboard boxes and then, the following day when the meat is solidly frozen, bring it back home to your own freezer.

Still another option is freezer storage lockers, which are available for rent in most large cities on a weekly, monthly, or yearly basis. The hunters who usually avail themselves of these services are those who have recently collected

Meat	*Refrigerator Storage Time (38°–40°F)*
Steaks	2–4 days
Roasts	2–4 days
Tenderloins	2–4 days
Deerburger	1–2 days
Sausage containing suet	1–2 days
Sausage containing pork	3–7 days
Stew meat	1–3 days
Leftover cooked meat	4–5 days

Type of Meat	*Freezer Storage Time (0°F or lower)*
Large roasts	9–12 months
Small roasts	8–10 months
Large, barded roasts	6–8 months
Small, barded roasts	5–6 months
Steaks (round, sirloin tip)	8–10 months
Steaks (tenderloin)	6–8 months
Stew meat	6–8 months
Deerburger	6–8 months
Sausage containing suet	3–4 months
Sausage containing pork	1–3 months
Leftover cooked meat	2–3 months

a large elk or moose. Faced with the prospect of having to freeze and store as much as 600 or 700 pounds of meat, even a jumbo-sized chest freezer is inadequate. So they rent a freezer locker downtown and periodically transfer large quantities of the meat to their home freezer. Since this approach can be a bit costly, it generally is not the first choice of deer hunters. On the other hand, if you kill two or three deer some particular year, there may be no other alternative.

As to how long various cuts of meat can remain in your freezer, the following chart offers a good guideline.

In examining the above chart, note that small packages of venison should be eaten first, as they will tend to lose their moisture more quickly than roasts and other large cuts. Keep in mind as well that in all cases the fat content of the meat plays a major role in its freezer life. For example, if you eliminate the "barding" of roasts—the addition of bacon or fat to help tenderize them during cooking—you can extend the freezer life of those roasts by about two months; tenderizing can later be achieved, then, through "larding" or injecting the meat with fat just prior to cooking. Obviously, labeling your packages with the type of meat and date frozen is important.

But also keep in mind that the above chart is only a suggested guideline (you may recall my experience described earlier with an 18-month-old roast that tasted delicious). Therefore, whether your venison has been in your freezer a long time, or just a brief period, always allow your eyes and nose to be the final judge. If the meat doesn't look just right when you defrost it, or has a peculiar odor, do not hesitate to discard it as you would any other suspect food.

How to Defrost Venison

Many housewives have fallen into bad habits when it comes to defrosting meats. Too tired after a long and harried day, they grab a meat package from the freezer just minutes before mealtime and hold it under a stream of warm tap water. Or, at the opposite extreme, they take the meat out of the freezer at breakfast time and let it sit on a drainboard all day, which allows the meat to reach room temperature by noon and then just sit there another six hours until dinnertime. Luckily enough, they get away with these abhorrent practices because domesticated livestock meats are so excessively treated with additives and chemicals that you can abuse them to no end and still expect them to be at least marginally edible.

Venison suffers greatly when mishandled in such ways. Lacking preservatives, artificial coloring agents and whatnot, venison requires—no, demands—tender loving care, but this can easily be accomplished with a little planning.

Simply think about what kind of meal you'd like to have the following day and take an appropriate package of venison from the freezer the night before. But do not let it sit out and defrost at room temperature! Place it in your refrigerator overnight. This way, it will properly defrost and yet all the while remain very cold and thereby suffer no deterioration whatever.

However, a critically important point must be inserted here. Before placing your venison in your refrigerator to defrost overnight, unwrap it. That's right, remove both the outer freezer wrapping paper and the inner cling-wrap. Next, place the meat in a collander seated over a pan. Finally, dampen a cloth or towel, wring it out thoroughly, and drape it over the meat.

Why is this procedure necessary? Because it prevents the meat, during defrosting, from soaking in the various fluids and juices being purged from the meat as a result of ice crystals eventually melting. If the meat is allowed to remain wrapped, and the created juices not allowed to escape and drain away, the meat is likely to have a stale, unpleasant taste.

Never defrost venison by letting it sit on a drainboard at room temperature. Instead, remove the packaging materials, place the meat in a colander sitting in a pan, cover with a damp towel, and allow it to defrost overnight in your refrigerator. This way the venison, which has no preservatives like domestic meats, will remain very cold, and stale juices and meltwater will drain away into the collection vessel.

A few other random things should also be mentioned. For one, venison does not always have to be entirely thawed prior to cooking. If you are going to oven-braise a roast, for example, it can go right into the oven still partially frozen. Likewise, burger or sausage that is to be merely browned in a skillet before being added to a casserole, can also go into the pan nearly frozen, as can steaks about to be slipped onto a griddle or charcoal grill. Just remember that in any of these cases you have to increase by one-third the cooking time stated in the recipe you're following. In other words, if a venison rump roast recipe calls for oven-braising for a period of 1½ hours, you can begin with a still partially frozen roast but must extend the cooking time to 2 hours.

Also keep in mind that no meat should be allowed to completely defrost and then be refrozen in its existing state. The key word here is "defrost," because meat that is still extremely cold and has visible ice crystals on its surface is not considered to be thawed yet and, if absolutely necessary, it can be returned to the freezer with no harm incurred.

However, completely thawed venison that is fully cooked can indeed be refrozen. In this case the key word is "cooked," because cooking so radically transforms the cellular structure of the meat it's like starting all over with fresh food. Consequently, if you defrost deerburger and make spaghetti sauce or perhaps a casserole from the burger, it's perfectly safe and acceptable to freeze leftover sauce or casserole for future use; even leftover rump roast can be frozen for later use.

When defrosting such cooked foods, again do not allow them to sit and thaw at room temperature. Take them out of the freezer early and let them defrost overnight, in their storage containers, in your refrigerator.

CHAPTER 14

Failsafe Venison Cookery

I
T CONSTANTLY amazes me how our senses can play tricks on us, particularly when it comes to the cooking and eating of various types of foods.

One of the most startling experiences I've ever had occurred during a postgraduate experimental psychology class. One day, our professor asked for volunteers to participate in a very unusual experiment. Only five hands were raised and mine, admittedly with a good deal of trepidation, was one of them. Naturally I was astonished when the professor said the experiment would be taking place in his home, and to show his appreciation we were invited to enjoy a sumptuous T-bone steak dinner.

As it happened, we all showed up at the appointed hour but quickly became suspicious when, upon entering the prof's front door, we were promptly blindfolded. Then we were lead into a room and seated before the dinner table and I could smell the wafting, intoxicating aroma of broiled T-bones being placed before us.

"Don't worry," the prof said, "you're getting exactly what I promised. On each of your plates there is a prime beefsteak cooked to perfection, along with mashed potatoes, green beans, and a glass of milk. I realize that in being blindfolded you may have a bit of difficulty cutting your meat and eating, so just do the best you can, and enjoy."

As knives and forks went to work, everyone agreed the food was superb but then, about halfway through our meal, the professor instructed us to remove our blindfolds and that is when we all received the shock of our lives. The steak dinner was exactly as had been claimed, but the professor had neglected to tell us one very important thing. He had added common, harmless, food-coloring dyes to our various dinner items.

Our steaks were a sickening, greenish-yellow color! The mashed potatoes were blue! The green beans were bright red and the milk, incredibly, was black!

"Don't just sit there gawking," the professor laughed. "Finish your meals."

Well, right then and there two people lost their appetites, claiming the food looked positively gross and was not fit to eat. One person actually began saying his steak didn't smell just right and he thought maybe he had gotten a bad piece of meat. The girl sitting beside me cupped her hand over her mouth and then made a hasty exit for the bathroom. I thought the whole thing was hilarious and promptly set to the task of not only polishing off my own steak but then attacking the abandoned one on the girl's plate next to me.

Obviously, the purpose of the experiment was to demonstrate how conditioned we all become and, hence, how strongly many of our attitudes and beliefs are influenced by our sensory perceptions (the way we see, hear, feel, smell, and taste things).

The relationship this bears to the cooking and eating of venison should be patently clear because venison looks very much like beef. This is particularly the case with chunks of prime stew meat, tenderloin, round steaks, and rolled shoulder and rump roasts.

Since venison looks so much like beef, many first-timers make the mistake of trying to cook it like beef, and afterwards they expect it to taste like beef! In trying to cook their venison as they would beef, they often ruin it. And when they taste the venison and it doesn't have the beef flavor and texture their tastebuds have told them to anticipate, an alarm bell rings. They curl their lips and begin suspecting the meat is spoiled. Or they comment about its "wild and gamey" flavor.

Actually, all that has happened, as in the psychology experiment, is that they've become honest, innocent victims of their own sensory deception. In most cases, as the proverb goes, time heals all wounds, and they overcome their initial prejudices and find there are few things as delicious as venison. Others are not always so lucky.

Characteristics of Venison

There are two things venison and beef have in common. Both are red meats and both provide mighty good eating. We could make the same analogy between apples and oranges. Both are fruits, both are round in shape, both are vaguely similar in color, and both are delicious. But you certainly wouldn't expect them to taste the same, so why make the same mistake with venison and beef?

One of the major differences between venison and beef, which influences the flavors and textures of the two meats and therefore how you cook them and how they subsequently taste, is the difference in the fat content of the two animals.

Beef, by content, possesses 25.1 percent fat, while venison possesses only 4 percent fat. This is due to the distinctly different diets and lifestyles of the two animals. Not only that but a very high percentage of the fat found in beef steers is woven interstitially throughout the tissue fibers, while nearly all of the small amount of fat possessed by deer is layered across the front shoulders, down the back and across the rump. It should also be noted that venison contains about 5 percent more protein than an equal quantity of beef.

For comparative purposes, here are beef tenderloin steaks and venison tenderloin steaks on a charcoal grill. Note the vast difference: the beef contains a substantial amount of marbling fat, the venison almost none at all. Venison, nevertheless, can be just as tender as the beef if cooked properly.

These figures lead to the following generalizations. Overall, the tissue structure of beef is relatively fine grained and marbled, and actually quite bland tasting. Conversely, venison is overall more coarsely grained, very lean (possessing minimal marbling), and due to the diets of deer just a tad on the tangy, robust, slightly pungent side.

As a result of the high fat content in beef, the longer you cook it, as a general rule, the longer the internal fat has a chance to break down the tissue's cellular structure and therefore the more tender the meat becomes.

But since venison is already a lean, dry meat, the longer you cook it, as a general rule, the drier and tougher it becomes. In short, there is very little in the way of internal basting or lubricating fat to seep throughout the tissue fibers as they cook and subsequently break them down. Not only that, but by the time the deer is 1½ years old, its musculature has long since "hardened off," that is, individual tissue fibers have greatly compacted themselves. Therefore, if you take the extremely lean, hardened-off musculature of a deer and attempt to cook it as you would beef, you'll need a linoleum knife to slice your venison.

Not to worry, though, because whatever the problem, there always is some type of solution, or perhaps several of them, at hand. One remedy that greatly helps to tenderize deer meat is properly aging the venison (see Chapter 8). Also, as described in Chapter 10, fat can be added to the venison through the techniques of larding and barding. And very shortly I'll discuss cooking techniques recommended for specific cuts of meat that are sure to make them tender beyond belief. But right now, let's look at still two other interim procedures that can be enacted upon your venison before it makes its journey to your stove or oven.

Marinades and Tenderizers

What makes meat tender? Well, as noted above, interstitial marbling plays a very important part but is not the entire explanation; an even greater role is played by the 25 different categories of enzymes found in all types of meats. Enzymes are chemical ferments that, through a process known as oxidation, work on proteins, carbohydrates, and fats in meats to break down the connective tissue, reducing it to a gelatinous consistency. This process not only makes meat tender but also enhances its flavor and "juiciness" through the release of water held in the meat.

Because of differences in their chemical constitution and the related activity of enzymes, animal fats vary considerably in their tendency to oxidize. Pork fat, for example, oxidizes much faster than beef fat; hence, the enzymatic breakdown of connective tissue is more complete, and this is why a pork roast is invariably far more tender than a beef roast.

Venison fat, on the other hand, oxidizes very slowly and, aggravating the situation, there is not much interstitial marbling to begin with. Consequently, if cooked like pork or beef, venison can be as tough to chew as a rubber conveyor belt. All of this is exactly why, in larding or barding venison, I recommended the use of bacon or salt pork, with the next best bet being beef suet.

In the absence of these pork-fat or beef-fat additives, you can take a chemical approach to tenderizing venison by using any of countless marinades. Don't let the word "chemical" scare you away because in this context I'm referring to natural ingredients, not synthetic compounds created in a laboratory.

A *marinade* is a liquid bath in which otherwise tougher cuts of venison are allowed to soak for a predetermined length of time before being cooked. Shoulder roasts, neck roasts, blade roasts, and similar cuts are the ones most frequently given marinating treatments.

There are literally hundreds of popular marinade recipes to choose from, but all share the common bond of possessing some type of highly acidic or highly enzymatic ingredient such as vinegar, wine, salt brine, whole milk, buttermilk, or baking soda. All of these greatly accelerate the otherwise slow enzymatic oxidation process that breaks down connective tissue and makes it tender.

The dozens of combinations of remaining ingredients commonly found in marinades simply add to the venison their own unique flavors. The two exceptions to this rule are "milk" and baking soda marinades, which do not impart any flavors whatsoever. This is a terrific situation for the hunter planning to marinate some cut of venison. He can enhance the flavor of the venison with any number of potions. Or, he can accomplish the same goals of marinating and all the while retain the exclusive flavor of the venison with nothing competing or detracting from its uniqueness.

Following are the marinade recipes I rely upon most.

Marinade #1

1½	cups vinegar	1	teaspoon thyme
¾	cup vegetable oil	1	teaspoon black pepper
2	cups water	2	cloves
3	slices onion	1	large bay leaf
1	carrot, pared and diced	1	tablespoon salt
2	small garlic cloves, crushed		

In a large saucepan, bring all of the ingredients to a boil while stirring continually, then reduce the heat and slowly simmer for 15 minutes. Turn the heat off and allow the marinade to cool. Meanwhile, use an ice pick to randomly punch holes in your venison roast. Place the roast in a glass or plastic bowl (never use a metal bowl with a marinade), pour the marinade over the top of the meat until it is entirely covered, cover the bowl, then place it in your refrigerator for 24 hours. Turn the meat once every 6 or 8 hours. The following day, remove the roast, pat dry with paper toweling, then use your favorite cooking recipe.

Marinade #2

2	cups dry red wine	1	medium carrot, diced
¼	cup vinegar	½	teaspoon black pepper
1	cup water	1	bay leaf, broken
½	cup vegetable cooking oil	2	stalks celery, chopped
1	small onion, chopped	1	tablespoon parsley flakes

Mix all of the ingredients thoroughly, pour over venison in a glass or plastic bowl, cover with a lid, then refrigerate for 24 hours, turning the meat frequently.

Marinade #3

1 quart cold water
3 tablespoons salt

3 tablespoons vinegar

Thoroughly mix the ingredients, then pour over venison in a bowl and soak in your refrigerator overnight. The next day, remove the venison from the marinade and rinse thoroughly under cold tap water before proceeding with your favorite recipe.

Marinade #3 is a basic brine marinade that should be discarded after use. However, Marinade #1 and Marinade #2, after using, can be stored in a glass jar in your refrigerator for up to three months and reused whenever you like. Also, it's perfectly acceptable to vary the first two marinade recipes in accordance with your own tastes. In place of the dry red wine in Marinade #2, you can add white wine or a robust burgundy. Other common marinade ingredients include a splash of lemon juice, diced green pepper, ginger, soy sauce, sugar, orange juice, allspice, tarragon, Worcestershire sauce, and even beer or a touch of bourbon. So feel free to experiment and you're certain to discover specific marinade flavors you like better than any other.

As mentioned earlier, there are two marinades that impart no flavors of their own. Both are very simple to make.

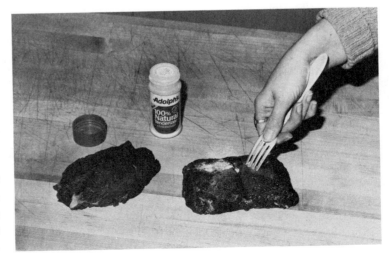

Using a commercial meat tenderizer is the easiest method of tenderizing meat. To assure good results, sprinkle the tenderizer all over the meat, pierce deeply with a fork, and place in refrigerator for 30 minutes per half inch of thickness.

One is the baking soda marinade, prepared by mixing one quart of cold water, ½ cup baking soda, and 1 teaspoon salt. Blend the three ingredients together until the soda and salt are dissolved, then pour the liquid over the meat in the usual way and place in your refrigerator overnight.

To use milk as a marinade (buttermilk is preferred to whole milk, but both are suitable with no residual flavors of their own imparted to the venison), simply place the meat in a bowl, cover with milk, and refrigerate overnight.

In addition to marinades for tenderizing venison, commercial meat tenderizers, which are available in all grocery stores, do a splendid job. With these, you gain the advantage of being able to begin cooking almost immediately because there is no delayed soaking period as with marinades.

These tenderizers are saltlike, crystalline compounds made entirely from natural ingredients and contain active enzymes that attack a meat's connective tissue and break it down. Adolph's Meat Tenderizer is perhaps the most widely recognized brand name and its active ingredient is a vegetable enzyme called "papain," obtained from the papaya melon. Other companies use bromelin and ficin enzymes with equally good results.

Regardless of the particular brand name you elect to use, for the enzymatic action to occur efficiently, it is important to sprinkle the tenderizer evenly over all sides of the meat at a rate of 1 teaspoon per pound. Then the meat should be pierced deeply with a fork and, prior to cooking, allowed to sit in your refrigerator for 30 minutes for each half-inch of thickness. Thus, an inch-thick steak, sprinkled on both sides, should stand for one hour.

Here's a special trick very few know about. If you'd like to enhance the flavor of a venison roast by using a marinade, but you don't have time to

Meat mallet can be used to tenderize venison cuts, and also shape them into uniform sizes and thicknesses.

allow the roast to sit in your refrigerator overnight, do this. Add 2 tablespoons of meat tenderizer to each cup of prepared marinade, mix thoroughly, and pour over your roast, and you can cut your marinating time down to two hours!

Finally, still another way to tenderize various cuts of meat is by pounding them with a mallet or hammer. This technique is especially well-suited to "flat" cuts of meat such as round steaks. In looking at a meat hammer, you'll note the head has two faces, one of which is smooth and flat and the other revealing sharp, pyramidal-shaped points. It's the sharp, many-pointed side of the hammer head that you want to use to tenderize the meat, but one word of caution. Do not unmercifully pound the meat into mush.

All that's necessary is inflicting several light taps of the hammer head on one side of the meat, then flip it over and similarly treat the other side. This light pounding slightly cuts the surface muscle fibers of the meat, and at the same time sends disintegrating shock waves deeper into the meat, both of which disrupt the tissue structure just enough to allow subsequent enzymatic action to more effectively take place.

Incidentally, the other end of the hammer head, which is flat and smooth, is a dual-purpose tool. It can be used to shape the meat so it is of uniform thickness and therefore will cook more evenly. And, it is used to force flour and other ingredients into the meat when preparing certain recipes such as Swiss steak.

Cooking Methods

The tenderness of a given cut of venison depends upon a variety of factors, many of which have already been examined in detail. Foremost is the particular cut of meat itself that predetermines how easily it will yield to knife and tooth. In fact, this is true whether it's the musculature of deer, beef steers, hogs, or any other animal species. As a result, various parts of any animal's anatomy are best treated by entirely different cooking methods.

As a general rule, with less tender cuts of venison (such as shoulder roasts and round steaks) it is necessary to use a combination of moist heat, a low temperature, and a relatively long cooking time. Braising (such as for pot roasts and Swiss steak) and cooking in liquid are two examples.

Conversely, with far more tender cuts of meat (such as tenderloin steaks and rump roasts), dry heat, a moderate to high temperature, and a much shorter cooking time will produce the desired tenderness. Roasting, broiling, pan-broiling, and panfrying are examples here.

In the following chapters I'll discuss these methods individually, and offer a wide assortment of mouth-watering recipes ideally suited to each technique. Meanwhile, I should say a few words about that relatively new breed of food preparation called "microwave cooking," which in my opinion is basically ill-suited to the cooking of venison.

This is not to say that microwave ovens do not have a rightful place in modern kitchens; they do indeed produce excellent results when certain types of foods are being prepared. The fact that microwaves allow very *fast* food preparation is undoubtedly their main selling point, but fast doesn't necessarily mean better and perhaps this explains the results of a recent, nationwide consumer survey. The poll revealed that 65 percent of the people who have acquired microwave ovens in the last ten years are now rather disappointed with their purchases. And consequently, they now only infrequently use microwaves for cooking meat, except when time is very short, preferring overwhelmingly to use conventional ovens instead.

There are several drawbacks to microwave ovens, not the least of which is their $800 to $1,200 price tags (for the better models). Also, electronically cooked roasts have a very high shrinkage factor, and when cooking venison, compared to beef, the situation is even more apparent and discouraging because shrinkage entails the loss of moisture which, in turn, results in the meat being less tender than otherwise. Furthermore, since microwave frequencies often do not penetrate a roast uniformly, there may be variations in the "doneness" of the meat. This does not pose such a great problem when preparing a beef roast, as some seated at the dinner table are sure to prefer their meat well done while others may ask for a slice that is medium rare. But as explained in more detail in the next chapter, venison should *never* be roasted to the point of being well done.

Along the same line, it always is imperative that the internal temperature of a venison roast never be allowed to exceed 140°–150°F. Accomplishing this with a conventional oven is relatively easy because time is on your side. That is, it takes a conventional oven quite a while to increase a roast's internal temperature one degree at a time, which allows you to leisurely monitor its progress and simultaneously coordinate the cooking of other foods to be served with the roast. But since a microwave cooks the meat with such extraordinary speed, there is very, very little margin for error; consequently, depending upon the size of the roast, as little as only two minutes too long in the microwave oven can spell the difference between a roast that is cooked to perfection and one that is overdone, tough and dry.

Finally, foods cooked solely in microwave ovens do not brown, so that meats characteristically reveal a raw, grayish-pink, rather unappetizing appearance. This is the last thing you want, especially when planning to serve your venison to already skeptical first-timers who have not dined on deer meat before. If you doubt the meat's appearance alone could precipitate such unfavorable reactions, recall what happened when my college classmates saw greenish-yellow T-bone steaks on their plates!

To remedy this deficiency of microwave ovens, many cooks have been known to take their meat out of the microwave before it is fully cooked and transfer it to their conventional oven for the remainder of the cooking, where it will then brown nicely. To me, this seems absurd. Why not just use the conventional oven for the entirety of the cooking in the first place?

On a brighter note, microwave ovens do have advantages for those who live such hurried (harried?) lifestyles that they want to spend an absolute minimum amount of time in their kitchens. In such cases, I would not really care to share their venison roasts with them, but microwave ovens do indeed produce splendid results when merely heating up leftovers or preparing casseroles, stews, meat pies, and similar dishes.

CHAPTER 15

Steaks, Roasts, and Chops

AS MENTIONED in the last chapter, the tenderest cuts of venison a deer possesses are generally cooked by dry-heat methods, at a moderately high temperature, and for lesser periods of time than other cuts. Falling into this category are meat cuts such as the tenderloin steaks (call them "chops" if they are bone-in steaks), rump roasts, sirloin tip roasts, and sirloin tip steaks.

The recipes in this chapter, then, invariably call for roasting, broiling, or panfrying these tender cuts. However, these are only the most usual methods and a number of recipes in this chapter will utilize tender cuts but call for other cooking techniques. For example, not long ago I invented a delicious Venison Teriyaki recipe in which tenderloin meat is sliced very thin, then steamboiled in either a wok or high-sided skillet before being ladled over a bed of rice.

But before listing my favorite recipes, a few rules of thumb pertaining to dry-heat cooking methods will get you started.

Roasting is accomplished by placing the meat (fat-side up if the top is draped with bacon) on a rack in an open, shallow roasting pan. The rack holds the roast out of the grease, and the bacon or other fat dribbles down slowly and bastes the roast as it cooks.

It is imperative that a meat thermometer be used to monitor the cooking progress of the roast. Insert the thermometer so the bulb is in the center of the thickest part of the meat and ensure that the bulb does not touch bone or the bottom of the roasting pan. A venison roast should be cooked only until it is medium-rare to medium on the inside, with a slight blush of bright pink to the meat's color. Forget that you may like your beef roasts well done. Venison is not beef!

If you look at your meat thermometer, you'll see a graduated temperature scale paired to the desired "doneness" of various types of meat such as beef, pork, and fowl. Venison won't be listed on the scale, meaning that you have to go by temperature alone and to achieve a roast that is medium-rare to medium you should allow it to cook until its internal temperature registers 140°–150°F (by comparison, a well-done beef roast has an internal temperature of 160°–170°F).

Ideally, your roasting pan should sit on the middle shelf-rack in your oven and the temperature dial of the oven should be set at 300°–350°F, depending upon the size of the roast. Very large roasts (more than six pounds) should be cooked at the lower temperature and mid-sized roasts (two to five pounds) at the higher temperature. You should never use a dry-heat cooking method with roasts smaller than two pounds because they will turn out tough and dry, so always use a roast of ample size; if it's larger than what your family can consume at one meal, the leftovers can be served the following day in sandwiches or soups.

Broiling is another dry-heat cooking method, but this technique generally is reserved for tenderloin steaks or sirloin tip steaks. Steaks to be broiled should be at least ¾ inch thick, but not more than 1½ inches thick. Turn

Two common thermometers with probes that are inserted deep within the meat and a typical oven thermometer (center) used to verify the oven's thermostat reading.

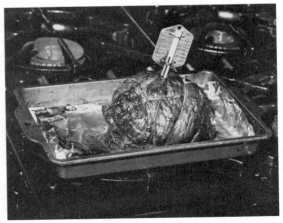

Place thermometer into thickest part of the roast and cook the meat until temperature registers 140° to 150°F.

your oven's regulator dial to "broil," or to its highest setting (generally, 500°F), and remember that for effective broiling at such high temperatures the oven door should be left slightly ajar.

Place your venison steaks on the rack of your broiler pan so the created juices can drain away (otherwise, they may flame up) and situate the pan so the meat will be from two to five inches from the heat source. Here is where each cook will have to temper his decisions with good judgement because the heat output of gas broilers, compared to electric, can vary quite a bit; also, thicker steaks should be placed farther away from the heat than thin ones.

Broil the steaks just until their top sides begin to brown, then flip them and broil on the other side for about one-half the previously allotted time. You may wish to barely slice into one of the steaks to check its progress. Some claim this practice is anathema, that cutting into steaks will allow their juices to escape. Well, a small amount of juice may indeed escape, but better that than relying purely upon guesswork and often cooking your steaks so long they are dry and tough.

I strongly advise never cooking a venison steak beyond the point of medium-rare, as this stage is when it is at its tender and juicy best.

Pan-broiling is a splendid method of cooking steaks but few people are familiar with it. A heavy, cast-iron skillet or griddle is necessary; it should be *very* sparingly brushed with just a bit of cooking oil. One-half teaspoon of oil should be plenty to prevent the meat from sticking; if you add more than this you are no longer pan-broiling but panfrying.

Lay your steaks in the pan and then merely cook them over very low heat. Since the meat is in direct contact with the skillet or griddle, it is essential to turn the meat occasionally to ensure even cooking. The steaks are ready to serve when they are slightly brown on both sides and pink and juicy in the middle.

Panfrying is similar to pan-broiling in that a heavy skillet or griddle is used. However, substantially more cooking oil is added to the skillet and the meat is cooked at a much higher temperature. While pan-broiling is ideally suited to thick steaks, panfrying is best accomplished with thinner steaks and also those which have been floured or breaded.

Panfrying typically results in the outer surfaces and edges of steaks achieving just a bit of crispness, which enhances the flavor of the meat. Yet, in achieving this desirable result there may be some sacrifice of tenderness. So, beforehand, you may desire to treat your meat (especially sirloin tip steaks) to a dose of commercially prepared meat tenderizer.

One thing to guard against in panfrying is a burner temperature that becomes so hot your fat or grease begins to smoke. Another axiom of panfrying is to turn the meat frequently to ensure even cooking but, still again, venison steaks should never be cooked beyond medium.

Finally, it is absolutely essential, no matter which cooking method you decide to use, that your intended serving platter be preheated. I like to simply slip my platter into the oven for five minutes before serving a roast or steaks.

The necessity of a hot platter has to do with the fat content in venison compared to beef. Beef has a good deal of interstitial fat, or marbling, which gets extremely hot during cooking and therefore helps to retain the temperature of the meat long afterwards. Because venison does not have as much fat woven between its tissue fibers, it cools very fast.

It stands to reason, then, that if you remove a venison roast from the oven, or steaks from a broiler or skillet, and place the meat on a cold platter that has come straight from the cupboard, you're in for an unpleasant experience. The meat will become cold well before everyone has finished his meal, and when venison becomes cold it loses a good deal of its tenderness. A hot serving platter significantly delays all of this.

Now let's look at a number of recipes that call for roasting, broiling, pan-broiling, or panfrying the tender cuts of venison sure to please. Keep in mind that you can vary any of the following recipes, especially those calling for roasts, by first soaking your venison in a marinade (see Chapter 14).

Sautéed Steaks or Chops

4 inch-thick steaks or chops   Lawrey's Seasoned Salt
¼ cup butter (½ stick)

Melt the butter in a skillet, then blend in 1 teaspoon of the seasoned salt. Place the steaks in the pan and cook them slowly over medium heat until they are browned on all sides and pink and juicy in the middle. Serves 4.

Spicy Deer Steaks

2 pounds tenderloin or sirloin
   tip steak
   marinade

3 tablespoons butter
3 tablespoons cooking oil
   flour

Select a marinade of your choice from Chapter 14, pour it over the steaks in a bowl, and refrigerate overnight. The following day, remove the steaks, drain, and pat dry with paper towels. Flour the steaks well, then panfry in a skillet containing the butter and cooking oil. Serves 4.

Georgia-style Steaks

2 pounds tenderloin steaks or
   chops, cut thick
1 cup catsup
1 tablespoon salt

1 tablespoon chili powder
2 tablespoons tarragon
1 onion, chopped
⅓ cup A-1 Steak Sauce

In a skillet, sear the steaks in just a bit of cooking oil on medium-high heat. Meanwhile, place the remaining ingredients in a saucepan and over low heat bring the mixture to a boil, stirring continuously. Transfer the steaks to a shallow roasting pan, pour the sauce over the top and bake for 1½ hours at 350°. Serves 4.

Venison Teriyaki with Rice

2 pounds tenderloin steak sliced into thin strips
3 tablespoons olive oil
3 tablespoons soy sauce
½ teaspoon garlic powder
1 tablespoon lemon juice
1 tablespoon brown sugar

2 cups uncooked Minute Rice
1 4-ounce can mushrooms
1 cup green peppers, sliced into strips
1 cup beef broth or beef bouillon

1. Slice tenderloin or sirloin-tip steak into strips.

2. In a wok or high-sided skillet, stir-fry the venison in olive oil until it is almost cooked.

Add the olive oil and soy sauce to a wok or high-sided skillet, then stir in the garlic, lemon juice, and brown sugar. Heat the wok or skillet on medium-high heat until the liquid begins to steam. Add the tenderloin strips and stir-fry them until they are almost cooked. Meanwhile, prepare the Minute Rice according to the instructions on the package. Now add to the wok or skillet the mushrooms (drained), green peppers, and beef broth. Turn the heat down to medium, cover, and slowly cook until everything is steaming hot. Then ladle over a bed of rice on a preheated platter. Serves 4.

3. Blend in mushrooms and peppers, then broth. Turn the heat down, cover, and slowly steam until everything is cooked through.

4. Serve over a bed of rice. Delicious!

Venison Teriyaki #2

2 pounds tenderloin or sirloin
   tip steak
1 cup beef broth
½ teaspoon garlic powder
½ cup soy sauce

½ cup chopped onion
2 tablespoons lemon juice
1 teaspoon seasoned salt
2 tablespoons brown sugar

Slice the steak into thin strips and place in a glass or plastic bowl. Combine the remaining ingredients, mix well, pour over the meat, and refrigerate overnight. The following day, drain the meat and broil the strips for 3 to 5 minutes, turning them frequently and basting them with the sauce remaining in the bowl. Serve with any combination of "go-withs" of your choice (see Chapter 21). Serves 4.

High-country Buttermilk Venison

2 pounds tenderloin or sirloin
   tip steaks
   cooking oil

1 cup buttermilk
   flour

Cut the steak into thick cubes, then pound each with a meat hammer so it is no more than ½ inch thick. Place the meat in a bowl and cover with the buttermilk. Allow the steak to soak for 2 hours, then dredge the pieces in flour and panfry. Serves 4.

1. To make High-country Buttermilk Venison, cut meat into cubes, then pound them flat with a meat hammer.

2. Marinate the venison in a bath of buttermilk.

3. Dredge venison pieces in flour; then panfry in bubbling hot oil until tender.

4. Serve buttermilk steaks on a preheated platter. Excellent go-withs include butternut squash and camp-fried potatoes.

Pepper Steak

2 pounds tenderloin or sirloin
   tip steak
1 teaspoon black pepper

1 teaspoon garlic powder
olive oil

Blend the black pepper and garlic powder, then gently pound the mixture into both sides of the steaks with your meat hammer. Place the steaks on a broiler pan and broil 3 to 5 inches from the heat source, basting occasionally with the olive oil. Serves 4.

Pepper Steak Supreme

4   large tenderloin or sirloin
   tip steaks
   black pepper

2   tablespoons butter
2   tablespoons olive oil
1½ ounces brandy

Sprinkle just a bit of black pepper on both sides of the steaks and then gently pound it into the meat with your hammer. Add the butter and olive oil to a heavy skillet and sear the steaks on both sides over medium-high heat. Turn the heat down to low and continue cooking the steaks until they are medium-rare inside. Meanwhile, warm the brandy in a small saucepan. When the steaks are ready, transfer them to a preheated platter and pour the juices from the pan equally over the tops of them. Bring the platter to the table and, before your guests, pour the brandy over the top of the steaks and ignite it; be careful, and use a long stick-match because the brandy may flare up slightly. Allow the brandy to completely burn itself out, then serve. Serves 4.

1. Pepper Steak Supreme: Begin by pounding black pepper into sirloin tip steaks.

2. In a skillet, sear the steaks in butter and olive oil, then turn the heat down and continue cooking.

3. Meanwhile, warm a bit of brandy.

4. Transfer steaks to a platter, pour brandy over them and ignite. Allow flames to die out before serving.

Venison Italiano

2 pounds tenderloin or sirloin
    tip steaks
½ cup olive oil

½ teaspoon garlic powder
½ teaspoon Worcestershire
    sauce

Thoroughly blend the olive oil, garlic powder, and Worcestershire sauce in a bowl. Then use the mixture to baste your steaks as you broil them in the usual manner. Serves 4.

Steaks in Port Wine

4 large tenderloin or sirloin
    tip steaks
6 tablespoons butter
1 teaspoon salt
½ teaspoon black pepper

1 8-ounce can mushrooms
2 teaspoons lemon juice
¼ cup water
¼ cup port wine
4 thick slices French bread

In a high-sided skillet, melt the butter and stir in the salt and pepper. Now, sauté the mushrooms, then transfer them to a platter in your oven to keep them warm. Next, cook the steaks in the butter until they are browned on the outside and pink on the inside, turning them frequently and dribbling just a bit of lemon juice on each. Now transfer the steaks to the platter in your oven to keep them warm. To the drippings in the skillet, add the water and the wine and stir continuously until the mixture comes to a boil, then quickly reduce the heat. Meanwhile, toast the French bread. To serve, arrange the toasts on a hot platter, set a steak on top of each, pour the wine sauce over the tops of the steaks, then sprinkle on the mushrooms. Serves 4.

Cracker-fried Steaks

4 large chops or sirloin tip
   steaks
2 eggs, well beaten

1 cup saltine crackers, finely
   crushed
cooking oil

Dip each steak into the beaten egg, roll in the cracker crumbs, then pound very gently with a meat hammer. Dip the steaks a second time in the egg, then roll again in the cracker crumbs. Fry in a skillet until the cracker coating has a toastlike appearance, no longer! Serves 4.

Burgundy Chops

4 large chops or sirloin tip
   steaks
2 cups buttermilk
6 tablespoons butter
1 onion, chopped
1 cup Burgundy

1 8-ounce can tomatoes,
   drained
1 teaspoon salt
½ teaspoon black pepper
1 cup sour cream

Place the chops or steaks in a bowl, pour the buttermilk over the top, and marinate overnight in your refrigerator. The following day, drain the chops and pat dry with paper towels. In a high-sided skillet, brown the chops on both sides in the butter, then add the onion and cook until it is clear. Now add the tomatoes and the Burgundy, reduce the heat to low and continue cooking until the meat is tender. Transfer the meat to a platter and set it in your oven to keep warm. Then stir the salt, pepper, and sour cream into the ingredients remaining in the pan until a thick sauce is created. Pour the sauce over the steaks and serve. Serves 4.

Tenderloin Cheese-Steaks

2   pounds tenderloin or sirloin
    tip steaks
2   eggs, beaten
½   teaspoon salt

¼   teaspoon black pepper
1   cup seasoned breadcrumbs
¼   cup grated Romano-
    Parmesan cheese

Thoroughly mix the salt and pepper with the beaten eggs. In a separate bowl, thoroughly blend the breadcrumbs with the grated cheese. Dip the steaks individually in the egg batter, then roll in the bread crumb and cheese mixture. Fry in just a bit of cooking oil over medium-high heat until the exterior breading is golden brown, turning frequently. Be careful not to allow the breading to burn. Serves 4.

Bourbon Steaks

4   large chops or sirloin tip
    steaks
¼   cup butter
¼   cup bourbon

½   cup chicken broth
½   cup heavy cream
1   teaspoon salt
½   teaspoon black pepper

Don't worry about the whiskey in this recipe because you'll be burning off its alcohol content, leaving only a residual flavor of the bourbon. Begin by browning the steaks in the butter in a high-sided skillet, then tilt the pan and pour off the butter. Lower the flame under the skillet, add the bourbon, and then light it with a match. When the flame dies out, transfer the steaks to a platter and place in your oven to keep warm. Add the chicken broth, cream, and salt and pepper to the pan and stir the mixture continuously until it is thick. Then pour the sauce over the steaks and serve. Serves 4.

Venison Cantonese

2 pounds sirloin tip steak, sliced in thin strips
2 teaspoons meat tenderizer
4 tablespoons cornstarch

¼ cup sherry
6 large onions, sliced
¼ cup cooking oil

Mix together the tenderizer and cornstarch and thoroughly dredge the steaks, then gently pound them with your meat hammer. Place in a deep dish and pour the sherry over the top and let stand for 15 minutes. Meanwhile, separate the onion slices into rings and fry in the cooking oil until they are clear in the middle and crisp around the edges, then transfer them to a plate in your oven where they will stay warm. In the same skillet, now fry the thin strips of steak for 5 or 6 minutes, stirring continually. Place the onion rings on top of the meat strips, toss gently, and serve. Serves 4.

Easy Roast Venison

1 3-pound rump roast

8 strips bacon

Use one of the tenderest rump roasts you have. Drape the top of the roast with the bacon strips, held in place with toothpicks. Or, in preparing a rolled rump roast, drape the meat with the bacon before you make your string ties. Insert a meat thermometer in the thickest part of the meat, set it on a roasting pan, then place in an oven preheated to 350°. The roast is finished when its internal temperature reaches 145°. Transfer the roast to a hot serving platter and remove the bacon. Slice the roast very thin. Then slice the bacon into squares and sprinkle over the top of the meat slices. Finally, take any remaining pan juices and pour over the meat. Serves 4 (with enough leftovers for sandwiches the next day).

Stuffed Holiday Venison

2 large round steaks, ¾ inch thick
½ teaspoon salt
¼ teaspoon black pepper
¼ cup flour
3 cups breadcrumbs

1 medium onion, chopped
1 stalk celery, chopped
1 green pepper, chopped
½ cup butter
½ teaspoon paprika
bacon strips

Shape the steaks with your meat mallet until they are only ¼ inch thick and rectangular, using a knife to trim them as necessary. Blend the salt, pepper, and flour and very gently pound it into the steaks with your hammer. In a bowl, mix all the remaining ingredients to form a stuffing, using as much water as necessary to make it moist and thoroughly kneading the stuffing with your hands. Lay the steaks end to end on a flat surface. Lay your stuffing in the center of one of the steaks, then spread it out somewhat to the edges. Next, roll the meat from one end to the other. What you'll have is a barrel-shaped affair with the meat on the outside, wrapped around the stuffing on the inside. Tie in several places with cotton string to hold everything together. Set the rolled, stuffed roast in a lightly greased roasting pan and completely cover it with bacon strips. Bake for 1 hour in an oven preheated to 325°. Serves 4.

Stuffed Holiday Venison looks like this just before going into the oven. It's a unique recipe that is as delicious to eat as it is easy to make.

Deutschfleisch

1 3-pound rump roast
1 teaspoon dried onion flakes
½ teaspoon allspice

¼ teaspoon salt
¼ teaspoon black pepper
   gingersnap cookies

Insert a meat thermometer in the roast, then place it on a roasting pan. In a bowl, blend the onion flakes, allspice, salt, and pepper. Sprinkle this mixture evenly over the roast. Then carefully layer the entire roast with the gingersnap cookies (this is tricky but works out okay if you begin by first propping them up around the bottom perimeter of the roast). Place in an oven preheated to 325° and bake until the internal temperature of the roast is 145°. Remove the cookies and discard, then slice the roast thinly and serve on a preheated platter. Serves 4–6.

Iron Range Venison Roast

1 3-pound rump roast
1 teaspoon fennel seed
1 teaspoon sage

1 teaspoon sugar
1 teaspoon salt
½ teaspoon black pepper

This recipe comes from northern Minnesota's famous mining region. Take a rolled rump roast and remove the string ties so you can open the meat. Spread the venison out as much as possible and make numerous scoring cuts across the meat with a knife. In a bowl, thoroughly blend all the remaining ingredients, then sprinkle over the meat. Roll the meat back up into its original shape and make new string ties. Insert a meat thermometer, drape the roast with bacon, and set in a shallow roasting pan. Roast at 325° until the internal temperature registers 145°. Serves 4–6.

Steak Sandwiches

Venison tenderloin, particularly the mini-tenderloins from that part of the backbone inside the chest cavity, make superb steak sandwiches. I like to take these mini-tenderloins and pound them flat with a meat mallet so they are uniformly about ½ inch thick. Then either broil them, pan-broil them, or panfry them, for the most delicious sandwiches your crew ever enjoyed.

Any tenderloin steak, sirloin tip steak, or rump roast left over from a meal can also be served as sandwiches the following day. It's fine cold, after sitting overnight in your refrigerator. But you may prefer to slice the steak or roast into very thin strips, then place the meat in a skillet with just a bit of cooking oil over medium-high heat. Cover the pan and let the meat become very hot as you occasionally stir and toss it.

We like to serve our steak sandwiches on fancy steak rolls with just a light touch of horseradish or other conventional sandwich fixin's, but they are equally delicious when served between slices of buttered rye toast.

CHAPTER 16

Pot Roasts and Braising

IN THE LAST CHAPTER we looked at dry-heat cooking methods designed chiefly for very tender cuts of venison. Now let's shift gears and look at moist-heat cooking methods designed for not-so-tender cuts that need a bit of assistance if they are to provide toothsome fare.

I'm talking here about venison cuts from the front legs of the deer (shoulder roasts, blade roasts, arm roasts) and certain portions of the rear legs (such as the round steaks). Also included in this category are rolled roasts made from the neck meat. The best way to cook these cuts is to braise them.

Braising is traditionally done in a pot or pan on top of the stove or in the oven. The idea is to cook the meat in some type of closed environment so that steam is trapped within the vessel and softens the meat's connective tissue. The steam comes from a small amount of liquid added to the cooking vessel in accordance with the particular recipe you're following. Generally the liquid is water, vegetable juice, soup, or wine.

Two things I particularly like about cooking pot roasts or using a braising recipe are that you often can put potatoes, vegetables, and other items right in with the meat, which vastly simplifies meal preparation, and you frequently obtain a rich, sumptuous gravy as a special bonus.

5-Minute Pot Roast

1 2-pound shoulder or neck
   roast
1 cup water

1 envelope dry onion soup mix

This is the fastest, easiest pot roast I know how to make and, happily, one of the most delicious. Place your roast in the center of a square sheet of heavy-duty aluminum foil and bring the edges up around the sides to form a pouch. Pour one cup of water over the top of the roast, then sprinkle on the dry soup mix. Now pinch together the edges of the foil to form a tight seal to trap steam, and place the pouch in a shallow roasting pan. Place in a 325° oven for 1½ hours. When you open the pouch to slice the meat you'll find it tender beyond belief and as a special surprise you'll have a good quantity of perfect gravy you can ladle over noodles or potatoes. As with all venison, remember to serve on a hot platter. Serves 4.

1. Place the roast in the middle of a sheet of foil and bring up the edges to form a pouch.

2. *Pour in 1 cup of water and sprinkle the roast with a package of dry soup mix (above). Add salt and pepper if you wish.*

3. *Pinch the foil edges together to form an airtight seal (right) and carefully set the package in a shallow roasting pan.*

4. *Not only is the roast incredibly tender, but you also obtain a good quantity of perfect gravy.*

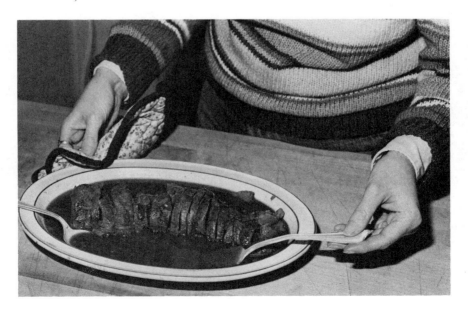

Spicy Pot Roast

1 3-pound shoulder or neck roast	1 cup tomato sauce
2 onions, chopped	½ teaspoon poultry seasoning
1 teaspoon garlic powder	¼ teaspoon nutmeg
4 tablespoons butter	¼ teaspoon cinnamon
¼ cup vinegar	¼ teaspoon allspice

1. *Chop onions and sauté them with garlic in melted butter. Then transfer the onions to a plate where they will stay warm.*

2. *In the same pan, sear the roast until it is brown on all sides.*

In a skillet, sauté the onions and garlic in the butter, then transfer to a plate where they will stay hot. In the same skillet, sear the roast until it is brown on all sides. Transfer the meat to an oven-proof pot, spoon the onions over the top, pour the vinegar and tomato sauce into the pot, then sprinkle the seasonings on top of the meat. Cover the pot with a lid and cook slowly in a 300° oven for 2 hours or until the meat is very tender. After placing on a hot platter and slicing, pour the juices from the pot over the roast. Serves 4 (with leftovers for sandwiches the next day).

3. Transfer the roast to an oven-proof pot, spoon the onions over the top, then add seasonings and spices. Cover the pot and bake slowly for 2 hours.

4. Transfer the roast to a hot platter and slice. Pour savory pan juices over the top and serve.

Burgundy Roast Venison

1	4-pound venison roast	1	large onion, sliced
1½	cups Burgundy	1	medium-sized, brown-in
	salt and pepper		cooking bag
3	tablespoons butter		

Place the roast in a glass bowl, pour the Burgundy over the top, then refrigerate overnight. Remove the roast, pat dry, sprinkle with salt and pepper, then dot with pieces of butter. Lay several onion slices inside your cooking bag, then set the roast on top. Place the remainder of the onion rings on top of the roast, then pour the Burgundy marinade into the bottom of the bag. Seal the bag and make several knife slits in the top according to the package instructions. Place the bagged roast in a shallow pan and cook 2½ hours at 300°. When the roast is tender, transfer it to a serving platter, and place back into the oven to keep warm. Meanwhile, pour the liquid from the bag into a pan and thicken with just a bit of cornstarch dissolved in water to make a gravy. Pour the gravy over the roast and garnish with the onions. Serves 4–6.

Indian Summer Roast

1	3-pound shoulder roast	1	medium-sized oven cooking
	salt and pepper		bag
½	teaspoon nutmeg	1	cup apple cider
¼	cup flour		

Sprinkle the venison roast with a bit of salt and pepper and then rub it into the meat with your fingers. Now sprinkle the nutmeg on top of the roast. Shake the flour inside the oven bag, carefully set the roast inside, then pour the apple cider into the bottom of the bag. Close the bag with a twist-tie and make six inch-long slits on the top, then roast in a 325° oven for 2 hours. Transfer the roast to a hot plate, slice, then pour the cider gravy over the top. Serves 4–6.

Pot Roast Elegante

1 2-pound shoulder or neck
   roast
  salt and pepper

1 medium can condensed
   "cream" soup
1 onion, sliced

In a skillet, brown the roast on all sides in a bit of cooking oil. Transfer the roast to a pot or oven-tempered glass casserole dish and sprinkle on a bit of salt and pepper. Pour on top of the roast and around the sides the can of condensed soup (cream of mushroom, cream of celery, or some other favorite). Lay the onion slices on top, cover with a lid, and slow cook at 325° for 1½ hours. Transfer the roast to a hot platter, slice, then pour the gravy from the cooking pot over the top. Serves 4.

Pot Roast Italiano

1 2-pound shoulder or neck
   roast
1 medium can condensed
   "cream" soup
½ cup dry red wine

2 tablespoons parsley flakes
½ teaspoon thyme
1 bay leaf, crumbled
  salt and pepper

In a skillet, brown the roast on all sides in a bit of cooking oil. Transfer the roast to a pot or oven-tempered casserole dish. In a bowl, blend the soup (I like cream of mushroom) with the wine and then pour the mixture over and around the roast. Sprinkle the seasonings on top of the roast, cover, and place in a 325° oven for 1½ hours. Transfer the meat to a hot platter, slice, pour the sauce over the top and serve. Serves 4.

Hungarian Pot Roast

1 3-pound shoulder or neck
   roast
1 large clove garlic
   salt and pepper
1 onion, chopped
2 carrots, sliced thick

½ teaspoon oregano
½ teaspoon parsley flakes
1 stalk celery, chopped
1 cup beef broth or bouillon
1 teaspoon Hungarian paprika
½ cup sour cream

Slice the garlic clove into thin slivers, then insert them into thin slits made in the roast with a knife. Rub the roast with salt and pepper, then brown the roast in a skillet using a bit of oil (preferably olive oil). Place the roast in a pot and add all the remaining ingredients except the sour cream. Cover the pot and with the burner on low heat slowly simmer the roast for 1½ hours or until it is tender. Transfer the roast to a hot platter and slice, then ladle the vegetables over the meat, using a slotted spoon. Add the sour cream to the broth in the pot, turn the heat up, and cook until the sauce is steaming, then pour over the slices of pot roast. Serves 4.

All-In-One Pot Roast

1 2-pound shoulder or neck
   roast
   salt and pepper
4 potatoes, cut into large
   chunks

4 carrots, cut into large
   chunks
1 can green beans, drained

In a skillet or deep pan, sear the roast on all sides until it is brown, then transfer to a pot. Pour hot water into the pot until it comes up halfway on the side of the roast. Sprinkle with salt and pepper, cover the pot with a lid and begin slow cooking with the heat turned on low. After 45 minutes of simmering, place the potato chunks in the pot. After another 30 minutes, add the carrots and green beans. Continue to simmer until the potatoes are tender. Transfer the meat to a hot platter and slice. Use a slotted spoon to transfer the vegetables to a hot dish. Then pour the "gravy" over the pot roast slices. Serves 4.

Tangy Pot Roast

1 3-pound roast (your choice
   of cut)

1 envelope dry onion soup mix
   Worcestershire sauce

Place the roast in a pot or glass casserole dish. In a bowl, mix just enough water with the dry soup mix to create a paste, then brush it over the roast. Sprinkle the entire roast liberally with Worcestershire sauce, then pour 1 cup of hot water into the bottom of the pot. Cover and place in a 275° oven for 2 hours or until the roast is tender. Transfer to a hot platter and slice, then pour the sauce over the top. Serves 4–6.

Curried Pot Roast Supreme

1 2-pound shoulder or neck
   roast
1 clove garlic
1 tablespoon curry powder

1 cup beef broth or bouillon
2 tablespoons soy sauce
   salt and pepper

Slice the garlic into thin slivers, then push these into slits you've made in the roast with a knife. Rub the curry powder into the roast. Set the roast on a square of heavy-duty aluminum foil and bring up the sides. Blend the beef broth with soy sauce and pour over the roast, then sprinkle with salt and pepper. Pinch and seal the edges of the foil to prevent steam from escaping, then set the works on a shallow roasting pan. Place in a 325° oven for 1½ hours. Transfer the pot roast to a platter, slice, then pour the sauce from the foil pouch over the venison. Serves 4.

Venison Sauerbraten

1 2-pound shoulder or neck
   roast
½ teaspoon black pepper
5 whole cloves
2 bay leaves, crushed
1 cup vinegar (or dry red
   wine)

6 carrots, cut into thick
   chunks
6 small white onions
2 stalks celery, cut into thick
   chunks
1 tablespoon sugar
10 gingersnap cookies, crushed

Place the roast in a glass or plastic bowl. Add to the bowl the pepper, cloves, bay leaves, and vinegar (or wine). Then add to the bowl as much cold water as necessary to completely cover the meat. Allow the meat to marinate in your refrigerator for 2 days, turning it frequently. Remove the meat, pat dry, and brown on all sides in a skillet with a bit of olive oil. Transfer the pot roast to a deep pot, add the vegetables, and 2 cups of the marinade. Cover and simmer on low heat for 1½ hours. Transfer the meat and vegetables to a hot platter. Then stir the sugar and crushed gingersnaps into the marinade in the pot to make a sauce. After slicing the meat, ladle the sauce over the top and surround with the vegetables. Serves 4.

Crabapple Venison Roast

1 3-pound shoulder roast
   salt and pepper
½ pound salt pork

¼ cup orange juice
2 tablespoons lemon juice
¼ teaspoon allspice

Rub a bit of salt and pepper into the roast with your fingers. Place the roast in a deep, greased pan and cover the meat with thin slices of the salt pork. Turn the oven temperature up to 450° and sear the venison (this should take about 15 minutes). Reduce the heat to 350°, remove the salt pork, cover the pan, and continue cooking the roast for 1 hour. Every 15 minutes, baste the roast with a mixture of the orange juice, lemon juice, and allspice. As the roast continues to cook, make the following glaze.

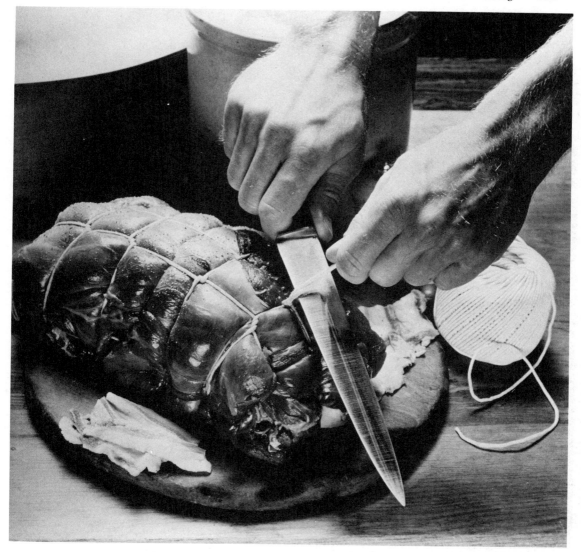

1. Ideal cut for Crabapple Venison Roast is a large rolled shoulder, draped with bacon slices or pieces of salt pork. Sear the meat in the oven at high temperature, then lower the heat and continue to cook slowly (continued next page).

Crabapple Roast Glaze

2 tablespoons melted butter   ½ cup crabapple jelly
2 tablespoons orange juice

2. Prepare a mixture of lemon juice, orange juice, and allspice, and periodically baste the roast.

Place all of the ingredients in a small saucepan and simmer over very low heat until the mixture begins to steam. After the roast has cooked for 1 hour, continue cooking another 30 minutes, basting the roast every 10 minutes with the glaze. Transfer the roast to a hot platter and slice. Serves 4.

3. During the final half-hour of cooking, baste the roast with a glaze made of butter, orange juice, and crabapple jelly.

Honey-glazed Pot Roast

1   3-pound shoulder roast
½   cup water
½   cup white wine
1   onion sliced

1   teaspoon salt
½   teaspoon black pepper
½   teaspoon garlic powder

Place the venison in a pot or roasting pan, then pour in the water and wine and lay the onion slices around the roast. Blend the salt, pepper, and garlic and sprinkle over the meat. Cover the pot with a lid and cook at 300° in your oven for 2 hours. Meanwhile, prepare the following glaze.

Honey Roast Glaze

¼   cup butter
¼   cup honey
2   teaspoons lemon juice

½   cup orange juice
½   teaspoon rosemary

Place all the ingredients in a small saucepan and simmer over low heat until the mixture begins to steam. During the last half-hour the roast is cooking, baste it frequently with the glaze. Transfer the pot roast to a platter, slice very thin, garnish with the onions and serve. Serves 4–6.

Pot Roast Surprise

1 2-pound roast (your choice
   of cut)
  flour
4 tablespoons butter
4 tablespoons cooking oil

3 cups sour cream
½ teaspoon salt
¼ teaspoon black pepper
¼ cup honey

Dust the roast with flour, then brown on all sides in a skillet containing the butter and cooking oil. Place 1½ cups of the sour cream in a deep glass baking dish, set the pot roast on top, and sprinkle with the salt and pepper. Pour the honey over the top of the roast, cover the dish with a lid, and place in a 300° oven for 1 hour. Then add the remaining sour cream and continue cooking ½ hour longer. Transfer the roast to a platter, slice, then pour the sauce over the top. Serves 4.

Creamed Sirloin Tips

2 pounds sirloin tip steak
  meat tenderizer
1 onion, finely chopped
2 tablespoons butter

2 tablespoons flour
½ cup sour cream
1 4-ounce can mushrooms

Sprinkle meat tenderizer over the steaks, then gently pound it into the meat with the sharp edge of your meat hammer. Allow the steaks to sit for 1 hour. In a skillet, sauté the onions in the butter until they are clear. Now, use a knife to cut the sirloin tip steaks into triangular-shaped wedges and sear these in the skillet with the onion until the venison is brown on all sides. Reduce the heat to low, add ½ cup water, cover the pan, and slowly simmer for ½ hour. Meanwhile, stir the flour into the sour cream. When the meat is tender, add the cream mixture and mushrooms to the skillet, cover, and allow to slowly bubble for another 20 minutes. The creamed sirloin tips can be served as-is, or ladled over a bed of noodles. Serves 4.

1. *Braised Round Steak is both tender and flavorful. After treating the steak with meat tenderizer, use a meat mallet to shape the steaks to uniform thickness. Pound as much flour into steaks as they'll hold.*

2. *In a skillet, sear the steaks on both sides until they are lightly browned; then add 1 cup water, cover, reduce heat and simmer for one hour.*

3. *Onion rings are a delicious accompaniment to Braised Round Steak. By merely adding green pepper, onions, and tomatoes to the pan while the steak is cooking, the recipe becomes Venison Swiss Steak.*

Braised Round Steak

2 pounds round steak	flour
meat tenderizer	salt and pepper

Sprinkle both sides of the steak with meat tenderizer, pierce deeply with a fork, then let stand 1 hour. Gently pound the steaks to uniform thickness with a meat mallet, using the sharp end to drive the tenderizer deep into the meat. Sprinkle a bit of salt and pepper into a modest quantity of flour, then gently pound the flour into the steak with the smooth side of your meat hammer. In a skillet, brown both sides of the meat in cooking oil. Then add 1 cup water, cover, reduce the heat to very low and slowly simmer for 1 hour. Serves 4.

Venison Scallopini

2 pounds round steak	1 teaspoon parsley flakes
6 tablespoons olive oil	1 teaspoon salt
1 teaspoon garlic powder	½ teaspoon black pepper
1 12-ounce can tomatoes	4 slices mozzarella cheese
1 teaspoon oregano	

Cut the round steaks into four equal portions. In a skillet, blend the garlic powder into the olive oil, then brown the steaks on both sides over medium-high heat. Add the tomatoes and sprinkle the seasonings over the tops of the steaks. Reduce the heat to very low, cover the pan, and slowly simmer for 45 minutes. Spoon the tomatoes and juices onto an oven-proof platter, arrange the steaks on top, then lay a slice of mozzarella cheese on top of each of the steaks. Slide the dinner platter into an oven preheated to 400° until the cheese is melted and just barely beginning to reveal a trace of browning. Serves 4.

Tomatoed Deer Steak

2   pounds round or sirloin tip
      steak
    flour
1   onion, chopped
6   tablespoons bacon
      drippings

1   cup dry red wine
1½ cups beef broth or bouillon
¼   teaspoon thyme
3   tablespoons tomato sauce

Gently pound the flour into the steak with a meat hammer. Sauté the onions in the bacon drippings. Then, in the same skillet, brown the meat on both sides. Add half the wine and half the beef broth, bring to a boil, then reduce the heat to low and continue to cook 5 minutes. Turn the steak, cover the skillet, and continue cooking for 1½ hours. When the steak is tender, transfer it to a platter and place it in your oven to keep warm. Now add the remaining wine, broth, and the thyme and tomato sauce to the pan, turn the heat up slightly and stir until a smooth, bubbly sauce is created. Ladle the sauce over the steak and serve. Serves 4.

Steak 'N Mushrooms

2   pounds round steak or
      sirloin tip steak
2   tablespoons olive oil
2   tablespoons butter

1   onion, chopped
2   teaspoons flour
½   cup sour cream
1   cup mushrooms

Blend the olive oil with the butter in a skillet, then sauté the onions until they are clear. With a slotted spoon, remove the onions and briefly set them aside. Now, in the same pan, sear both sides of the steak until it is brown. Spoon the onion on top of the steak, add ½ cup hot water, cover, and simmer over low heat for 20 minutes. Blend the flour with the sour cream, then add this along with the mushrooms to the pan, cover, and slowly simmer another 20 minutes. Transfer the meat to a hot platter and ladle the mushroom sauce over the top. Serves 4.

Texas Red Whiskey Deer Steaks

4 large sirloin tip steaks
1 onion, finely chopped
   tarragon vinegar
½ teaspoon Tabasco sauce
½ teaspoon Worcestershire
   sauce

2 teaspoons chili sauce
1 teaspoon wet mustard
½ cup bourbon

Place the steaks and onion in a skillet and pour in tarragon vinegar until the steaks are barely covered. Simmer over low heat for 20 minutes. Add all the remaining ingredients, except for the bourbon, and continue to cook until the sauce becomes thick. Now spoon half of the sauce into a shallow pan, arrange the steaks on top, then spread the remaining sauce on top of the steaks. Pour the bourbon over the steaks and cook, uncovered, in a 350° oven for 1 hour. Serves 4.

Barbecued Round Steak

2 pounds round steak
2 tablespoons butter
2 tablespoons cooking oil
1 onion, chopped
2 stalks celery, chopped
1 medium can tomato soup

1 cup beef broth or bouillon
2 tablespoons brown sugar
4 tablespoons Worcestershire
   sauce
2 tablespoons soy sauce
2 tablespoons lemon juice

Blend the butter and cooking oil in a skillet and sauté the onion and celery, then set aside briefly. In the same skillet, brown the round steak. In a separate saucepan, add all the remaining ingredients and simmer for 15 minutes. Place the browned steak in a deep casserole dish, spoon the sautéed onions and celery over the top, then pour the barbecue sauce over all. Cook, uncovered, for 1½ hours in a 350° oven. Serves 4.

Venison Swiss Steak

2 pounds round steak or
   sirloin tip steak
½ teaspoon salt
¼ teaspoon black pepper
   flour

1 green pepper, chopped
2 onions, sliced
1 8-ounce can tomatoes

Blend the salt and pepper with a little flour, then gently pound the mixture into both sides of your steak with a meat hammer. Now cut the meat into four equal portions. In a skillet containing several tablespoons of oil or fat, brown the meat on both sides. Add the pepper, onion, and tomatoes (with packing juice), cover the pan, reduce the heat to low, and slowly simmer for 1 hour. Check after one-half hour and add a bit of water to the pan if necessary. Serves 4.

CHAPTER 17

Soups and Stews

T HE EXACT ORIGIN of venison stew is unknown, but undoubtedly it dates back to the first primitive uses of fire and food cooked in clay vessels. However, it wasn't until the medieval 14th-century reign of King Henry that *stuwe* acquired its official name to identify the nature of the feast. Stews have not really changed much since then, the reason being, I suppose, because it's difficult to improve upon something that's already good to begin with.

Nevertheless, a few points having to do with the innate characteristics of stews are worth remembering. Without meaning to burst the bubbles of self-proclaimed gourmets, I can say right off that a stew is really nothing more than a thick soup. Or, on behalf of those who might find themselves tempted to debate such ridiculous syntax, you could look at it another way and say that soups are really nothing more than thin stews.

With that resolved, it would be incredibly easy to fill the remaining pages of this book with literally thousands of recipes for soups and stews. But that would be pointless because the prolific number of such recipes is more illusory than real. By adding a pinch of thyme, subtracting the celery, splashing the pot with just a hint of sherry, or whatever, I could sit here and concoct numerous untried variations of soups and stews. Yet none of those recipes would be so individually unique that they could really qualify as "new."

Be it known, therefore, that when any particular recipe finds its way to the table, its basis is unquestionably one that already has been tried before,

Soups are really nothing more than thin stews made on short notice by dicing their ingredients.

despite any claims by the chef that it is his original, secret version. Just smile approvingly, as though you believe every word of it, and let him have his fun, because that's what soups and stews are really all about.

Aside from soups merely being thin stews, and stews really being thick soups, there are a few other minor differences in their personalities.

For one, the typical assortment of vegetables comprising a soup are generally diced while those going into stews are generally cubed or "chunked." The reason for this is that soups traditionally are made on short notice and designed to be eaten just as quickly. Hence, you want to as speedily as possible see to the shotgun marriage of all their various ingredients.

Stews, on the other hand, are long-term love affairs that are best eaten only after hours of slow simmering and which even fare better the following day, the day after that, or after sitting in one's freezer for several weeks. Consequently, the use of small-sized, diced vegetables, as in soups, would inevitably see the stew transform itself into an amalgam of mush; thick chunks of vegetables hold together longer to help the stew retain its integrity.

Another difference between soups and stews is that soups typically have a broth color ranging from semi-clear to amber, while stews characteristically reveal a rich, dark, gravy-like color. The reason for this is that in preparation of soup the venison chunks are either placed in the soup pot raw to steam-cook, or they are just briefly seared in a bit of cooking oil before going into the pot. But in preparation of stew, the venison chunks are usually first dredged with flour and then are browned well in a skillet.

Stews are really nothing more than thick soups made with chunks of meat and vegetables and allowed to simmer slowly a long while to harmonize their flavors.

In either case, hunters intent upon impressing others with their cooking prowess commonly make the mistake of using very tender cuts of venison in their soups or stews. It all sounds logical enough, but remember that the most delectable soups and stews are those that have very slowly bubbled away on the burner in order to harmonize their individual ingredients. And such lengthy cooking will have the effect of turning already tender cuts of venison into soft, limp meat lacking all character and personality.

A far better approach is to use tougher cuts that will hold together through the duration of the cooking and only later become tender. Ask any experienced butcher or restaurant chef which portion of an animal's anatomy makes the best soup or stew and he'll not hesitate to say "brisket meat." It easily retains its shape, texture, and conformation well after it has reached the stage of becoming "tender," while many other cuts do not. The next best bets are neck meat, flank meat, and lower leg meat. Already-cooked leftovers from other cuts also can be used in stews if cooking time is reduced.   It should be emphasized, however, that there is no specific length of time any soup or stew should be allowed to cook. As long as the meat and vegetables are tender, the soup or stew is ready to eat when you are! But there are a few other rules of thumb regarding the actual cooking. Foremost, never allow a soup or stew to come to a rolling boil because this will cause the meat to shrink, the vegetables to wilt, and the spices to commit suicide. What you want is an almost arthritic simmer, which reveals faint wisps of steam rising from the potion as tiny bubbles barely pop on the surface.

Don't allow the large number of stew recipes to befuddle you; most are basically the same. The basic ingredients for most stews are meat chunks, vegetables, and assorted seasonings. To show how simple stews are to make, and how universal the approach, let's invent a fast, delicious one that doesn't even have a name.

1. Flour venison cubes and brown them in a skillet. Flour gives stews their typical rich, brown, gravy-like color and consistency, compared to soups, which are clear to amber colored.

2. Transfer the browned venison cubes to a stew pot and sprinkle with a little basil and thyme; salt and pepper to taste. Add enough canned beef broth to cover the meat.

3. Simmer stew, covered, for about an hour; then blend in vegetables of your choice. Potatoes, carrots, green beans, mushrooms, onions . . . whatever. This is the beauty of concocting a stew. Since you can use whatever you happen to have on hand, no two creations are ever exactly the same, unless you are following a specific recipe. The reason you add the vegetables late in the simmering is to prevent them from overcooking and becoming mushy.

4. A perfect no-name stew that is sure to delight everyone. Try inventing a stew of your own, or follow the time-tested recipes in this chapter.

If there is any doubt as to the proper cooking temperature, use a clip-on thermometer designed for pot cooking and adjust the dial on your burner so that the soup or stew temperature remains within a range of 170°–180°F.

Of course, neither soups or stews should be allowed to cook so long their liquid content begins to evaporate significantly. This is more commonly a problem with stews than soups, particularly when the stew is reheated time and again over a period of days. Adding a bit of water, stock or wine is the recommended prescription.

In launching now upon the task of revealing my favorite soup and stew recipes, I've headed the list with *chili* since, technically speaking, it is a stewlike creation. However, I'm not referring here to the type of civilized chili described in Chapter 11. That recipe was a modern American household version utilizing deerburger, tomatoes, beans, and whatnot. It's a sumptuous dish, to be sure, but it's about as far from "authentic" chili as Tucson is from Manhattan.

Throughout the desert Southwest, where chili originated more than a century ago, the only protein available to poor country folks was jackrabbit, whitetail and mule deer, and upon rare occasion the meat from an old, range-fed steer. During that era it was quite difficult to keep meat from spoiling and the steer meat, particularly, was often so tough even the haunches had to be attacked with a Bowie knife. Chili powder was therefore used as both a preservative and flavor enhancer and, simultaneously, a moist-heat cooking method was employed to make the meat tender.

Chilis, then as now, are the fruits of a woody plant called *Capsicum frutescens;* after being dried they are pulverized into a powdery substance known as "molido." Depending upon where the chilis are grown, and at what stage in their development they are harvested, the molido powder may have a flavor running the gamut from very mild to three-alarm (which, if you haven't inferred, means very, very hot).

I like chili hot enough that it has a noticeable "bite" to it, but not so hot that it burns. Yet since chili molido powder can vary, you may have to experiment a bit to learn exactly how much is just right. Do this by adding a little to your chili, letting it simmer a while, tasting it, then adding a little more if you like.

If real chili molido powder is not available in your local grocery store, conventional chili powder is an adequate substitute. But since this breed of chili powder contains cumin, garlic, oregano, and salt in addition to the molido, omit those ingredients from the following recipe. Also, since the amount of molido is a bit diluted, so to speak, increasing the degree of "hotness" of your prepared chili should *not* be accomplished by adding more of the chili powder but instead sprinkling in a bit of red cayenne pepper.

Authentic Mexican-American Chili

2   pounds venison
2   tablespoons chili molida
        powder
1   garlic clove, chopped

1   large onion, chopped
½   teaspoon oregano
½   teaspoon cumin
1   teaspoon salt

(Note: If instead of molida you use regular chili
powder, omit the cumin, garlic, oregano, and
salt, and add 1 teaspoon red cayenne pepper)

Cut venison into inch-square cubes, then brown them in a Dutch oven
or pot containing just a little lard or fat. When the meat chunks are browned
on all sides, spoon off as much of the fat as possible. Sprinkle the chili molida
powder on top of the meat, stir thoroughly, then reduce the heat to very
low, cover the pot, and allow the seasoning to cook into the meat for 20
minutes. Now add to the pot just enough water to cover the meat, and then
add the remaining ingredients. Cover the pot again and continue simmering
for an absolute minimum of 1 hour. Authentic chili is one dish that improves
after being allowed to cool overnight before being reheated the following
day. Serves 4.

Stormy Weather Soup

1   pound venison, cubed
3   carrots, diced
4   potatoes, diced
2   onions, diced
2   bell peppers, diced
1   large can tomatoes
3   celery stalks, diced

1   large can V-8 juice
2   tablespoons Worcestershire
        sauce
2   teaspoons Tabasco sauce
    salt and pepper to taste

In a skillet, brown the venison cubes in a bit of lard or fat, then transfer
to a large pot. Cover the meat with cold water, then add the remaining
ingredients and slowly simmer for 1 hour. Serves 4.

Venison Minestrone

1½ pounds venison, cubed
4   quarts water
4   cups dry pinto beans
1   large onion, sliced
6   carrots, chopped
6   stalks celery, chopped
6   tablespoons olive oil
1   large can tomatoes

3   potatoes, cubed
2   teaspoons garlic powder
2   tablespoons basil
½   cup chopped parsley
½   cup macaroni, cooked
½   head cabbage, chopped
     Parmesan cheese

Place the beans in a deep bowl, completely cover with cold water, and allow to soak overnight. Simmer the meat in 1 quart of cold water until it is tender, then refrigerate overnight. The following day, drain the beans and add them to the pot containing the venison and broth and simmer 2 hours or until the beans are tender. Meanwhile, in a deep skillet, sauté the onion, carrots, and celery in the olive oil. When the vegetables are fully cooked, add the can of tomatoes and simmer until the liquid is almost evaporated, then add this skillet of vegetables to the soup pot along with 3 quarts of water. Allow the soup to simmer for 1 hour, then add the potatoes, garlic, basil, and parsley and allow to simmer for 1 hour longer. Just before serving, stir the macaroni and cabbage into the soup, cover and let sit for at least 5 minutes. After ladling the soup into bowls, sprinkle about 1 tablespoon grated Parmesan cheese on top of each. Serves 4 (with plenty left over that you can freeze or reheat the next day).

Savory Bean Soup

1 pound leftover venison cut
   into cubes
1 8-ounce can tomato sauce
1 large can tomatoes
2 tablespoons dried onion
   flakes
10 cups water

1 medium can red kidney
   beans
½ cup uncooked Minute Rice
½ teaspoon chili powder
2 teaspoons salt
½ cup shredded American
   cheese

Add all of the ingredients, except the rice and cheese, to a deep pot and simmer on low heat for 1 hour. Five minutes before serving, stir in the rice. Ladle the soup into bowls, then sprinkle the cheese on top of each. Serves 4 very generously.

Low-Cal Delight

1½ pounds venison, cubed
2 bay leaves
½ cup chopped onion
1 cup chopped cabbage
5 carrots, chopped
5 stalks celery, chopped with
   leaves

1 large can Italian tomatoes
2 cubes beef bouillon
1 tablespoon Worcestershire
   sauce
   salt and pepper to taste

Place the cubed venison in a large pot, cover with cold water, and bring to a boil. Immediately turn the heat down and continue simmering, skimming off any foam that appears. Add the bay leaves, celery, carrots, onions, and cabbage and cook over low heat for 2 hours. Remove the bay leaves, add the tomatoes, Worcestershire sauce, and bouillon cubes and simmer ½ hour longer. Serves 4.

Venison and Barley Surprise

1 pound venison, cubed
1 cup uncooked barley
2 quarts cold water
2 stalks celery, chopped with
    leaves

2 carrots, chopped
1 teaspoon salt
½ teaspoon marjoram
½ teaspoon thyme

Brown the venison in a skillet containing a bit of olive oil, then transfer to a deep pot. Prepare the barley according to the instructions on the package, then thoroughly rinse and add to the pot. Stir in the remaining ingredients and allow to slowly simmer over low heat for 1 hour. Serves 4 generously.

Hunter's Soup

2 pounds venison, cubed
2 quarts of water

seasonings
vegetables

This famous soup is variously known as hunter's soup, cupboard soup, or "whatchagot" soup and no two recipes ever turn out exactly the same because the ingredients consist of whatever you can "hunt" around for and find in your cupboard. But don't let this imply that "hunter's soup" is only a half-hearted endeavor; on the contrary, it can be so delicious you'll deeply regret you didn't jot down the recipe ingredients as you threw them into the pot. Begin by adding two pounds of cubed meat to the pot and then the water. Heat just until the soup begins to boil, then quickly turn down the burner and begin simmering, ladling off any foam that appears on the surface. Now add whatever vegetables you have. Some unique ones I've used that have added tantalizing flavors have been turnips, squash, and red cabbage. As to the spices, the ones most commonly used are thyme, marjoram, basil, parsley, salt, and pepper. Add them in ¼ teaspoon amounts at a time until you achieve just the right, proportional flavor you like. Once, I added to our soup pot a package of frozen broccoli spears and a can of condensed cream of mushroom soup, and I'll take an oath the soup was positively ambrosia. You can also throw in a handful of beans (red, kidney, or pinto, after they have soaked in water), rice, wide noodles, macaroni, or any other odds and ends you happen to have on hand. Enjoy!

Crockpot Venison Stew

1½ pounds venison, cubed
3   potatoes, cut into chunks
1   turnip, cut into chunks
3   stalks celery, cut into
      chunks
2   onions, quartered

3   carrots, cut into chunks
½   teaspoon salt
¼   teaspoon black pepper
¼   teaspoon thyme
¼   teaspoon oregano

This is a perfect all-day stew that can be allowed to endlessly slow-simmer in a crockpot, beanpot, or Dutch oven. Flour the meat and then brown it in a skillet containing a modest amount of fat. Transfer the meat to your crockpot, add the remaining ingredients, then pour in just enough water to cover everything. Let the stew cook on very low heat for at least 3 hours. After the first 2 hours of cooking, you may have to occasionally add ¼ cup water. Serves 4, whenever they happen to straggle in.

Venison Cider Stew

2   pounds venison, cubed
1   teaspoon dried onion flakes
2   teaspoons salt
¼   teaspoon thyme
¼   teaspoon nutmeg

3   potatoes, cut into chunks
4   carrots, cut into chunks
1   apple, chopped
1   cup tart apple cider

Brown the venison in a skillet, sprinkling on the onion, salt, thyme, and nutmeg while stirring continually. Transfer the seasoned meat to a crockpot or stew pot, add the vegetables and apple, then pour the cider over the top. Slow-cook on very low heat for at least 3 hours. If too much of the liquid begins to evaporate, replenish it with a mixture of ½ cup water blended with ½ cup cider. Serves 4.

Missouri Venison Stew

3	pounds venison, cubed	1½	teaspoons salt
1½	cups hot water	1	teaspoon black pepper
1	cup dry red wine	3	potatoes, cut into chunks
1	teaspoon mixed marjoram, thyme, basil	3	carrots, cut into chunks
1	teaspoon dried parsley flakes		

Roll the meat in flour, then brown in a skillet containing a bit of fat or bacon drippings. Add the meat to your stew pot along with the hot water, wine, herbs, and salt and pepper. Cover the pot and simmer for 2 hours. Then add the potatoes and carrots and simmer 1 hour longer, adding more hot water if needed. Serves 4 very generously.

Hunter's Stew

1½	pounds venison, cubed	4	carrots, cut into chunks
1	teaspoon salt	2	4-ounce cans mushrooms
½	teaspoon black pepper	3	tablespoons soy sauce
2	onions, quartered	½	teaspoon ginger
4	potatoes, cubed		
3	stalks celery; cut into chunks		

Season the meat with the salt and pepper, then roll in flour and brown in a skillet. Transfer the meat to a stew pot, add the remaining ingredients, then cover with water. Simmer for 2 hours or until the vegetables are tender. Serves 4.

Savory Venison Stew

2 pounds venison, cubed
¼ cup bacon drippings
2 onions, cut into chunks
2 carrots, cut into chunks
2 stalks celery, cut into
   chunks

2 10-ounce cans beef broth
2 cups dry red wine
2 bay leaves, crumbled
   salt and pepper to taste

Dust the meat with flour and brown in a skillet containing the bacon fat, then transfer both the meat and remaining bacon drippings to a stew pot. Add the remaining ingredients, cover the pot, and slowly simmer for at least 2 hours. Serves 4.

Venison Bourguignon

2 pounds venison, cubed
3 onions, cut into chunks
½ cup bacon drippings
2 cups Burgundy
1 large can beef broth

¼ teaspoon thyme
¼ teaspoon marjoram
1 teaspoon salt
½ teaspoon black pepper
1 pound fresh mushrooms

Sauté the onions in a skillet containing the bacon drippings until the onion chunks are brown around the edges, then transfer to your stew pot. In the same skillet, now brown the brisket meat after dusting it with flour. Add the remaining ingredients (except the mushrooms) to the stew pot, cover, and simmer on low heat for 3 hours. Add the mushrooms during the final ½ hour of cooking. Serves 4.

Deutschstu

2 pounds venison, cubed
¼ cup bacon drippings
2 teaspoons lemon juice
½ teaspoon Worcestershire
   sauce
1 teaspoon garlic powder

2 bay leaves, crumbled
¼ teaspoon paprika
¼ teaspoon allspice
12 small white onions, whole
4 carrots, cut into chunks
3 potatoes, cut into chunks

Flour the venison cubes, then brown in the bacon drippings. Transfer the meat and remaining drippings to your stew pot, sprinkle on the seasonings, then cover with hot water. Slowly simmer for 2 hours. Then add the vegetables, cover the pot, and simmer 1 hour longer. Serves 4.

Venison Herb Stew

1½ pounds venison, cubed
1 onion, chopped
3 tablespoons butter
1 large can condensed
   tomato soup

1 cup water
1 teaspoon garlic powder
¼ teaspoon basil
½ teaspoon seasoned salt
¼ teaspoon black pepper

In a skillet, sauté the onion in the butter until it is clear. Transfer the onion to a stew pot, then lightly brown the venison cubes in the same skillet, adding a bit more butter if necessary. Place the meat and seasonings in a stew pot, stir in the remaining ingredients, and simmer 2 hours, adding just a bit more water if necessary. Serves 4.

Quickie Venison Stew

2 pounds venison, cubed
4 potatoes, cut into chunks
1 large can cut green beans

2 carrots, cut into chunks
1 onion, chopped
1 envelope dry onion soup mix

Brown the venison in a skillet containing a bit of cooking oil. Transfer the meat to your stew pot along with the other ingredients, cover with water, and simmer over low heat 1 hour. Let each guest add salt and pepper to his own taste. Serves 4.

Red Whiskey Stew

1½ pounds brisket meat, cut
    into cubes
6   tablespoons flour
1   teaspoon salt
1   teaspoon black pepper
1   teaspoon garlic powder
¼   cup cooking oil

1   onion, chopped
1   large can beef broth
2   teaspoons brown sugar
3   ounces bourbon whiskey
1   package frozen mixed
    vegetables
1   large can cut green beans

Blend together the flour, salt, pepper, and garlic powder, then dredge the venison with the mixture. In a skillet containing the cooking oil, brown the venison chunks and onion simultaneously. Transfer the meat and onion to your stew pot, add the beef broth and enough water to cover the meat. Just barely bring to a boil, then quickly reduce the heat and simmer 1 hour. Now add the brown sugar and bourbon, cover and cook 1 hour longer. Now add the vegetables and cook 1 hour longer. Serves 4.

Creamy Venison Stew

2   pounds venison, cubed
¼   cup bacon drippings
1   onion, cut into chunks
3   cups canned tomatoes,
        with liquid

2   cups evaporated milk
2   tablespoons vinegar
¼   teaspoon paprika

In a skillet, brown the venison and onions in the bacon fat. Transfer the meat and onion to a stew pot, add the remaining ingredients, and simmer over low heat 2 hours, adding just a bit of water if necessary. Serves 4.

Winter Day Stew

2   pounds venison, cubed
¼   cup bacon drippings
1   onion, cut into chunks
2   carrots, cut into chunks
2   stalks celery, cut into
        chunks
1   4-ounce can mushrooms
3   potatoes, cut into chunks

2   medium cans beef broth or
        4 cups bouillon
1   cup port wine
2   tablespoons Worcestershire
        sauce
1   teaspoon brown sugar
½   teaspoon cloves
½   teaspoon cinnamon

In a skillet, brown the venison and onion in the bacon drippings. Transfer the onion and venison to a stew pot, add the remaining ingredients and simmer 3 hours. If the stew becomes too thick, add more beef broth. Serves 5 very generously.

CHAPTER 18

Casseroles and Meat Pies

IT IS UNFORTUNATE that a vast majority of deer hunters, particularly those of the male genre, are intimidated by the thought of making a venison casserole or meat pie. Although both *sound* somewhat complicated and time consuming, they are actually easy to prepare and exceedingly delicious.

A *meat pie* is really nothing more than a thick, stewlike concoction baked in a relatively shallow dish with something on top of it. That "something" might be a standard pie crust, but it can also be a topping of biscuits, or a heavy sprinkling of breadcrumbs or crackercrumbs.

A *casserole* is a similar stewlike meal that often has rice, noodles, or potatoes stirred in and then is baked in a relatively deep dish, often with a sprinkling of cheese, onion rings, or croutons on top. But it can also mean a recipe simmered in a skillet on top of the stove and then merely ladled over a bed of rice or noodles on a hot platter.

The favorable attributes of casseroles and meat pies are almost too many to list, but I will describe a few of their more noteworthy advantages and characteristics.

Generally, a casserole or meat pie is a "one-pot" meal. What I mean is, it's an all-encompassing main dish that in a single cooking vessel contains meat, vegetables, starches, and everything else customarily thought to constitute a balanced meal. Consequently, you don't have to worry about preparing a number of side dishes to accompany this feature attraction as you would if preparing a venison roast. This isn't to say you can't have several small additions if you so desire, but they aren't entirely necessary and in most cases need only be simple things such as a fruit cocktail, relish dish, or perhaps a fresh loaf of hard-crusted bread.

Another advantage of casseroles and meat pies is that their cooking time is usually one hour or less. This means you can use tender cuts of venison if you choose, with no worry that they will turn into mush. Yet since casseroles and meat pies involve moist-heat cooking you can also use lesser cuts of venison with the full assurance they will be tender—cuts such as shoulder meat, brisket, neck meat, and round steak. We do advise cubing them slightly smaller than you'd ordinarily do in making a stew.

In my family, however, we like to use already cooked, leftover venison in our casseroles and meat pies. For example, if we enjoyed a rump roast for dinner one evening or two before, likely as not there will be leftover meat that just isn't sufficient enough for a second meal in its own right. But if it's cooked in conjunction with other foods in a casserole or meat pie, invariably there's plenty for a hearty meal. This explains why, in many of the recipes to follow, I may not specify a particular cut of venison but only the quantity of meat required. In these cases, the reader can use whatever he happens to have on hand with the assurance of success.

Easy Venison Casserole

1½	pounds deerburger	½	teaspoon black pepper
1	onion, chopped	¼	teaspoon oregano
1	stalk celery, chopped	1	package frozen tiny, tender peas
2	8-ounce cans tomato sauce		
2	teaspoons flour	1	package "tube" biscuits
1	4-ounce can mushrooms	1	cup shredded mild cheddar cheese
1	teaspoon salt		

Brown the deerburger in a skillet, then stir in the onion and celery and cook over low heat until the onions are clear. Drain off any grease, then stir in the flour, tomato sauce, seasonings, mushrooms, and peas. Pour this into a deep casserole dish. Arrange the biscuits on top, then sprinkle on the cheese. Bake at 350° for about 20 minutes (be careful that the biscuits and cheese topping do not burn). Serves 4.

Venison Moussaka

1½ pounds deerburger
2   cups cooked green beans
1   8-ounce can tomato sauce
½   teaspoon garlic powder
⅛   teaspoon cinnamon
2   eggs, slightly beaten
1½ cups small-curd cottage
      cheese

2   tablespoons ripe olive juice
¼   teaspoon nutmeg
½   cup grated Parmesan-
      Romano cheese
ripe olives, sliced

Rub butter over the entire inside of a deep glass casserole dish, then arrange a thick layer of the green beans in the bottom. In a skillet, brown the deerburger and drain off any grease that forms. Now stir into the deerburger the tomato sauce, garlic powder, and cinnamon. Spoon this mixture evenly over the green beans. In a bowl, blend the eggs, cottage cheese, olive juice, and nutmeg, then spread this over the mixture in the casserole dish. Sprinkle the cheese over the top and bake 30 minutes at 350°. Several minutes before serving, sprinkle the olive slices on top. Serves 4 generously.

Deer-Me Casserole

2   pounds venison, cubed
1   medium can condensed
      cream of mushroom soup
1   cup canned tomatoes, with
      juice

1   envelope dry onion soup
      mix
½   cup seasoned breadcrumbs

Arrange the meat cubes in the bottom of a casserole dish, then pour the mushroom soup (undiluted) over the top. Sprinkle on the dry onion soup mix, then pour the tomatoes and juice over the top. Cover the dish and bake at 325° for 2 hours. During the final 15 minutes of cooking, remove the cover from the dish and sprinkle the top of the casserole with the breadcrumbs. Continue baking until the breadcrumbs are nicely browned. Serves 4.

Venison Stroganoff

1½	pounds venison, cubed	1	tablespoon salt
	flour	¼	teaspoon black pepper
½	cup butter or margarine	1½	cups water
1	teaspoon garlic powder	1	cup mushrooms
1	onion, chopped	1¼	cups sour cream

In a skillet, melt the butter and then stir in the garlic powder. Flour the venison chunks and then brown them in the skillet. Add the onion, salt, and pepper, then stir in the water, cover the pan, and simmer slowly for 45 minutes. Now add the mushrooms and sour cream and continue to cook another 15 minutes, but do not allow the sauce to come to a boil. Traditionally, stroganoff is served over a bed of thick Pennsylvania Dutch noodles, but for variety you can use thin Oriental noodles or rice. Serves 4.

1. Flour the venison cubes, then brown them in melted butter or margarine. Now stir in seasonings.

2. When the meat is tender, blend in sour cream and mushrooms. Allow to cook another 15 minutes.

3. Ladle over a bed of thick noodles and serve.

West Texas Venison Casserole

2 pounds round steak or
   sirloin tip steak
¼ cup flour
1 teaspoon salt
½ teaspoon black pepper
¼ cup bacon drippings
1 stalk celery, chopped

3 onions, sliced
2 tablespoons Worcestershire
   sauce
2 cups tomatoes, with juice
1 8-ounce package wide
   noodles

1. Flour and brown round steak or sirloin tip steak.

Cut the venison into four 8-ounce pieces, then thoroughly dredge in a mixture of the flour, salt, and pepper. Brown the meat on all sides in a high-sided skillet containing the bacon fat. Add the celery and onions and continue cooking over low heat until the onions are clear. Add the other ingredients, cover the pan, and cook slowly for 1½ hours or until the meat is tender. Prepare the noodles according to the package instructions. Then place the noodles on a hot serving platter, carefully lay the four steaks on top, then pour the sauce from the pan over the top. Serves 4.

2. Add the other ingredients, slowly simmer, then serve over noodles.

Chicago!

1 pound deerburger
2 teaspoons butter
2 8-ounce cans tomato sauce
½ teaspoon salt
½ teaspoon Worcestershire
  sauce
1 8-ounce package cream
  cheese

1 8-ounce carton small-curd
  cottage cheese
¼ cup sour cream
1 small green pepper, chopped
¼ cup scallions, minced
1 6-ounce package wide
  noodles

In a skillet, brown the deerburger, then pour off any grease that forms. Stir in the tomato sauce, salt, and Worcestershire sauce, and allow to simmer on very low heat. In a separate bowl, blend the cream cheese, cottage cheese, and sour cream, then stir in the green pepper and just a bit of the scallions. Prepare the noodles according to the package instructions, drain thoroughly, then stir the noodles into the cheese blend. Butter the inside of a casserole dish, then spread the noodle-cheese mixture in the bottom. Spoon the meat and tomato sauce on top of the noodles and sprinkle with the remaining scallions. Bake at 350° for 45 minutes. Serves 4 generously.

Sausage Supreme

1 pound bulk venison sausage
1 onion, chopped
2 teaspoons Worcestershire
  sauce
1 teaspoon garlic powder
3 carrots, grated

1 8-ounce package "curly"
  noodles
1 medium can condensed
  cream of mushroom soup
½ cup Parmesan cheese

In a skillet containing just a bit of grease, brown the sausage, then stir in the onion and Worcestershire sauce. When the mixture just begins to bubble, stir in the garlic, then turn off the heat. Prepare the noodles according to the package instructions, then thoroughly drain them. Now stir the noodles, venison sausage, carrots, and soup together until they are well blended. Pour into a buttered casserole dish and bake in a 350° oven for 20 minutes. During the final 5 minutes of cooking, sprinkle the Parmesan cheese over the top. Serves 4.

Venison Steak Casserole

2 pounds round or sirloin tip
   steak
8 tablespoons flour
1 teaspoon salt
½ teaspoon black pepper
¼ teaspoon oregano
1 teaspoon garlic powder

¼ cup cooking oil
6 potatoes, sliced
2 onions, sliced
2 carrots, sliced
1 green pepper, cut into strips
3 cups beef broth or bouillon

Cut the steak into serving-sized pieces. Then blend together the flour, salt, pepper, oregano, and garlic powder. With a meat mallet, pound about one-half of this mixture into both sides of the steaks. Now brown the steaks in a skillet containing the cooking oil. Lay a number of pieces of the steak in the bottom of a glass casserole dish until it is covered. On top of the steak, arrange a layer of potatoes, onions, carrots and pepper slices. Sprinkle on top some of the remaining seasoned-flour mix, then add another thin layer of steak meat until you've used all of the ingredients. Pour the beef broth over the top, cover the dish, then bake at 350° for 30 to 45 minutes or until the vegetables are tender. Serves 4 generously.

Mexicali Rose

1 pound deerburger
2 4-ounce cans whole green
   chilies
2 eggs
½ cup flour

1 teaspoon salt
1⅓ cups milk
1 pound cheddar cheese,
   grated

In a skillet, brown the deerburger, then pour off any grease. In the bottom of a casserole dish, place a layer of chilies. Place a thin layer of deerburger on top, then a thin layer of the cheese. Now place another layer of chilies, deerburger, and cheese on top of the first. In a bowl, thoroughly blend the eggs, flour, salt, and milk, then pour the mixture over the top of the layers in the casserole dish. Bake uncovered at 350° for 30 minutes or until a custard-like topping forms. This is a mildly hot dish. Serves 4.

Country Casserole

1 pound deerburger or bulk
   sausage
1 onion, chopped
1 green pepper, chopped
1 16-ounce can baked beans
1 8-ounce package elbow
   macaroni

½ cup tomato juice
½ teaspoon salt
½ cup grated mild cheddar
   cheese

1. In a skillet, brown the burger or sausage, then stir in onion and green pepper. When the vegetables are cooked, stir in beans, tomato juice, and seasonings.

2. Blend in the cooked macaroni.

In a skillet, brown the deerburger in a bit of cooking oil, then stir in the onion and green pepper and continue to cook on low heat until they are tender. Stir in the beans, tomato juice, macaroni, and salt and mix thoroughly. Pour into a casserole dish and bake in a 400° oven for 20 minutes or until the casserole begins to bubble. Then sprinkle the cheddar cheese on top and bake 5 minutes longer. Serves 4. (For an entirely different taste treat, use the same recipe but substitute some of your own venison sausage for the deerburger.)

3. Transfer to an oven-proof pot and begin baking. When the casserole begins to bubble, sprinkle cheese on top and bake until cheese melts.

4. Country Casserole is a hearty meal for winter nights that is fun to make.

Hungarian Casserole

1 pound venison, cut into
   small cubes
3 tablespoons olive oil
3 tablespoons butter
½ teaspoon salt
¼ teaspoon black pepper
½ cup water

½ cup dry red wine
1 pound fresh mushrooms
1 onion, chopped
1 8-ounce package noodles
1 cup sour cream
¼ cup crackercrumbs
¼ cup grated Parmesan cheese

In a skillet, blend the olive oil and butter, then thoroughly brown the venison cubes on all sides. Stir in the salt, pepper, water, and wine, then reduce the heat, cover the pan, and let simmer for 30 minutes. Meanwhile, in a separate pan, brown the mushrooms and onion in just a bit of olive oil. Prepare the noodles according to the package instructions, then drain well. Pour off all but ⅓ cup of the stock from the pan in which the venison has been simmering. Now stir into the pan all the ingredients along with the sour cream. Use a large spoon to transfer the ingredients to a buttered casserole dish. Blend the crackercrumbs and cheese and sprinkle on top, then bake at 400° for 20 minutes. Serves 4 very generously.

Rio Grande Venison with Noodles

1 pound deerburger
   cooking oil
1 green pepper, chopped
1 onion, chopped
2 stalks celery, chopped
1 small can red kidney beans
1 16-ounce can tomatoes,
   with juice

1 4-ounce can mushrooms
½ teaspoon chili molida
1 teaspoon salt
½ teaspoon black pepper
1 8-ounce package noodles

In a deep skillet, brown the deerburger in a bit of cooking oil. Stir in the pepper, onion, and celery, then reduce the heat, and simmer until they are tender. Add the remaining ingredients (except the noodles), stir thoroughly, cover the pan, and slowly simmer for 30 minutes. Meanwhile, prepare the noodles according to the package instructions, then drain. Place the noodles on a hot platter and ladle the meat and vegetable sauce over the top. Serves 4.

Cheddar-Noodle Casserole

1 pound venison, cut into cubes
1 small onion, minced
1 stick margarine
1 4-ounce can mushrooms
1 bay leaf, crumbled
1 teaspoon Worcestershire sauce

1 8-ounce package noodles
1 cup milk
1 teaspoon salt
¼ teaspoon black pepper
½ cup grated cheddar cheese
1 cup seasoned croutons

In a skillet, brown the venison cubes in 2 tablespoons of the margarine, then stir in the minced onion and cook over low heat until it is clear. Drain the mushrooms and set aside, pouring the packing juice from the mushroom can into the skillet with the meat and onions. Add the Worcestershire sauce and bay leaf, stir well, cover the pan, and simmer on low heat for 30 minutes. Prepare the noodles according to the package instructions, then drain. Stir the remaining margarine into the hot noodles until it is melted, then stir in the venison cubes, pan juices, milk, salt, and pepper. Transfer to a buttered casserole dish, then sprinkle the cheddar cheese on top. Now sprinkle the croutons on top. Bake at 325° for 1 hour. Serves 4.

Tenderloin Delight

6 tenderloin steaks, ¾ inch
   thick
   cooking oil
½ teaspoon salt
¼ teaspoon black pepper
3 tablespoons butter
3 tablespoons flour

1 cup milk
¾ cup crumbled blue cheese
3 tablespoons chopped green
   pepper
3 tablespoons chopped
   pimento
1 8-ounce package noodles

In a skillet, brown the steaks on both sides in a bit of cooking oil, sprinkle with salt and pepper, turn the heat very low and allow the steaks to continue to cook. Meanwhile, prepare the noodles according to the package instructions, then thoroughly drain. Prepare a cheese sauce by melting the butter in a saucepan, then stirring in the flour, milk, and cheese. Cook over low heat until the sauce begins to thicken. Thoroughly mix together the noodles, cheese sauce, pepper, and pimento, then spoon into a buttered casserole dish. Arrange the tenderloin steaks on top, pushing them down gently so they are barely imbedded in the noodles. Bake at 350° for 30 minutes. Serves 4 very generously.

Venison Provençale

2 pounds round steak or
   sirloin tip steak
2 tablespoons flour
2 teaspoons blended herb
   seasoning
1 teaspoon salt
½ teaspoon black pepper

½ teaspoon garlic powder
¼ teaspoon nutmeg
2 tablespoons dried onion
   flakes
3 carrots, sliced thinly
1½ cups beef broth or bouillon
2 cups Minute Rice

Blend the flour, herb seasoning, salt, pepper, garlic powder, and nutmeg, then pound this into both sides of the steak. Cut the steak into cubes, then thoroughly brown them in a skillet with a bit of oil or fat. Add the onion flakes, carrots, and beef broth. Turn the heat low, cover the pan, and slowly simmer for 1 hour. Prepare the rice according to the package instructions, transfer to a hot platter, then ladle the venison and sauce over the top. Serves 4. (As a slight variation of this dish, substitute ½ cup dry red wine for ½ cup of the beef broth, and serve over noodles.)

Venison Casserole Melissa

2	pounds venison, cubed	1	tablespoon Hungarian paprika
¼	cup flour		
1	teaspoon salt	½	cup water
½	teaspoon black pepper cooking oil or fat	1	tablespoon tomato paste
1	onion, chopped	1	cup sour cream
1	teaspoon garlic powder	1	8-ounce package noodles seasoned croutons
1½	cups dry red wine		

Blend the flour, salt and pepper, dredge the venison cubes, then brown in a skillet with a bit of oil. Stir in the onion, garlic, paprika, wine and water, turn the heat low, cover the pan and simmer slowly for 1 hour. Stir in the tomato paste, add just a little hot water if the casserole seems too thick, cover and simmer slowly another hour. Prepare the noodles according to the package instructions, then drain. Stir the sour cream into the casserole sauce in the skillet, cover and let bubble for 5 minutes. Lay a bed of noodles on a hot platter, ladle the casserole sauce over the top, sprinkle with a generous amount of croutons and serve. Serves 4.

Quick Meat Pie

3 cups venison stew   pastry crust

This recipe is perfect for making use of leftover stew, and considering the wide number of stew recipes to choose from you can prepare an equal number of Quick Meat Pie variations. Begin by placing your stew in a saucepan and simmering it uncovered until it becomes very thick, stirring in just a pinch of flour now and then to speed things up. Meanwhile, prepare the pie crust recipe below.

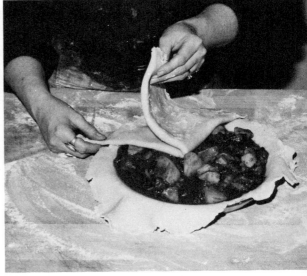

1. After mixing and rolling out the pie crust, lay it in a pie plate and sprinkle it with breadcrumbs. Then ladle your stew into the pie plate.

2. Drape pie crust over top of stew. Note how the crust, after being rolled out flat, is folded into quarters, laid on top of the pie filling, then unfolded. This evenly distributes the crust and prevents it from tearing.

3. *With the top pie crust in place, make flutes around the edge of the pie plate by using your fingers to pinch together the edges of the top and bottom crusts.*

4. *A perfect meat pie, ready for the table.*

Burgundy Pie Supreme

1 pound venison, cut into
  cubes
1 cup Burgundy
3 tablespoons butter
1 large onion, minced
2 cups hot water
1 teaspoon salt

½ teaspoon black pepper
2 carrots, sliced
1 large potato, diced
2 stalks celery, diced
2 tablespoons flour
1 egg yolk
  Easy Meat Pie Crust

Place the cubed venison in a bowl, pour the Burgundy over the top, and marinate in your refrigerator for 4 hours, then drain the meat. In a skillet, melt the butter, add the onion and venison cubes, and brown while continually stirring. Now stir in the Burgundy marinade, hot water, salt, and pepper. Cover the skillet, reduce the heat to low and simmer for 1 hour or until the meat is tender. Now stir in the carrots, potato, and celery, cover the skillet and simmer another 30 minutes. Blend the flour into ½ cup hot water, then stir this into the skillet, turn the heat up slightly and continue to stir until the mixture thickens. Pour the meat, vegetables, and sauce into a deep pie plate or casserole dish. Then cover with Easy Meat Pie Crust, pinching and "fluting" it around the edges. Make six or eight small knife slits in the pie crust. In a bowl, blend the egg yolk with 1 tablespoon of water, then brush over the top of the pie crust. Bake at 350° for 30 minutes or until the crust is nicely browned. Serves 4.

Easy Meat Pie Crust

1⅓ cups flour
½ teaspoon salt

½ cup shortening
3–4 tablespoons cold water

Blend the flour and salt in a bowl, then cut in the shortening thoroughly with a fork. Sprinkle in the water, 1 tablespoon at a time until the dough is moistened and there is no flour clinging to the inside of the bowl. Gather the dough into a ball and then shape into a flattened "round" on a floured work surface. Dust a rolling pin with flour and begin rolling the dough until it is as round as possible and just slightly larger in diameter than your pie plate. Now gently fold the dough into quarters.

Lightly butter the inside of your pie plate, then spoon in the venison stew and spread it around so it is equally distributed. Lay the pie crust on top of the stew and gently unfold it so the four quarters now form a round that entirely covers the pie plate. Pinch the edges of the crust around the diameter of the plate. With a knife, make numerous slits in the top of the crust. Bake in a 425° oven for 15 minutes or until the crust just begins to brown. Now turn the oven temperature down to 350° and bake 15 minutes longer. Serves 4.

Occasionally you may like to make a meat pie with a double crust—that is, one on the bottom and one on top as with a conventional berry or fruit pie. In this case, simply make a double quantity of Easy Meat Pie Crust, divide it in half and after rolling it out lay the first half in the bottom of your pie plate. Sprinkle on top of this ¼ cup of dry breadcrumbs, which will prevent the stew or other meat pie ingredients from making the bottom crust soggy. Then proceed as usual in laying the second pie crust dough on top and pinching together around the edges.

Deerburger Pie

1 pound deerburger	1 medium can cut green beans
1 onion, chopped	1 medium can condensed
¾ teaspoon salt	tomato soup
¼ teaspoon black pepper	1 tube biscuits

In a skillet, lightly brown the deerburger in a bit of fat or oil, then stir in the onion and continue to cook until it is clear. Now stir in the salt, pepper, beans, and soup. Pour the mixture into a greased casserole dish. Place in a 350° oven and begin baking for about 30 minutes. When the casserole begins to bubble, cover the top of it with the biscuits, turn the oven temperature up to 375° and continue baking another 15–20 minutes or until the biscuits are done. Serves 4.

Fancy Venison Pie

2   cups venison, cubed
      cooking oil
1   medium can condensed
      tomato soup
¾   cup water
2   tablespoons flour
1   teaspoon salt
¼   teaspoon rosemary

¼   teaspoon black pepper
1   teaspoon garlic powder
1   onion, chopped
2   potatoes, cubed
2   carrots, cubed
      Easy Meat Pie Crust
½   cup shredded cheddar
      cheese

In a skillet, brown the venison cubes in the cooking oil, then pour off the grease. In a large bowl, blend the soup, water, flour, salt, rosemary, pepper, and garlic. Then blend in the onion, potatoes, carrots, and venison cubes. Pour into a deep casserole dish. Now prepare your Easy Meat Pie Crust, but before sprinkling in the water in the usual way work the cheddar cheese into the dough. After rolling out the pie crust, lay it on top of the meat filling in the casserole dish and carefully press it around the edges. Bake for 20 minutes at 400°, then turn the oven down to 350° and bake 20 minutes longer, being careful not to allow the crust to burn. Serves 4.

Cedar Creek Venison Pie

2   cups venison, cubed
      cooking oil
3   tablespoons butter
3   tablespoons flour
1   teaspoon salt
½   teaspoon black pepper
¼   teaspoon thyme
¼   teaspoon marjoram

1   cup beef broth
½   cup cream
1   small onion, chopped
1   stalk celery, chopped
1   package frozen peas and
      carrots
1   potato, diced
      pie crust or breadcrumbs

In a skillet, brown the venison cubes in the cooking oil, then pour the oil off. Add the butter to the skillet and when it is melted, stir in the flour, salt, pepper, thyme, and marjoram. Continue to cook over low heat for 5 minutes. Now stir in the beef broth and cream, raise the heat just a bit and continue to cook until the mixture bubbles. Now stir in the vegetables until the mixture comes to a bubble again. Pour the mixture into a casserole dish and cover the top with Easy Meat Pie Crust, a thick layer of breadcrumbs, or seasoned croutons. Bake at 400° for 20 minutes, then turn the heat down to 350° and bake another 20 minutes, being careful not to allow the pie crust or other topping to burn. Serves 4 generously.

Steak and Mushroom Pie

1	pound round or sirloin tip steak	4	tablespoons flour
6	tablespoons cooking oil	2	tablespoons sherry
4	tablespoons butter	1	tube biscuits
1	pound fresh mushrooms, sliced		

Cut the steak meat into chunks. In a skillet, add the cooking oil and 2 tablespoons of the butter. Then brown the steak. Now, turn the heat down low and sauté the mushrooms in the same pan. Transfer the meat and mushrooms to a pie plate. To the drippings in the skillet, add the remaining butter and stir in the flour. Then stir in just a bit of water, turn the heat up and continue to stir until a smooth gravy is created. Now stir in the sherry. Pour this gravy over the meat and mushrooms, then begin baking at 400° for 45 minutes. Fifteen minutes before the pie is finished, lay the biscuits on top and continue baking until browned. Serves 4.

It's difficult to decide whether Hunter's Favorite Pie is technically a meat pie or a casserole. Just call it delicious.

Hunter's Favorite Pie

2 pounds venison, cubed
2 tablespoons butter
2 onions, diced
1 teaspoon garlic powder
1 large can tomatoes
1 tablespoon paprika
¼ teaspoon red cayenne pepper

1 bay leaf, crumbled
¼ teaspoon thyme
1 cup beer
3 carrots, sliced thinly
1 package frozen peas
1 tube biscuits

In a skillet, brown the venison in the butter. Then stir in the onions, garlic, tomatoes, seasonings, and beer. Cover the pan and simmer slowly for 1 hour. Stir in the carrots and peas, cover, and simmer 15 minutes longer. Transfer the mixture to a deep pie plate or casserole dish and arrange biscuits on top. Now bake at 425° for 15 minutes or until biscuits are nicely browned. Serves 4.

CHAPTER 19

Venison Liver, Heart, and Other Variety Meats

SOME PEOPLE dislike liver and heart; others regard them as fare beyond compare. Still others detest the flavor of liver or heart from beef steers and calves but find those taken from deer and other big-game animals quite palatable.

Often, I think, the animosity harbored by many people toward liver and heart is simply an unfavorable—and predictable—reaction to the way the meat was handled before it was cooked, and indeed, the *way* it was cooked. Hopefully, I can remedy both problems by describing proper care procedures, desirable cooking methods, and recipes that do these meats justice.

For those who nevertheless continue to object to the flavors of liver and heart, I suggest a final attempt at reconciliation by cutting the meat into small cubes and adding it to soups and stews. This practice will somewhat camouflage the flavors of liver and heart and in fact make them downright tasty. And in these days of spiraling inflation, this sure beats allowing such a large quantity of edible meat to go entirely to waste by leaving it in the field as crowbait.

Still there are those who, no matter what the recipe or method of cooking, simply will not allow their forks to touch liver or heart. Their opinions should be respected, yet such beliefs are, at best, flimsy excuses for wasting these meats. To these hunters I say, take the time to remove the liver and heart

300

from the deer during field-dressing operations and bring them out of the woods. Likely as not there are partners in camp who would like to have them, and if not then perhaps neighbors back home.

Liver Care and Recipes

Liver is the world's single richest source of iron for the diet, but it is a very fragile and highly perishable foodstuff. It must be speedily removed from the deer carcass and then just as quickly cleaned and cooled. Otherwise, it will spoil in a matter of hours.

The reader may recall from an earlier chapter my strong advice about returning to camp and immediately cutting the liver into several large chunks and soaking them in a bath of cold saltwater. This has the effect of rapidly chilling the meat while simultaneously drawing out any remaining blood and fluids. The liver should then be refrigerated and, ideally, eaten within one or two days since fresh liver tastes much better than that which has been stored longer.

You're entirely right if you've inferred from this that freezing liver results in a less than superb dining experience at some later time. This isn't to say that liver cannot be frozen. It can indeed, but several things must be tended to. First, the liver should be sliced into pieces no more than ½ inch thick— never should liver be frozen whole or in large pieces—and each slice should be subjected to repeated saltwater baths until such time as the water remains clear. Then the liver should be double-wrapped as explained in Chapter 13. Unlike other venison cuts, liver has a very limited lifespan in a freezer and should therefore be consumed within one to two months. Finally, while fresh liver can be fried or broiled as-is, liver that has been frozen and then defrosted should probably be doctored up a bit with certain recipe ingredients if the dining adventure is to be eventful.

One other thing. With the exception of those specific recipes calling for some type of moist-heat cooking method—braising, casseroles, stews, and the like—liver should never be overcooked. When panfrying, sautéing, or broiling liver, do not let the meat progress beyond "medium" in its doneness or it will become so tough and flavorless everyone will politely find an excuse for leaving the table. When tested with a knife, liver that is ready to eat will be brown on the outside, perhaps a bit crispy around the edges, but distinctly pink on the inside with juices flowing freely. *Depending upon the thickness of the individual liver slices being prepared, this often means as little as one minute of cooking time on each side.*

Also, of course, like all venison, liver is at its best when piping hot and served on a hot platter to help retain its temperature.

Liver and Onions

2 pounds liver	butter
4 onions	cooking oil
flour	

Slice the liver into thin slabs. Then slice the onions and sauté them in a skillet with butter until they are tender. Remove the onions from the skillet and place on a hot plate to stay warm. Now flour the liver slices. Add a bit of cooking oil to the same skillet, turn the heat to medium-high and cook the liver slices quickly until they are brown on one side. This will probably take only 1 minute. Flip the liver pieces and cook momentarily on the other side. Transfer the liver to a preheated platter, then ladle the cooked onions over the top. Serves 4.

1. To make Liver and Onions, cut the liver into thin slices. Flour the slices and set them aside.

2. Meanwhile, in a skillet, sauté the onions in butter until they are tender.

Liver with Bacon and Onions

2 pounds liver   flour
10 strips bacon   butter
4 onions

In a skillet, begin cooking the bacon. Be sure the heat is not too high or the bacon drippings will scorch the inside of the pan. While the bacon is cooking, slice the onions and sauté them in butter in a second pan. When the bacon and onions are finished, remove them to a hot plate to stay warm. Now, flour the liver slices and cook them in the pan containing the bacon drippings. Transfer the cooked liver to a preheated platter, then place the onion and bacon on top. Serves 4.

3. Transfer the onions to a plate where they will stay warm. Add a bit of cooking oil to the same skillet and fry the liver.

4. Transfer the cooked liver to a hot serving platter, spoon the onions on top, and serve. This is a traditional first-night-in-camp recipe.

Fancy Venison Liver

2 pounds liver
2 eggs, beaten
1 teaspoon Worcestershire
  sauce
1 teaspoon Lawrey's Seasoned
  Salt

1 teaspoon Lawrey's Seasoned
  Pepper
flour
crackercrumbs

Slice the liver into ¼-inch-thick slabs. In a bowl, blend the eggs with the Worcestershire sauce. On a flat work surface, blend the salt and pepper with enough flour to coat the liver. Dip each liver slice into the egg batter, then roll in the seasoned flour. Now, dip each liver slice into the egg batter again, and this time press crackercrumbs all over the liver slices. Fry quickly in either cooling oil or butter. Then transfer to a hot platter and serve. Serves 4.

Liver, Onions, and Ham

1½ pounds liver
½ pound ham
4 onions
½ teaspoon salt

½ teaspoon black pepper
½ cup flour
2 tablespoons butter
½ cup water

Cut the ham into small cubes and begin frying in a skillet with a bit of cooking oil. While the ham is cooking, cut the liver into cubes and dredge in a mixture of the flour, salt, and pepper. Add the butter to the skillet with the ham and when it is melted, stir in the liver cubes. Cook over low heat 5 minutes. Now stir in the onions and water, cover the pan, and let cook another 10 minutes or until the meat is tender. Serves 4 generously.

Baked Liver with Stuffing

1½ pounds liver   1   cup beef broth or bouillon
1   package prepared stuffing

Slice the liver very thinly, then mix the stuffing according to the package instructions. Lay small amounts of stuffing on top of each of the liver slices, roll up, and secure in place with skewers or toothpicks. Lay the stuffed liver rolls in the bottom of a buttered casserole dish, pour in the beef broth, cover, and bake for 30 to 40 minutes at 350°. Occasionally baste the meat rolls with juices from the casserole. Serves 4.

Liver with Rice and Cheese

1   pound liver   ½   pound Muenster cheese
2   cups Minute Rice, cooked   1   cup breadcrumbs
3   cups water   flour
½   pound Swiss cheese   butter

Prepare the rice according to the package instructions. Meanwhile cut the liver into cubes, dust with flour, and cook in butter until medium-rare in the center. Transfer the liver cubes to a plate where they will stay warm. In the skillet where the liver cooked, stir in the water and just a bit of flour and stir continuously over medium-high heat to make a gravy from the pan drippings. Mix together the rice, liver, and gravy, then transfer to a casserole dish and bake 10 minutes at 375°. Grate the cheese and sprinkle over the top of the liver casserole and continue baking until the cheese begins to melt. Now, sprinkle the breadcrumbs over the top and continue to bake another 5 to 7 minutes. Be careful the breadcrumbs are not allowed to burn. Serves 4.

Hunter's Liver

1 pound liver	½ teaspoon black pepper
1 cup milk	6 tablespoons butter
1 cup water	1 teaspoon parsley flakes
1 cup flour	1 teaspoon lemon juice
1 teaspoon salt	½ cup light cream

Blend the milk and water together, then soak the liver in the mixture for 1 hour. Mix the flour, salt, and pepper, dust the liver slices with the seasoned flour, then fry in the butter in a skillet. Transfer the cooked liver to a hot plate to stay warm. Add the parsley flakes and lemon juice to the pan and stir over medium-high heat until the juices begin to bubble. Now stir in the cream. When the sauce is very hot, ladle over the liver slices. Serves 4.

Savory Liver Stew

1½ pounds liver	2 potatoes, cut into chunks
bacon strips	2 carrots, cut into chunks
2 onions	2 stalks celery, cut into
1 cup dry red wine	chunks
1 cup beef broth or bouillon	1 teaspoon salt
1 bay leaf, crumbled	½ teaspoon black pepper

In a skillet, lightly brown the onion slices in butter or cooking oil, then transfer to a casserole dish. Begin frying the bacon in the same pan and when it is almost done cook the liver in the same (the liver should be cut into strips). Transfer the liver and bacon to the casserole dish, pour in the wine and beef broth, sprinkle in the bay leaf pieces, cover, and bake at 350° for 1 hour. Now add the vegetables, salt, and pepper; cover and continue baking another hour until the potatoes are tender. Remove the liver, bacon, and vegetables, placing everything on a hot platter to stay warm. Then set the casserole dish on a burner, sprinkle in just a bit of flour and stir to make a sauce. Pour the sauce over the liver and vegetables. Serves 4.

Liver with Onions and Mushrooms

1½ pounds liver
2 onions, sliced
1 cup mushroom slices
3 tablespoons butter

3 tablespoons cooking oil
flour
¼ cup vermouth

In a skillet, blend the cooking oil and butter, then sauté the onions and mushrooms. Slice the liver, dredge it with flour, then push the onions and mushrooms around the rim of the pan and begin cooking the liver in the middle. When the liver is cooked, transfer it to a hot platter where it will stay warm. Now stir the vermouth into the pan juices and stir with the onions and mushrooms until everything is piping hot. Ladle the sauce over the liver slices and serve. Serves 4.

Liver 'N Kraut

1½ pounds liver
flour
salt and pepper

cooking oil
4 cups sauerkraut

Blend a bit of salt and pepper with a modest quantity of flour, dredge the liver slices, then fry in cooking oil. Transfer the liver slices to a fresh pan, toss in the sauerkraut until everything is well mixed, cover the pan, and simmer over low heat until the kraut is hot. Drain off most of the kraut juice, then transfer the kraut and liver to a hot serving platter. Serves 4.

French Broiled Liver

1½ pounds venison liver   French salad dressing

Slice the liver very thinly, place in a glass bowl, cover with French salad dressing and allow the meat to marinate for 2 hours. Remove the liver slices from the bowl and shake to remove excess salad dressing, then arrange in a single layer on a broiling pan. Sprinkle lightly with salt and pepper if you wish, then broil in your oven for about 4 minutes per side or until the liver is lightly browned on the outside and pink in the middle. Serves 4.

German-fried Liver

1½ pounds liver   1   teaspoon pepper
2   cups white wine   1   teaspoon salt
1   onion, diced   ½   cup flour
2   teaspoons Worcestershire
     sauce

In a bowl, blend the wine, onion, and Worcestershire sauce, then soak the liver in the mixture for 1 hour. Remove the liver slices, shake off excess liquid, dredge with a mixture of the flour, salt, and pepper and fry in the usual way in butter or cooking oil. Serves 4.

Liver Parmesan

1½ pounds liver
1   cup white wine
¼   cup seasoned breadcrumbs

¼   cup grated Parmesan
     cheese

Place liver slices in a bowl, cover with the wine, and let sit for 1 hour. Remove the slices and shake off excess liquid, then dredge in a mixture of the Parmesan cheese and breadcrumbs. Next, fry in the usual way in cooking oil or butter. Serves 4.

Liver Soup Supreme

1 pound liver
3 medium cans cream of
   asparagus soup

seasoned croutons

Cut the liver into small cubes, then sauté in a skillet in melted butter. Prepare the soup according to instructions on the can. When the soup is very hot, stir in the cooked liver cubes and continue simmering 5 minutes. Ladle the soup into bowls and sprinkle seasoned croutons on top. Serves 4 generously.

Venison Heart

Unlike any other edible part of a deer's anatomy, the heart is both an organ and a muscle. And unlike the hearts of domesticated livestock, which laze around pastures and feedlots, the hearts of big-game animals are so well exercised they can be quite tough if not cooked long and slowly, preferably using a moist-heat cooking method. The one great disadvantage of preparing deer heart for a meal is that they're generally only large enough to serve two, unless you accompany the heart with a main side dish such as chef's salad or vegetable casserole, in which case you can "stretch" a single heart to serve three or four. An even better idea, next time you're sharing a camp with several partners, is to ask your pals to save their deer hearts for you, if they don't care to eat them themselves.

As with liver, a venison heart should be removed from the animal as quickly as possible, trimmed of restraining ligaments and other unwanted matter, then soaked in a bath of cold saltwater. In your freezer, venison heart will keep about one month longer than venison liver, but it is always much better when eaten fresh. Before using any recipe, be sure to remove the pericardial sac, if you haven't already done so. This is a thin, membranous pouch housing the heart organ which can be easily pulled away with your fingers.

Several of the following heart recipes, by the way, call for the use of a pressure cooker. Since pressure cookers vary in accordance with different capacities and designs, it would be wise to read your owner's manual to see if any special instructions or precautions apply to your particular model.

Tender-fried Deer Heart

1 heart	¼ teaspoon tarragon
¼ cup flour	¼ teaspoon basil leaves
½ teaspoon garlic powder	

Place the heart in a pressure cooker along with 2 cups of water and cook for 30 minutes. Remove the heart, drain, and allow to cool slightly. Then slice the heart into circles. Blend the flour and spices (sprinkling in just a bit of salt and pepper if you like), dredge the heart pieces, then fry in a skillet until brown all over and crisp around the edges. Serves 2.

1. *Core the heart to remove the inside chambers; place the whole heart in a pressure cooker with 2 cups of water and cook for 30 minutes. Then remove the heart, drain, and slice into rings.*

2. *Blend the flour and spices, then dredge the pieces of heart.*

3. *Fry the hearts slices until they are brown and crispy around the edges.*

4. *Even those who claim they do not care for heart will love this dish.*

Savory Heart

1	heart	½	teaspoon soy sauce
	water	1	small onion, minced
½	teaspoon garlic powder	1	small bay leaf, crumbled
¼	teaspoon Worcestershire sauce	¼	teaspoon sweet basil

Place the heart in a pressure cooker, add enough water to come up halfway on the heart, then add the remaining ingredients. Cook for 20 to 30 minutes. Transfer the heart to a hot serving platter, slice very thin, then ladle several tablespoons of the pan juices over the top. Serves 2.

Braised Heart

2	hearts	½	teaspoon parsley flakes
8	slices bacon	6	tablespoons sour cream
1	stalk celery, chopped	1	teaspoon salt
1	carrot, chopped	½	teaspoon pepper
1	onion, chopped		

Cut the bacon into small squares, then begin frying them in a skillet. Add the celery, carrot, onion, and parsley and sauté over low heat. When the vegetables are lightly browned, add the heart slices. When the heart begins to brown, sprinkle with salt and pepper, add 2 cups water, cover the pan, and cook slowly on low heat until the heart is tender. Meanwhile, prepare your choice of noodles, rice, dumplings, or mashed potatoes. Stir the sour cream into the skillet with the vegetables and heart and turn the heat to medium-high until everything is bubbling briskly. Then ladle the contents of the skillet over your rice or noodles. Serves 4.

Joe Brunneti's Liver and Heart

1 pound venison liver
1 heart
2 eggs, beaten
1 cup flour

1 tablespoon garlic powder
½ teaspoon sweet basil
½ teaspoon sage

Slice the liver and heart into ⅜-inch-thick strips. In a bowl, blend the flour, garlic powder, and basil. Dip the strips of venison in the beaten egg, dredge with the flour-seasoning mix, then place in a skillet and fry with a bit of cooking oil until the liver and heart is barely pink inside. During the final 5 minutes of cooking, sprinkle the sage on top of the meat. Serves 4 generously.

Delicious Heart Sandwiches

1 heart
2 bay leaves, crumbled
1 small onion, diced

salt and pepper
water

Place the heart in a saucepan, cover with water, then add the bay leaves, onion, and salt and pepper. Bring to a boil, then reduce the heat, cover the pan, and slowly simmer for 3 hours. Remove the heart, drain, then set on a plate in your refrigerator overnight. The following day, slice the heart very thin and make sandwiches with whole wheat bread or rye bread, spreading on just a touch of spicy mustard, mayonnaise, or horseradish. Serves 3.

Heart Casserole with Rice

1 heart
   water
2 tablespoons dehydrated
   vegetable flakes
1 teaspoon salt

½ teaspoon black pepper
½ teaspoon poultry seasoning
1 cup Minute Rice

Place the deer heart in a pressure cooker, add enough water to come up halfway on the side of the heart, and cook 30 minutes. Transfer the heart to a hot plate where it will stay warm. Begin preparing the rice according to the instructions on the package. Meanwhile, to the juices still in the pressure cooker, stir in the vegetable flakes and seasonings, turn the heat to medium-high and stir continuously, adding just a pinch or two of flour to thicken the juice into a gravy. On a preheated platter, lay a bed of rice, slice the heart and lay it on the rice, then pour the gravy over the top. Serves 2.

Stuffed Deer Heart #1

1   heart
1½ cups prepared stuffing mix

bacon strips

Use a knife to "core" the heart, removing the inner walls that form the chambers. Prepare the stuffing according to the package directions, then pack it into the heart. Wrap the heart with the bacon strips, holding them in place with toothpicks. Place in a baking dish and pour about ½ inch of water in the bottom. Bake at 325° for 2½ hours. Serves 2.

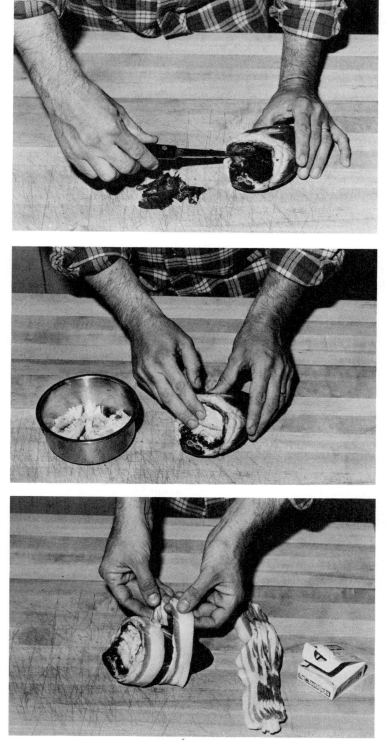

1. *To make Stuffed Deer Heart, first core the heart to remove the inside chambers.*

2. *Pack the heart with a prepared stuffing mix of your own choice.*

3. *Wrap the heart with bacon strips secured with toothpicks, then bake the heart in a dish containing a bit of water in the bottom. Deer hearts are rather small and each will serve two.*

Stuffed Deer Heart #2

1 heart
1½ cups prepared stuffing mix
¼ teaspoon thyme
¼ teaspoon poultry seasoning
¼ teaspoon black pepper

4 tablespoons tomato sauce
1 cup beef bouillon
1 bay leaf, crumbled
½ teaspoon garlic powder

Core the inside of the heart, removing the walls forming the chambers, to create a large pocket. Prepare the stuffing mix according to the package instructions. Then knead into the stuffing the thyme, poultry seasoning, and pepper. Pack the cavity of the heart with the stuffing. Place the heart in a deep saucepan. Blend the tomato sauce with the beef bouillon, then stir in the crumbled bay leaf and garlic. Pour this into the saucepan with the heart, cover, and simmer over low heat for 2 to 3 hours or until the heart is tender. Serves 2.

Heart O'Deer

1 heart
1 cup dry red wine
2 tablespoons vinegar
1 small onion, diced

1 teaspoon wet mustard
1 bay leaf
1 teaspoon salt
½ teaspoon black pepper

Mix all the ingredients together, then soak slices of the heart in the marinade for 3 hours. Remove the heart slices, shake to eliminate excess marinade, then dredge in flour and fry in a skillet in butter for 5 minutes per side. Serves 2.

Hearty Heart

1	heart	1½	cups water
1	envelope dry beef vegetable		flour
	soup		salt and pepper

Slice the heart ½ inch thick, dredge with flour, then brown in a skillet containing butter, cooking oil, or bacon drippings. Sprinkle on just a touch of salt and pepper if you like. Now sprinkle on top of the heart slices the dry soup mix. Add the water to the skillet, cover, and simmer over very low heat until the heart is tender. Transfer the heart slices to a hot serving platter, then ladle the soup over the top. Or, if you like, you can prepare a bed of rice or wide noodles, lay the cooked heart slices on top, then ladle the soup over everything. Serves 2.

Other Variety Meats

Venison liver and heart are known as *variety meats,* but there are several others as well that are sure to add a unique flair to your dining adventures. Tongue, for example, despite its rather unappetizing appearance, is looked upon by some as gourmet fare. So are venison kidneys. And then there are venison ribs, which can be cooked almost the same as you would spareribs or beef shortribs.

Tongue Sandwiches

1   deer tongue
2   bay leaves, crumbled
½   teaspoon garlic powder

¼   teaspoon sweet basil
1   teaspoon salt
½   teaspoon black pepper

Use a stiff-bristled brush to scrub the outside of the tongue thoroughly with cold water. Place in a pressure cooker with one or two cups water, stir in the seasonings, and cook for 30 minutes. When the tongue is tender, use tongs to remove it from the hot liquid, and quickly plunge it into a pan of very cold water. This will allow you to remove easily with your fingers the tongue's rough-textured outer sheath. Refrigerate the tongue overnight. The following day, slice the meat very thin and make sandwiches with rye bread, spreading on just a bit of spicy mustard or horseradish if you like. Superb! Serves 2.

Spicy Hot Tongue

1   deer tongue
1   lemon, sliced
1   teaspoon mixed pickling
      spices

2   teaspoons salt
½   teaspoon black pepper

After cleaning the tongue, place it in a saucepan and barely cover it with water. Add the seasonings, cover the pan and simmer over low heat until the tongue is tender (2–3 hours). Slice thin and serve while hot, or refrigerate and make sandwiches the next day. Serves 2.

Sautéed Kidneys

4 deer kidneys
¼ cup butter
1 small onion, minced
½ teaspoon salt

¼ teaspoon black pepper
¼ teaspoon marjoram
2 tablespoons lemon juice

Slice each kidney in half lengthwise, then use a knife to cut out the inner membrane. Soak the kidney halves in salted water for 1 hour. Now cut the kidneys into thin slices and sauté in the butter with the onion. When the kidneys begin to lightly brown, stir in the remaining ingredients and continue to simmer several minutes longer. Transfer the kidneys to a hot plate where they will stay warm and add just a bit of water and a pinch or two of flour to the pan drippings, stirring continually to make a light gravy. Place the kidney slices back in the pan. Then prepare a bed of rice or noodles, and pour the sautéed kidneys and sauce over the top. Serves 2.

Kidney Supreme

4 deer kidneys
¼ cup butter
1 onion, chopped
1 cup mushroom slices
2 tablespoons sherry or dry
   red wine

1 teaspoon salt
¼ teaspoon black pepper
¾ cup heavy cream
1 tablespoon arrowroot

Slice the kidneys in half lengthwise and with a knife remove the inner membrane and any fat. Soak the kidneys several hours in a bath of cold saltwater. Now cut the kidneys into small cubes. In a skillet, sauté the kidneys in the butter along with the onion and mushrooms. Then stir in the wine, salt, and pepper. Cover the pan and continue cooking over low heat for 30 minutes. Meanwhile, blend the arrowroot with the cream. When the kidney pieces are tender, stir the cream into the pan and continue to cook until a thick sauce is created. Ladle over a bed of noodles or rice. Serves 2.

Easy Venison Ribs

2 rib plates   1 bottle Open Pit Barbecue
                                              Sauce

Place the ribs in a roasting pan, cover with the barbecue sauce, and bake at 325° for 1½ hours. Serves 4.

When taken from large deer, venison ribs are quite tasty. In summer, they can be split into two and charcoal broiled.

Broiled Ribs

2   rib plates
1   tablespoon cooking oil
1   tablespoon Worcestershire
       sauce

2   tablespoons soy sauce
½   teaspoon garlic powder

The ribs can be broiled whole, or you may wish to slice them into two-rib sections. Place on a broiler pan and adjust your oven rack so the ribs will be no closer than 6 inches from the heat source. Begin broiling the ribs and baste frequently with a sauce made by blending the remaining ingredients. Serves 4.

In winter, whole rib plates baked very slowly, especially in some type of sauce, are delectable.

CHAPTER 20

Cooking Your Venison Outdoors

T HERE ARE only a few things I enjoy more than reaching into my freezer for a package of venison with a favorite recipe in mind. One is cooking venison while enjoying the companionship of close friends in an old hunting camp. And another is cooking venison outdoors, over a bed of glowing embers on a sultry summer evening, trying to contain my eagerness for yet another rapidly approaching deer season.

There is no mystery to cooking venison over a campstove, in a cabin in the outback, or over coals. In fact, dozens of the recipes already described can easily be prepared away from the comfort and convenience of your home kitchen. All that's necessary is a bit of planning so that you have the required ingredients and cooking equipment. I will say, however, that some of the more complicated recipes are best reserved for home use. When you're away from home and faced with rather primitive cooking facilities, and when you've just spent a long day hiking or hunting or engaged in some other outdoor activity, the last thing you want to come face to face with is an evening meal that entails 15 different ingredients and half a dozen mixing or cooking steps.

If you've read between the lines, you've probably already guessed that one-pot meals are perfectly tailored to outdoor cooking. This means soups, stews, easy casseroles, and pot roasts. It also means using a cast-iron Dutch oven whenever possible.

It's the nature of cast iron to take heat slowly, hold it for long periods, and distribute it evenly. This makes for relatively failsafe cooking because, after all, campstoves and campfires don't have temperature dials. Moreover, you can't plan your meals by the clock since there is no telling how long it may take to drag a deer back to camp or hike cross-country from some distant hunting location. In all of these cases, it's a smug feeling indeed to know that even though no one else is back in camp, dinner is cooked and hot and waiting, and even if you're an hour or two late nothing will burn.

If the weather is favorable, I often use a Dutch oven to prepare delicious pot roasts with all the trimmings and the meal is slow-simmered to perfection *below ground*. It's a simple trick, and usually one of the first mastered by those who have recently acquired a Dutch oven. Here's how it's done.

An eight-quart Dutch oven is perfect for a camp of four to six hunters, and you'll need a roast that weighs in the vicinity of four or five pounds. You can use a rump roast if you like, but since this is a moist-heat cooking method, a shoulder roast or even a neck roast will come out sinfully tender.

The first order of business is to use a shovel to dig a hole in the ground. It should be slightly larger in diameter than the size of your Dutch oven, and about two feet deep. Meanwhile, a robust fire of hardwoods should be

One of the best utensils for outdoor cooking is a failsafe Dutch oven. Get the authentic kind made of heavy cast iron with a flange around the lid for holding coals.

burning down to coals. Or, if it's more convenient, use charcoal. If my hunting partners and I are cooking all of our meals over an open fire, we usually prepare our evening meal right after breakfast, using whatever coals happen to be left over from the morning cooking.

Liberally brush the inside of your Dutch oven with grease, lard, cooking oil, or bacon drippings. Now set the Dutch oven on your coals and when the grease becomes hot, sear the roast on all sides. Now lay in the Dutch oven, on top of the roast and around the sides, whatever vegetables you happen to have on hand. Generally, I throw in large chunks of potatoes, carrots, several quartered onions, and upon occasion perhaps turnips, celery, or peppers. Now add about one-half cup water and sprinkle lightly with seasonings of your choice such as salt, pepper, or just a touch of thyme, marjoram, basil . . . whatever you have.

Place the lid on your Dutch oven and momentarily set it beside the hole you've dug in the ground. Next, shovel about one-third of your coals into the bottom of the pit. Using the wire bail on your Dutch oven, lower it into the pit so it is sitting directly on top of the glowing embers. Shovel the

To make a below-ground pot roast that will slowly simmer to perfection all day, first sear the roast on all sides, then add vegetables and seasonings.

remaining two-thirds of the coals on top of the Dutch oven's lid. Finally, shovel on top of the coals a layer of dirt. Careful, now. Not too much dirt. You don't want to smother the coals, just insulate them.

That's all! Nothing will overcook or burn. The pot roast and vegetables will v-e-r-y slowly cook to perfection over many, many hours. Eventually, of course, the coals will die out, but because everything is below ground and insulated, the pot roast dinner will remain piping hot for a long while. Exactly how long is uncertain and depends upon the type of coals you've generated and the quantity you've used.

Replace the lid and lower the Dutch oven into a pit on top of a small quantity of glowing coals. Then shovel more coals on top of the lid and cover with dirt.

After retrieving your dinner from the pit, clean off the top of the oven. You and your partners can straggle in hours late and still be assured of a piping-hot, sumptuous meal.

Usually, my hunting crew leaves camp early in the morning and returns around five or six o'clock in the evening. But sometimes we don't wander in until much later and our dinner is still hot. All that's necessary is to carefully scrape away the insulating layer of soil on top of the oven, grab the oven's wire bail and lift it out. A small whiskbroom is invaluable for cleaning soot and ashes from the top of the oven, and shortly after that we savor a dining event that is really fit for only dukes and earls.

Naturally, you can prepare a wide variety of meals in your Dutch oven. Use any one of the soup or stew recipes in Chapter 17, or try a simple casserole. You can even make a meat pie by simply removing the Dutch oven's lid, laying biscuit dough on top of your stew, covering with the lid again, and heaping fresh coals on top for several minutes.

As mentioned before, below-ground Dutch-oven cooking is ideal when everyone in camp plans to leave to go hunting. However, if you have a camp cook—someone who has already filled his tag and stays behind to chop wood and tend to other chores—it's much easier to merely set the Dutch oven on top of a campstove burner, at the edge of your fire pit, or on the hearth of your cabin fireplace.

From time to time, you may wish to undertake other types of outdoor cooking, or camp cooking, as well. Conventional cookware such as skillets, pots and pans can be used for pan-broiling, panfrying, sautéing, braising, or whatever. From time to time I even use heavy-duty aluminum foil, laying meat and vegetables in the center, wrapping it tightly, then burying the works in coals. Then too, cooking directly over coals is a splendid way of preparing tender cuts of venison such as tenderloin steaks, sirloin tip steaks, burgers, and even fresh liver. All of these efforts can not only be carried out in some wilderness camp but right over a conventional grill on your backyard patio.

In all cases, just remember a few essential bits of advice. First, when using a dry-heat cooking method, such as panfrying or broiling, use only your tenderest cuts of venison and never cook them beyond "medium." If it's a less tender cut, use a moist-heat cooking method such as braising. And no matter what cut is to be prepared, your venison should always be served on a very hot platter so that the meat will remain hot during the course of the meal.

Although dozens of the recipes already presented in this book can be prepared outdoors or in deer camp with a minimum of effort, the following are additional recipes specifically designed for outdoor or camp cooking.

Venison Sizzle Steaks

4 large tenderloin or sirloin
   tip steaks
4 eggs
½ teaspoon onion salt

½ teaspoon garlic powder
½ teaspoon black pepper
¼ cup butter

In a skillet, melt the butter over medium-high heat. In a bowl, thoroughly blend the eggs, onion salt, garlic powder, and black pepper. When the butter is hot, dip each steak in the batter, shake off any excess and lay the steaks in the pan. Begin frying the steaks over high heat but do not allow the butter to burn; if it begins to smoke slightly, turn down the burner or move the skillet away from the fire. With tongs, begin turning the steaks constantly. As soon as they are an even brown color on both sides, use your tongs to lift the steaks out and dip them in the egg batter again before placing them back in the pan for the remainder of the cooking. The steaks are ready to serve when they are medium-rare in the center. Serves 4.

Breaded Steaks

4 large tenderloin or sirloin
   tip steaks
1 teaspoon salt
½ teaspoon pepper

2 eggs, beaten
2 cups breadcrumbs
   cooking oil

Place the steaks in a skillet along with 1 cup water and slowly simmer them, covered, for ½ hour. Pour off the water, use paper towels to pat the steaks dry, then swab out the pan so it is clean. In a bowl, blend the salt, pepper, and eggs. Add cooking oil to the pan and turn the heat to medium-high. Dip the steaks in the egg batter and then coat them with breadcrumbs, pressing them into the meat as much as possible. Now fry the steaks in the pan until the breadcrumbs are crispy. Serves 4.

Venison Ragout

3	pounds venison shoulder meat	1	medium can tomato soup
6	tablespoons cooking oil	1½	quarts water
3	onions, chopped	2	teaspoons bourbon
3	teaspoons garlic powder	¼	cup beer
½	pound bacon, chopped	1	teaspoon salt
		1	large can mushrooms

Cut the meat into cubes, then brown the meat in a skillet containing the cooking oil, onions, garlic, and bacon. Add all the other ingredients except the mushrooms, cover, and simmer for 50 minutes. Stir in the mushrooms and simmer 10 minutes longer. This can be served over noodles, biscuits, rice, potatoes, or whatever you have on hand—even thick slices of homemade bread. Serves 4–6.

Braised Venison Steaks

4	tenderloin or sirloin tip steaks	½	teaspoon pepper
½	cup flour	½	cup water
1	teaspoon salt	1	cup red wine
		1	small can mushrooms

Dust the steaks with a mixture of the flour, salt, and pepper, then brown in a skillet containing cooking oil, fat, or bacon drippings. Add the water, cover the pan, and simmer until the steaks are tender. Now pour the wine over the steaks and continue to simmer until the wine is almost cooked away. Remove the steaks and place on a plate where they will stay hot. Make a gravy in the pan by adding just a bit of water and a pinch of flour to the drippings and stirring continually over high heat. Several minutes before the gravy is ready, stir in the mushrooms. Serves 4.

Kay Richey's Green Pepper Steak

2 pounds round steak
  salt and pepper
  cooking oil
2 cups beef broth bouillon
1 cup water
  cornstarch

1 green pepper
1 onion
1 large can mushrooms

Slice the round steak into thin strips, then season with salt and pepper and brown in a skillet containing a bit of cooking oil. Add the beef broth and water, cover, and simmer for 30 minutes until the meat is tender. Slice the pepper and onion and add them to the pan with the mushrooms and simmer 10 minutes longer. Thicken the gravy with cornstarch. Serve over rice, noodles, biscuits, or whatever you have. Serves 4.

Buttered Steaks

4 tenderloin or sirloin tip
   steaks

cooking oil
butter

Swab the inside of a skillet with just a tiny bit of cooking oil and then pan-broil your steaks over low heat at the edge of your cooking fire. When the steaks are almost done, paint them liberally with melted butter, then use tongs to transfer them to the grill directly over hot coals and sear them on both sides. This creates a very subtle, burned-fat flavor you otherwise get only when charcoaling beefsteaks. As usual, be careful you do not allow the venison steaks to cook beyond medium-rare or medium. Serves 4.

Mel Marshall's Venison Roll-ups

2	pounds round steak	½	teaspoon parsley flakes
2	cups breadcrumbs	1	teaspoon salt
1	stick margarine	½	teaspoon black pepper
3	cups mushrooms		meat tenderizer
1	onion, chopped		cooking oil
1	teaspoon garlic powder		

The round steak should be sliced thin. Then sprinkle the pieces with meat tenderizer and pierce deeply with a fork. Now use a meat hammer (in camp, a pop bottle works fine) to pound the meat out flat. Remove the stems from

1. *Sprinkle tenderizer on the meat and pierce it deeply into the steaks. Then pound the steaks thin with a meat mallet.*

2. *Remove the caps from the mushrooms and dice the stems, then chop the onions.*

the mushrooms and chop them along with the onion. Make a stuffing by kneading with your hands the breadcrumbs, margarine, mushroom stems, onion, seasonings, and as much water to make the stuffing moist. Lay a glob of stuffing in the center of each piece of round steak and roll up, securing each with toothpicks to hold everything together. In a large skillet or oval pan, sear the venison roll-ups in hot cooking oil until they are browned on all sides. Now reduce the heat by turning down the campstove burner or raking away some of the coals and continue to cook very slowly until the venison is tender. Meanwhile, in a separate pan, gently sauté the mushroom caps. Transfer the meat rolls to a hot plate, and surround them with the mushrooms. Serves 4.

3. Prepare the stuffing mix, place several spoonfuls onto steaks, roll them up, and secure with toothpicks.

4. Sear the roll-ups in a large skillet, rake some of the coals away and continue cooking on low heat until the meat is tender. In a separate pan, sauté mushroom caps and serve as a side dish.

Venison Shish Kabob

3 pounds tenderloin or sirloin
   tip steak
4 large onions, quartered
4 large tomatoes, quartered
4 green peppers, quartered

4 apples, quartered
Italian salad dressing
white wine
garlic powder

This is a fantastic, all-in-one meal that's perfectly suited to backyard or camp use, and if you've got kids they'll have great fun doing most of the work. In a deep pan, blend a bottle of white wine and a bottle of Italian salad dressing, then stir in just a little garlic powder. Meanwhile, on shish kabob skewers (or peeled, green willow branches) begin impaling chunks of venison, alternating the meat with the vegetables and fruit. As each skewer is finished, lay it in the pan to slowly marinate in the wine mixture, turning them frequently. The marinating time should be at least 45 minutes. Then carefully lay the kabobs on a grill over a bed of glowing coals. Every 10 minutes, rotate the skewers one-fourth turn, and use a brush to frequently baste the kabobs with more marinade from the pan. Total cooking time should be 45 minutes to 1 hour. Serves 4–6 very generously.

Savory Chunks O'Venison

1½ pounds venison round
   steak or sirloin-tip
1 cup buttermilk
1 teaspoon Worcestershire
   sauce

1 teaspoon salt
¼ teaspoon black pepper
¼ teaspoon garlic powder
   flour
   cooking oil

Cut the venison into one-inch cubes. In a bowl, blend the buttermilk, Worcestershire sauce, salt, pepper and garlic. Add the meat chunks to the bowl and allow them to soak for 1 hour, turning them frequently. Remove the chunks, shake off excess liquid, dredge with flour, then fry in cooking oil until medium-rare inside. Serves 4.

Making Venison Shish Kabobs is nothing less than pure fun. Use tenderloin steak, cut into chunks. Alternate the venison on skewers with onions, peppers, and tomatoes, then marinate in white wine and Italian salad dressing.

Baconed Tenderloin

4 large tenderloin steaks   garlic salt
8 strips bacon

Sprinkle both sides of the steaks lightly with the garlic salt. Then wrap each steak with 2 slices of bacon. Begin frying the steaks in a skillet, turning only once, until the bacon is cooked. Serves 4.

Grilled Ribs

6 pounds venison ribs   1 cup soy sauce
1 teaspoon garlic powder   ⅓ cup Worcestershire sauce

Blend the garlic, soy sauce, and Worcestershire sauce, then frequently paint the ribs as they cook over glowing coals. I like ribs to be slightly charred on the outside, which usually means 30 to 45 minutes cooking time. Serves 4.

Barbecued Ribs

6 pounds venison ribs   1 bottle Open Pit Barbecue
                                   Sauce

Begin broiling the ribs over coals. After they have cooked 5 minutes on each side, begin lightly basting with the barbecue sauce. Continue cooking another 20 to 25 minutes. Serves 4.

Foiled Again!

2 pounds deerburger
2 onions, sliced
4 potatoes, sliced

4 carrots, cut into chunks
4 slices American cheese
  salt and pepper

Lay out four large squares of heavy-duty aluminum foil. In the center of each arrange several potato slices. On top of this, lay a large half-pound deerburger patty. Now lay a slice of cheese on top of each piece of meat, another layer of potatoes, then onion slices and carrot chunks. Sprinkle the food lightly with salt and pepper. Cup the foil and in the bottom ladle about 2 teaspoons of water. Finally, bring up the sides of the foil and pinch and fold the edges securely to hold in steam. Arrange the foil pouches on top of a bed of coals and allow them to cook for 45 minutes. Then gently turn them upside-down and allow another 15 minutes cooking time. You don't need plates because everyone can merely peel back the edges of the foil and eat right from the makeshift container. Serves 4.

Breakfast Burgers

1 pound deerburger
½ pound bacon
1 onion, minced
1 teaspoon salt
½ teaspoon black pepper

⅛ teaspoon thyme
⅛ teaspoon marjoram
1 egg
1 cup breadcrumbs

Cut the bacon into very small pieces. Then place all of the ingredients in a bowl with the deerburger and knead thoroughly with your hands. Now form individual patties and fry in the usual way. Serve with eggs, fried potatoes, pancakes, hot coffee, and other traditional breakfast foods. Serves 4.

Supper Burgers

2 pounds deerburger
¼ cup breadcrumbs
1 onion, minced
2 teaspoons salt
¼ teaspoon chili powder

¼ teaspoon garlic powder
½ teaspoon black pepper
½ cup water
1 egg, beaten

In a bowl, thoroughly knead all of the ingredients together except the water. Begin frying the burgers in a skillet containing a bit of cooking oil. When the burgers are seared on both sides, turn the heat down, add the water, cover and slowly simmer for 1 hour. Serves 4.

Skillet Stew

2 pounds venison shoulder or
   round steak
   bacon drippings
1 large onion, sliced
   salt and pepper
3 cups tomatoes

2 potatoes, cut into chunks
1 small can evaporated milk
2 teaspoons vinegar or lemon
   juice
½ teaspoon paprika

In a skillet, brown the venison cubes in grease, then stir in the onion slices. Sprinkle lightly with salt and pepper, then turn down the heat. Add the remaining ingredients, cover, and simmer for 1½ hours. Serves 4.

Broiled Liver

1 pound deer liver
¼ cup olive oil
1 teaspoon garlic powder

2 teaspoons lemon juice
1 tablespoon butter
   salt and pepper

In a bowl, blend the olive oil, garlic, lemon juice, and butter. Now begin broiling slices of liver on a grill over coals. Frequently baste with the mixture in the bowl. Cook the liver only until it is pink inside, then salt and pepper to taste. Serves 4.

Hank Brower's Stew

2 pounds venison brisket,
   shoulder or neck meat
½ pound venison liver, cubed
1 large onion, sliced
4 tablespoons butter

2 potatoes, cut into chunks
2 teaspoons salt
1 teaspoon pepper
½ teaspoon marjoram
1 can beer

In a skillet, sauté the onion slices in the butter until they are clear, then transfer the onion to your Dutch oven. In the skillet drippings, brown the venison chunks and liver and then transfer them to the oven. Next, in the skillet again, stir together the salt, pepper, marjoram, and beer. Bring to a boil, then quickly pour this over the meat and potatoes in the Dutch oven. Cover the oven with its lid and set on a bed of coals with a shovelful of coals placed on top of the lid. Bake for 1 hour. Serves 4 generously.

Burger 'N Noodles

1½ pounds deerburger
1 medium can cream of
   mushroom soup
1 medium can cream of
   potato soup

1 8-ounce package wide
   noodles

Brown the burger in a skillet containing just a bit of bacon grease, cooking oil, or butter. Pour off the grease, stir in the 2 cans of soup and simmer on low heat for 30 minutes. Meanwhile prepare the noodles according to the package instructions. Transfer the noodles to a hot platter, ladle the burger and sauce over the top, and serve. Serves 4.

Broiled Liver Kabobs

1½ pounds venison liver   16   small onions
½   pound bacon

Cut the liver into one-inch-square cubes. Then impale the liver on skewers, alternating with rolled strips of bacon and small onions. Broil over coals, turning frequently and sprinkling with salt and pepper. Serves 4.

Venison Jerky

venison round steak   Liquid Smoke, *or* garlic powder
                                 and hickory smoked salt

This is an excellent snack for trail munching. Begin by slicing the round steak into strips. Brush the strips of meat with Liquid Smoke. Or, lay the meat in a dish, sprinkling alternate layers of the meat with the seasoning, and allow to marinate overnight in your refrigerator. The following day, place the jerky strips in a small sportsman's smoker. The required smoking time will vary but usually is 6 to 8 hours. The idea is not to cook the meat but merely dehydrate it. When the jerky is done it will have a coal-black appearance on the outside, but it will be chewy and flavorful inside. Since the meat is dried, it requires no refrigeration. Store it in zip-loc plastic bags in your cupboard.

1. Slice venison into strips.

2. Brush strips of meat with Liquid Smoke or sprinkle with seasonings and marinate overnight in your refrigerator.

3. Arrange venison strips in smoker. Required smoking time is usually 6 to 8 hours.

4. Finished jerky looks coal black but is not burned, only dehydrated. It requires no refrigeration and can be stored in jars or plastic bags.

Although this is the end of this chapter, other types of venison cookery outdoors or in camp are limited only by each hunter's imagination. If you have an electric or charcoal smoke-cooker, for example, it will produce splendid venison roasts. Numerous designs are presently on the market and each manufacturer even includes a booklet with recipe hints best suited to his particular model.

Rolled rump roasts can also be cooked on a spit if your outdoor barbecue grill boasts some type of revolving rotisserie arrangement. And in any store that sells outdoor cooking and picnic supplies, you're sure to find a wide array of latching grills, enclosed broiling baskets, and other camping tools specifically designed for cooking foods over coals or open fires. In using any of these, my friends and I also like to take advantage of wild foods that may be available on certain outings. On our western hunts, for example, we commonly bring back to camp a bit of sage gathered from sagebrush flats and sprinkle it on liver or in casseroles. Or, we gather hickory nuts or black walnuts, chop the meats, and add them to stews for a new and exciting taste treat. In temperate climates, early hunting seasons are also likely to reward observant outdoorsmen with any number of wild greens that can be added to soups or served as a garnish with almost any meat dish.

Even conventional cookbooks found in any home kitchen are likely to be valuable sources of new ideas for cooking venison at home or outdoors. Such books probably won't specifically mention venison, but beef, chicken, pork, lamb, veal, hamburger, and sausage recipes can nearly always be duplicated by merely substituting an appropriate cut of venison. Just keep in mind the unique properties of venison and gear your cooking procedures and cooking times accordingly.

---- CHAPTER 21 ----

Go-Withs

ANY VENISON DISHES, such as stews, casseroles, even shish kabobs, are entire meals in their own right. But often, especially if you're going to serve tenderloin steak or juicy rump roast, you can't just plop a slab of meat onto a dinner guest's plate and say, "okay pal, there it is." You have to serve a complete, balanced meal, and this usually means two or more side dishes, or as I call them, "go-withs."

There are several essential things to keep in mind when considering various accompaniments to any venison dinner. To begin with, cooking the venison itself is almost certain to require your full attention, so you don't want overly complicated side dishes that entail so much effort that your time is entirely monopolized and you're unable to enjoy your role as chef and host.

Similarly, since your venison should be the sole attraction of the meal, you don't want it to be up-staged by some other food. Since venison already is a robust, flavorful meat with a distinct character all its own, your selection of go-withs should merely complement the meat, not compete with it.

Following are a number of delicious side dishes I often rely upon to enhance venison dinners and at the same time provide meals that are nutritionally balanced. They're all guaranteed mouth-waterers, but I'll leave it up to your individual taste preferences as to which combinations might go best with the particular venison recipe you've chosen as the order of the day.

Potato Boats

4   Idaho baking potatoes   4   tablespoons butter
½   cup grated cheddar cheese   parsley flakes

Place the potatoes in a 375° oven and bake them for about 45 minutes. Remove them and very carefully make a lengthwise slit through the top of each. Use a teaspoon to carefully remove the potato from inside so as to not damage the outer skin. Place the globs of potato in a bowl, then mash in the cheese and butter until it is almost a creamy consistency. Now use the teaspoon to pack the potato back into the skins, again being very careful not to tear the skins. Sprinkle the tops of the potatoes with a bit of parsley, then place under your broiler for several minutes or until the potato-cheese-butter mixture just begins to brown. If you like, during the last minute of cooking, sprinkle on a bit of paprika for color. Serves 4.

Savory Potato Wedges

4   potatoes   1   envelope chicken-flavored
                                  Shake and Bake

Peel the potatoes, then slice into large oval or wedge-shaped pieces. Place several at a time in a plastic bag containing Shake and Bake coating mix and shake well until the pieces are well covered. Arrange on a cookie sheet, then bake at 375° for 45 minutes. Serves 4.

Camp-fried Potatoes

4 potatoes   3 onions
                              bacon drippings

This is a simple favorite of all time. Melt about ½ cup bacon drippings in a skillet. Slice the potatoes thin, then add them to the skillet. Cover the pan and cook over medium-heat for 30 minutes, stirring frequently. When the potatoes are almost cooked through, remove the lid, turn the heat to high and brown them on all sides, turning frequently. During the last 10 minutes of cooking, add onion slices to the skillet and toss with the potatoes so they are cooked and crisp around the edges but not overdone and mushy. Serves 4. (As a slight variation of this, fry 8 slices of bacon in a separate pan and when it is almost cooked, stir the bacon in with the potatoes.)

Charlie Hause's Grilled Spuds

4 potatoes, sliced lengthwise in   butter
    half   garlic powder

With a knife, score the cut-side of the potato halves, then use your fingers to rub butter into the scoring cuts. Now sprinkle lightly with a bit of garlic powder. Wrap each potato half in aluminum foil and place on top of your outdoor cooking grill. Cook for 45 minutes, turning frequently. Serves 4. (As a slight variation, substitute garlic salt, onion salt, seasoned salt, or just a pinch of marjoram and thyme.)

Parslied New Potatoes

16 new potatoes (red or white   ½ cup butter
    skins)   parsley flakes

Wash the potatoes, then boil them very gently for 25 minutes in two cups of lightly salted water. After the allotted cooking time use a fork to test for doneness. Then pour off nearly all the water and put the pan back on the burner, uncovered, until the remaining water evaporates. Add the butter and roll the potatoes gently until they are thoroughly covered with melted butter. Transfer to a hot serving platter and sprinkle parsley flakes on top. Let each dinner guest add his own salt and pepper. Serves 4.

Cheesy Potato Casserole

4 potatoes   ¼ cup milk
½ cup sour cream   8 slices bacon
1 teaspoon salt   ¼ teaspoon garlic powder
2 tablespoons butter   ½ cup sharp cheddar cheese

Wash and peel the potatoes, cut into chunks, then boil in lightly salted water until they are almost cooked. Drain off the water, then mash thoroughly with the sour cream, salt, butter, milk, and garlic. Fry the bacon until crisp, crumble into small pieces, then stir into the potatoes. Transfer the potato mix to a buttered casserole dish, sprinkle the cheddar cheese on top, then place in a 300° oven until the cheese melts and just begins to turn brown. Serves 4.

Potato Patties

4   cups mashed potatoes
2   eggs, beaten

½ cup chopped onion
    flour or breadcrumbs

Prepare the mashed potatoes in the usual way, or use leftovers from a previous meal. Place the potatoes in a bowl and thoroughly mix in the eggs and onion. Mold into hamburger-shaped patties, then dredge with flour or breadcrumbs. Fry slowly in a skillet containing melted butter (about 5 minutes on each side). Serves 4.

Scalloped Potatoes

6   potatoes, sliced thin
3   tablespoons butter
3   cups milk
2   tablespoons flour

1   teaspoon salt
¼ teaspoon black pepper
1   medium onion, chopped

In a bowl, make a sauce by blending the butter, milk, flour, salt, and pepper. Place half of the sliced potatoes in a greased casserole dish, and cover with one-half of the sauce and chopped onion. Place the remaining potatoes on top, then pour on top the remaining sauce and onions. Cover the dish and bake at 350° for 1 hour. Remove the lid and continue baking until the top begins to brown. Serves 4.

Crunchy Potato Casserole

4 large potatoes, sliced	1½ cups grated cheddar cheese
⅓ cup butter	2 teaspoons salt
1 cup cornflake crumbs	1½ teaspoons paprika

In a large, flat, rectangular pizza pan melt the butter in a 375° oven. Meanwhile, slice the potatoes into ½-inch-thick slices. Arrange the potato slices in the bottom of the pan, then turn once so they are coated on both sides with butter. Mix the remaining ingredients in a bowl, then sprinkle over the top of the potatoes. Bake for 30 to 40 minutes. Serves 4.

Fried Rice

4 tablespoons butter	1 teaspoon salt
1 cup uncooked rice	4 cups beef broth or bouillon

In a skillet, melt the butter, then begin gently frying the rice over medium-heat until it is lightly browned. Meanwhile, heat the beef broth in a saucepan until it is steaming. Now add the broth and salt to the skillet containing the rice, stir well, reduce the heat and slowly cook until the rice is tender and all of the liquid is absorbed. Serves 4. (As a slight variation, you can use brown rice, or substitute chicken broth for the beef broth, or you can add a pinch of thyme, basil, marjoram, rosemary, or savory.)

Easy Wild Rice

1 cup wild rice
5 cups cold water

1 teaspoon salt

Wash the uncooked rice in a pan of cold water and drain. Transfer the rice to a large saucepan, add the 5 cups of water and the salt, bring to a boil, cover, reduce the heat, and simmer 30 to 40 minutes until the brown grains have begun to puff open, showing their white insides. Transfer the rice to a collander and thoroughly rinse with very hot tap water. Now place the rice back in its pan, turn the heat to low and fluff the rice with a fork a few minutes until it is dry. Serves 4.

Wild rice must first be washed, then cooked for 30 to 40 minutes. Technically, it's not a real rice at all but a weed seed, but that does not make it any less delicious.

Fancy Wild Rice

1 cup wild rice
5 cups cold water
1 teaspoon salt

1 cup beef broth
1 cup sliced mushrooms

Wash the uncooked rice in a pan of cold water and drain. Transfer the rice to a large saucepan, add the 5 cups of water and the salt, bring to a boil, cover, reduce the heat, and simmer 30 minutes until the brown grains have split open, showing their white insides. Transfer the rice to a collander and thoroughly rinse with very hot tap water. Place the rice back in its pan, stir in the beef broth and mushrooms and simmer uncovered until the broth is almost evaporated. Serves 4.

Spanish Rice

1   cup Minute Rice
1   green pepper, chopped
1   onion, chopped
¼   cup bacon drippings
1   cup beef or chicken broth
2   cups tomato sauce

In a skillet, begin cooking and browning the rice, pepper, and onion in the bacon drippings. Now stir in the beef broth and tomato sauce, bring to a boil, quickly reduce the heat, cover the pan, and simmer 5 minutes until the rice is tender. Serves 4.

Broccoli-Rice Casserole

1½ cups water
1 onion, chopped
⅓ cup butter
1 package frozen broccoli cuts
1½ cups Minute Rice

1 medium can condensed mushroom soup
1 8-ounce jar Cheese Whiz
1 medium can french-fried onion rings

In a large saucepan, bring the water, onion, and butter to a boil. Add the frozen broccoli and simmer until it is thawed. Stir in the rice, turn the heat off, cover, and let stand 5 minutes. Now stir in the cheese and soup. Transfer to a buttered casserole dish and bake for 40 minutes at 325°. Top with onion rings and bake another 5 minutes. Serves 4 very generously.

Easy Baked Beans

2 1-pound cans pork & beans with tomato sauce
4 strips bacon
1 onion, chopped

2 tablespoons brown sugar
1 tablespoon Worcestershire sauce
1 teaspoon wet mustard

In a skillet, cook the bacon until it is crisp, then remove from the pan, crumble, and allow to drain on a paper towel. In the same pan, cook the onion in the bacon drippings until it is lightly browned. Now mix all of the ingredients together and transfer to a bean pot or casserole dish. Bake uncovered at 350° for 2 hours. Serves 4–6.

Timbales

1 cup cooked, flaked fish	½ teaspoon salt
2 cups Minute Rice, cooked	¼ teaspoon black pepper
2 eggs	cooking oil
⅛ teaspoon marjoram	

This is a great favorite when preparing combination fish and game dinners, and at season's end it's a splendid way to make use of that single fish still remaining in the deep freeze. Boil the fish in lightly salted water for 4 minutes, then remove and allow to cool. Next, flake and shred the meat with a fork. In a bowl, mix the fish thoroughly with the other ingredients, then drop large spoonfuls of the timbales onto a sizzling hot griddle wiped with cooking oil and fry just like pancakes until golden brown. As a slight variation, add ¼ cup chopped onion or chopped green pepper. Serves 4.

When preparing combination wild game dinners, with venison one of the several offerings, Timbales are fine go-withs, made from rice and any leftover fish.

Stir-Fried Vegetables

2 tablespoons olive oil	½ head cabbage, cut into large chunks
3 tablespoons soy sauce	2 onions, sliced thick
1 teaspoon Worcestershire sauce	1 cup mushrooms
1 teaspoon A-1 Steak Sauce	1 green pepper, sliced
½ teaspoon black pepper	1 package frozen broccoli spears
1 teaspoon garlic powder	

In a wok or high-sided skillet, blend the first six ingredients. Turn the heat to medium-high and when the liquid begins to steam add the cabbage and broccoli spears and toss gently for several minutes. Now add the sliced onions and sliced green pepper and continue tossing another 5 minutes. Add the mushrooms, cover the wok or skillet with a lid, reduce the heat to low and steam-cook 10 minutes, tossing frequently. The vegetables should be cooked through but not allowed to become mushy. Use a slotted spoon to transfer them to a hot serving dish. Serves 4.

Stir-fried vegetables cooked in an authentic wok add flair to any venison repast.

Our Favorite Acorn Squash

2 large acorn squashes, cut in
    half lengthwise

4 tablespoons brown sugar
4 tablespoons butter

Add ½ inch water to a flat cake pan. Lay the four squash pieces cut-side down in the water and bake for 30 minutes at 350°. Pour the water out of the pan and turn the squashes right-side up. In the center cavities of each, where the seed pouch previously was, place 1 tablespoon brown sugar and 1 tablespoon butter. Return the pan to the oven, turn the heat up to 375°, and continue baking for another 20 to 30 minutes until the squash is light bronze in color. Serves 4.

Our Favorite Acorn Squash is special because of the melted butter and brown sugar in the center.

Deep-fried Veggies

2 red tomatoes
2 green tomatoes
2 green peppers
1 pound whole, fresh
   mushrooms

1 cup pancake mix
1 egg
1 teaspoon salt
1 cup beer

Make a batter by blending the pancake mix, egg, salt, and beer. Let stand 5 minutes. Meanwhile, slice the tomatoes and peppers into rings. Dip the vegetable pieces individually in the batter, shake off any excess, then lay them in a large skillet containing bubbling hot cooking oil. Fry on both sides until golden brown, then drain on paper toweling and transfer to a hot platter. Serves 4.

Fried Onion Rings

3   large onions, sliced thick
1½ cups flour

1   can beer
    cooking oil

In a large bowl, blend the flour and beer. Then cover the bowl and allow to sit at room temperature for 3 hours. Dip onion ring slices into the batter, shake off excess, then lay in a large pan containing at least ½ inch of bubbling cooking oil. Cook onion rings about 2 minutes on each side or until golden brown. As each batch of onion rings is finished, transfer them to a paper towel to drain momentarily, then onto a plate in your oven to remain warm. Serves 4 generously.

Charcoal-grilled Sweet Corn

8 ears sweet corn in husks   salt and pepper
   butter

Very gently, pull back the cornhusks but do not entirely remove them. Now, strip away the silk and discard. Push the husks back into place as they previously were. Use a bit of string if necessary to tie the ends securely closed. Now soak the ears of sweet corn in a large pan of cold water, turning them frequently, for at least 5 minutes. Lay the ears of sweet corn on a grill several inches above a bed of glowing charcoal. Cook the ears 30 to 45 minutes, turning frequently, until the outer husks are charred black; don't worry about this blackness as the corn inside will be tender, sweet, and juicy. Let each guest peel away his own husks, then butter and season with salt and pepper. Be sure to have plenty of napkins on hand. Serves 4.

Perfect Cornbread

1 cup flour   1 cup yellow cornmeal
¼ cup sugar   2 eggs
4 teaspoons baking powder   1 cup milk
¾ teaspoon salt   ¼ cup shortening

In a bowl, blend the flour, sugar, baking powder, and salt, then stir in the cornmeal. Add the eggs, milk, and shortening, then blend with an electric beater for 1 minute (no longer!). Pour the batter into a greased 9 × 9 × 2-inch pan and bake in a 425° oven for 20 to 25 minutes until golden brown on top. Serves 4–6.

Secret to grilling corn is first to soak the ears in ice-cold water (top). Then place ears on a charcoal grill and cook until the husks are thoroughly charred. The corn, inside the protective husks, will remain tender and juicy.

Beer Bread

3   cups self-rising flour
3   tablespoons sugar
½   teaspoon salt
1   can beer

1   teaspoon dill seed
1   teaspoon dried onion flakes
    margarine
    cooking oil

In a bowl, thoroughly mix all of the ingredients except the margarine and cooking oil. Use the cooking oil to paint the inside of a cast-iron skillet. Shape the bread dough with your hands into a nice round and carefully lay it in the pan. Bake at 375° for 55 minutes. Now brush the top of the bread with melted butter or margarine and place back in the oven for 5 more minutes. Serves 6–8.

These recipes are by no means the only side dishes that go well with venison. They are merely easy-to-make favorites that my family and friends have found just different enough from standard accompaniments to make venison dinners especially eventful. Likely as not, you have many favorite go-withs of your own to add to this list.

INDEX

Index